S T A R   T R E K ®

C O O K B O O K

STAR TREK COOKBOOK

Ethan Phillips and William J. Birnes

POCKET BOOKS

New York   London   Toronto   Sydney

PHOTO CREDITS

Carin Baer: 149.
Bill Birnes: 222, 223.
Danny Feld: 186, 188.
Julie Dennis: 190.
Kim Gottlieb-Walker: 106.
Robbie Robinson: 3, 10, 23, 29, 34, 37, 62, 107, 115, 124, 133, 139,
143, 150, 155, 161, 167, 174, 179, 183, 197, 200, 219, 220, 230, 239,
247, 248, 251, 254, 256, 269, 278, 282, 301.
Fred Sabine: 95.
Alan Sims: 57, 58, 111, 121, 131, 263.

Line drawings by Patty Cresswell

An *Original* Publication of POCKET BOOKS

POCKET BOOKS, a division of Simon & Schuster Inc.
1230 Avenue of the Americas, New York, NY 10020

ISBN-13 978-0-671-00022-6
ISBN-10:   0-671-00022-5

First Pocket Books trade paperback printing January 1999

20 19 18 17 16 15 14

Book design by Richard Oriolo

Printed in the U.S.A.

To our talented, beautiful, kind, gracious,
"verray, parfit, gentil wives,"
Patty Cresswell and Nancy Hayfield:

> "I noot wher she be womman or goddesse,
> But Venus is it soothly, as I gesse."

Geoffrey Chaucer, *The Knight's Tale*

"O, pipius claw!

That hath such wonders to it."

—Unknown Klingon minstrel song from the 3rd edition of *The Uncollected Songs of Kahless,* ed. Jesse B. Yessmer and R. Strode (Canterbury: Oxbridge University at The Longwill Press, 11. 2247ff).

Contents

TWO · THE CREW OF THE *U.S.S. ENTERPRISE* 65

THREE · THE CREW OF THE *U.S.S. ENTERPRISE*-D 91

FOUR   LIFE ON DEEP SPACE 9   153

FIVE LIFE ON *VOYAGER* 255

S I X THE LOST RECIPES OF TALAX 287

Foreword

by Quark (as told to Armin Shimerman)

It isn't often that I give anything away for free—unless, of course, there's greater profit to be made later on. But I'm feeling unusually generous. Ethan Phillips, the actor (now, there's an unprofitable profession) who plays that delightful character Mr. Neelix on *Star Trek: Voyager,* had the temerity to ask me to write a few words for his *Star Trek Cookbook.* At first I just laughed. Not only at his absurd suggestion of charity, but also at the unbelievably garish makeup he was wearing. (There are things even I won't do for a living!!) But then I thought, why not? After all, we serve some of that same food (granted it's replicated) at Quark's Bar, Grill, Gaming House, and Holosuite Arcade (see the recipe Poulet Ferengè. I thought, why not get some free publicity for my place in exchange for a few brief minutes at the word processor. So without any further ado:

BUY THE BOOK! COOK THE FOOD! AND TELL YOUR FRIENDS! YOU'LL LOVE IT!

There, Ethan, I hope you're happy.

Introduction

by Neelix

"Mr. Neelix," Captain Janeway began, amazed at how I'd transformed her private dining room into a ship's galley and was serving out breakfast to the crew.

At first the captain was a little taken aback. She asked me to follow her to the bridge. I was to serve as scout extraordinary.

"Mr. Neelix," the captain explained, "you could be the most important person on board this ship, and we need your help to find our way home, but my dining room. . ."

If you want to know the truth, I considered my redesign of the captain's dining room something of an accomplishment. Ever since I joined the *Voyager* crew, I'd had nothing to do. Frankly, I was feeling as useful as a second pinkie until the captain chose to confide in me her deepest concerns. I was flattered, of course, and not a little humbled that Captain Janeway would share her thoughts with me about the morale of the crew, the building of an esprit de corps, and my prowess as a scout through these alien territories.

"Why that's no problem, Captain," I said. "In my travels throughout the quadrant I've encountered so many different cultures I must have a million different types of meals I can prepare. It didn't take me long at all to set up a galley and reroute the mess hall power conduits, and I'll learn everything about each member of the crew so I can make their favorite dishes as well."

"You could have asked me, Mr. Neelix," the captain said. And I could feel her bristle at the loss of her dining room, but I knew that in the end she would see it my way.

"You can trust me, Captain," I assured her. "You have found the right Talaxian to guide you through this quadrant. And, my cooking will accomplish wonders, just wait and see."

And that's how my assignment to the galley on *Voyager* was solidified. Plain old, companionable Neelix became Neelix: scout to the Delta Quadrant, trusted confidential adviser to Captain Janeway, occasional ambassador, ship's morale officer, but, most important, the chief cook. It was a hefty job, a big challenge to take on. I did not know the crew. But I could apply myself, just as I did to woo and win my beloved Kes.

I kept a careful record of all the meals I prepared in my galley and proudly offer in this cookbook some of the best and most notable dishes. The actual recipes have been reconfigured for humans using ingredients entirely from the planet Earth. You don't need to serve onboard a starship in order to cook the recipes I've prepared. In fact, this cookbook is the only complete gastronomical reference to all our adventures in the Delta Quadrant. So, in the grand tradition of Starfleet, these are my recipes from the *Starship Voyager,* whose seventy-thousand-light-year mission is to explore new worlds, seek out new civilizations, and, above all, to return home from where no Starfleet vessel has gone before.

THE CREW OF THE
U.S.S. VOYAGER

Chief Cook and Morale Officer

Straightening out what would become my galley and organizing the pots, pans, and various utensils, I knew that I must take Captain Janeway's admonitions to heart. I would be assiduous in my assignment. The crew's needs were my needs. I would live to serve—meals, that is.

But before I could begin preparing the dishes the crew would love, I needed to understand more about them, about what they liked to eat. So I decided to conduct a series of interviews, a kind of "away mission" to each crew member's palate. On this journey I came to learn many things, not only about the crew's tastes in food and things like traditional holiday meals and the concept of comfort food, but also about the crew as individuals. They shared with me their hobbies and hopes, their peccadilloes and pet peeves, their noble and varied reasons for being in Starfleet or the Maquis, and a little more than I wanted to know about different gastrointestinal ailments. It was an illuminating experience that I would later draw upon in many ways. As a chef, I could surprise them with a taste of home tucked away inside some alien morsel. And as morale officer, I now knew a little bit more about them, which would help me reach out in a personal way when they needed support and kindness. All in all, it was an inspiriting, stimulating, and very productive mission.

ENSIGN HARRY KIM

My first meeting was with Ensign Harry Kim. He actually sought me out first; he had a bad need for a bottle of soy sauce. I was able to accommodate him by giving him a jar of crushed Bothan brain fluid I'd had sitting around for years in my own private cargo, the saltiest extract in the quadrant. It had a caramelaceous enzyme added that made it very similiar to what he desired. The ensign was overjoyed! It started us chatting. This is a sweet, decent young fellow, overwhelmed at being so far from home, deeply missing his family, but brave and devoted to Starfleet. He told me he was from Earth, of Asian descent, and was quite knowledgeable about the cuisine of his heritage. I learned about soy, rice, plums, ginger, oyster sauces, sake, kimchi, rockfish, mirin, sushi, and wasabi. I came away with a substantial idea of what he liked, and what follows are some of the meals I've prepared on the ship just for Mr. Kim.

Garret Wang's Chicken and Sun-Dried Tomatoes

My character, Ensign Kim, loves twentieth-century Earth cuisine. It's fortunate for me that I like it, too. This is one of my favorite recipes because it combines my favorite spinach rotelle with sun-dried tomatoes (I like the imported kind for a treat every once in a blue moon) and fresh chicken breasts. This is a light dish that also makes a great luncheon entrée on a buffet table. Serves approximately four.

1 16-ounce package spinach or multicolored rotelle pasta
  (largest size)
2 to 3 boneless chicken breasts (skinless is optional)
16 ounces pesto sauce (packaged, from the refrigerator section
  of supermarket)
6-ounce jar sun-dried tomatoes in olive oil
2 tablespoons virgin olive oil
2 teaspoons garlic powder *or* 3 cloves garlic, crushed
salt and pepper to taste
grated Romano cheese, if desired

While pasta is cooking in boiling water, slice chicken breasts into long bite-sized pieces. Coat the cooking surface of a 12-inch skillet with olive oil, add garlic powder or crushed garlic cloves, and heat. When pasta is done, drain and set aside. Cook sliced chicken in the olive oil and garlic over medium heat, turning frequently until chicken pieces just turn brown. Do not burn. Drain sun-dried tomatoes and slice into thin lengthwise pieces. Combine pasta, cooked chicken, sun-dried tomatoes, and pesto sauce in a large mixing bowl or salad bowl. Toss thoroughly, cover lightly, and place in refrigerator. Serve well chilled. You may add some more olive oil and Romano cheese. This dish goes very well with a pinot grigio or Soave.

Ensign Kim's Rice Noodles in Milk

It didn't take me long to figure out that Ensign Kim is more of a nosher than an eater, but he goes for this dish in a big way. The noodles I use are actually slivered and pressed wokky intestines, and the "milk" is sap from the Pyrinthian *blacto* weed. Mr. Kim is not aware of this. In your galley, you can prepare a 16-ounce package of store-bought rice noodles from the Asian-foods section of your supermarket or any Asian-foods specialty store according to the package instructions. Drain, remove the portion you want to use, then refrigerate the rest.

In a microwavable bowl, add the noodles you want to use, enough milk (skim, reduced fat, or whole) to cover the noodles completely, a small pat of butter (optional), and maybe a dash of garlic salt, and heat on high in your microwave for a minute. Test to see if it is heated through, and if not heat for another 15 seconds, making sure that the milk doesn't boil over or form a skin. You can also serve with cinnamon instead of garlic salt.

Moo-Goo Ngow

Another recipe I prepare for Harry is Moo-Goo Ngow, my variation of a traditional Asian dish.

> 1 minced garlic clove
>
> 3 tablespoons cooking oil
>
> 1½ pounds round steak, cut in small pieces
>
> 3 tablespoons chopped onion
>
> 1½ cups beef bouillon
>
> ½ pound mushrooms, sliced
>
> 5 tablespoons cornstarch
>
> 1 tablespoon soy sauce
>
> 2 teaspoons water

Heat the oil in a large frying pan or, better, a wok or electric wok, until it's hot; then add garlic. Reduce heat and sauté about 2 minutes. Remove garlic. Add the steak and onion and sauté over an easy flame, stirring constantly until the meat is brown. Add the broth and mushrooms, and cook gently for 10 minutes. Make a thin paste by combining the soy sauce, water, and cornstarch; let it thicken for about a minute, then pour it over the stir-fried meat and mix it in. Keep stirring until the liquid thickens up. Serve meat and sauce over rice. Serves 4. Wow!

Mead

In addition to these traditional dishes I include a recipe for a special brew from Earth history: mead. Ensign Kim programmed the holonovel *Beowulf*, which is about an aging Danish king named Hrothgar who lives in a towering mead hall that is visited each night after the big beer bash by a monster named Grendel who gobbles up members of the king's retinue of warriors. Nobody among Hrothgar's hearth companions can vanquish the evil Grendel, until a troop of Geats led by Beowulf—a Saxon Kahless—lands on the shore of Hrothgar's kingdom. After a hand-to-hand battle even a Klingon would envy, Beowulf dispatches Grendel by yanking the monster's arm from its socket and sending him packing to the nether regions under a dark mere. In honor of that great battle, and Mr. Kim's glorious epic, I prepared the following recipe for the favorite drink of the Healfdanes, honey mead.

> **11 pints (22 cups) cold water**
>
> **¼ ounce peeled, sliced fresh ginger *or* 2 teaspoons ground ginger**
>
> **½ teaspoon brewer's *or* baker's yeast**
>
> **18 ounces clover *or* orange honey**
>
> **1 teaspoon freshly grated lemon peel**

In a large soup pot, bring the cold water to a boil. Add honey and reduce heat to a simmer. Slowly dissolve the honey in the simmering water, and when it is fully dissolved, bring the mixture back to a rolling boil. In the uncovered pot, let the honey mixture boil down to just over half its original volume as you skim any impurities—what the Anglo-Saxons called crud—from the surface of the water.

After about two hours, check for clarity. When the mixture is no longer cloudy and there is no more crud to skim, reduce heat to a slower boil and add the ginger. Brew for another half hour and add the lemon peel; let it boil a minute or so, and remove from the heat. Set aside to cool to lukewarm, then add the yeast.

Cover and let sit for 24 to 36 hours, while the fermentation process begins. Next, using thick, heavy, sealable mason jars, you will bottle the mixture, filling the jars only three-quarters full. Set the jars aside in a safe place while the fermentation continues and builds considerable pressure inside the containers. After about three days, it's time to refrigerate the bottles, taking care to handle them gently. Don't drop or bump the containers, because the pressure inside a container can cause it to explode. Refrigerate the mead for at least a week before drinking it. If you age it for a month, your mead, or meadu, as the Anglo-Saxon-speaking Spear Danes from Mr. Kim's epic holonovel called it, will be enough to turn any logic-spouting Vulcan into a swaggering Klingon thegn full of sound and fury and ready for battle.

Terran Pasta with Clam Sauce

I would also like at this time to thank Harry for being the only member out of the entire crew who professed a liking for pleeka rind and grub meal! He confessed this to Tom right before I passed out in the galley from Mylean DNA poisoning. I prepare this with the collagen fibers from the pleeka, a small Olipian reptile, and gooboo grubs, which nest in the hair of mature Alfarians. On Earth, spaghetti with clam sauce comes close. You have your choice of red or white clam sauce. Red is a tad more spicy because of the pepper; white is more tangy because of the requisite amount of garlic you need to add.

PASTA

1 16-ounce package #9 spaghetti or linguini

8 cups water

4 cloves garlic, crushed in a garlic press

1 tablespoon olive oil

While the clam sauce is cooking, boil the pasta in a large saucepan until soft enough to bite into it, but still firm, drain, crush four cloves of garlic into the pasta and stir, pour olive oil onto the pasta, stir through, and set aside until you are ready to add the clam sauce.

WHITE SAUCE

2 dozen shucked sliced raw littleneck clams *or* 3 cups shucked sliced raw chowder clams

8 cloves garlic, thinly sliced

¼ cup olive oil

2 teaspoons oregano

1 teaspoon dried parsley

salt and pepper to taste

In a skillet, sauté garlic cloves in the olive oil, but don't let them burn. Add the clams and simmer gently until they soften to the touch. Add the oregano and parsley and salt and pepper. Stir the clam sauce until all the flavors have blended, pour over the pasta, and completely stir through. Serves four.

RED SAUCE

2 dozen shucked sliced raw littleneck clams *or* 3 cups shucked sliced raw chowder clams

8 Italian plum tomatoes

6 cloves garlic, thinly sliced

½ cup olive oil

¼ cup red wine

3 teaspoons oregano

2 teaspoons red crushed pepper

1 teaspoon dried parsley

½ teaspoon sugar

salt and pepper to taste

In 1 tablespoon of olive oil, sauté tomatoes with 4 of the garlic cloves. After the tomatoes have cooked into a liquid, add the sugar, wine, pepper, oregano, and parsley; then cover and simmer slowly for at least 1 hour.

Now, using the remaining 2 sliced garlic cloves, prepare the clams as you did in the recipe for white clam sauce above. When the clams are ready, mix them into the tomato sauce and simmer for another ½ hour. Then pour some of the red clam sauce over the spaghetti and stir through. Leave enough clam sauce for your guests to add their own, as with the recipe for white clam sauce. Serves four.

Vulcan Mocha Ice Cream

Ensign Kim likes his sweets, sometimes even more than he professes to like Seven of Nine. When she refuses to be assimilated, Harry usually finds his way to the galley to immerse himself in a plate of my handmade Vulcan mocha ice cream. Harry loves Vulcan mocha; he loves ice cream, so I invented this dessert.

The easiest way to prepare this is to buy some chocolate ice cream from the store, stir in a finely ground, dark espresso or Kenya AAA coffee, (¼ cup coffee to 1 cup ice cream) and refreeze the mixture or simply whip it into an iced drink.

Or you can go completely wild and make the whole thing from scratch. Here's how:

⅓ cup high-quality unsweetened cocoa powder

⅓ cup sugar

½ cup sweetened condensed milk

1½ cups milk

1 teaspoon vanilla extract (use mocha syrup here if you find it)

1 cup whipping cream, chilled

⅛ teaspoon finely ground mocha coffee, for garnish

In the top half of a double boiler, combine cocoa, sugar, and condensed and regular milk; bring the mixture to a boil over direct heat, stirring constantly; then put the pan over water simmering in the bottom of the double boiler. Let the mixture cook for 30 minutes, stirring once or twice. When the cocoa has cooked thoroughly (with no powdery residue), dip the pan into a pan of cold water to cool it down quickly. Strain the mixture and pour into an ice-cream machine; add the vanilla extract (or mocha) and stir in the chilled cream. Follow your machines directions. Allow it rest in the refrigerator for about 20 minutes to soften before serving. Sprinkle a pinch of mocha coffee, ground to the consistency of turkish coffee, on top to make a decorative pattern.

COMMANDER CHAKOTAY

The next crew member I sought out was our first officer, Mr. Chakotay. I engaged him in a round of hoverball, and though I was new to the sport, I roundly beat him. This impressed him, and we had a somewhat easy chat over some cold *pejuta* in a small lounge on Deck 11. Though he was somewhat taciturn, I admired him a great deal, especially his deep pride in his Native American ancestry, which he rediscovered after joining Starfleet against his father's wishes. His tattoo is a sign of his honor to his father and his people.

The first officer is a fascinating and complex man, spiritual, skilled, and interested in many areas. He reveres all living things, and I learned an important fact right away: he will not eat any meat. Any idea I entertained of preparing jerky from his animal guide is completely out of the question. My favorite dish to make for the commander is a simple vegetarian stew. I always include dafkies in it; they are remarkably similar to corn kernels. Also, mushrooms, which he loves.

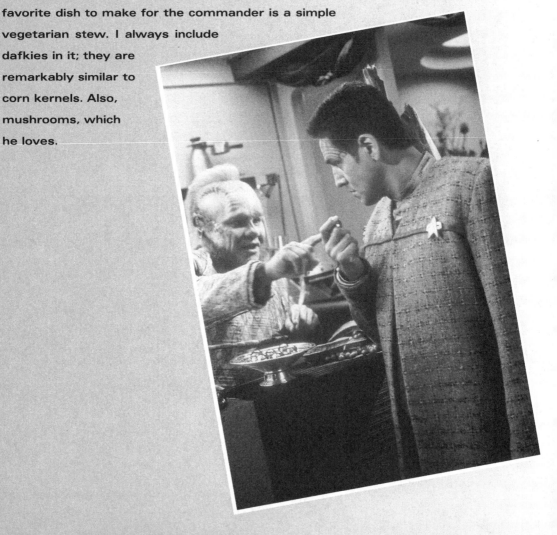

Robert Beltran's Chicken or Turkey Mole

Here is an adaptation of a Native American sauce so easy to prepare for turkey or chicken leftovers that even Neelix can whip it together. It's hot, though, because it's made with two bottles of red chili powder, so I suggest you complement it with either a mild polenta or cornmeal side dish or rice. Makes a great meal you can cook in a skillet over an open fire at the campsite or in your own backyard.

6 cups boiling water

2 4-ounce bottles Eagle Brand red chili powder (my favorite) *or*

> **1 cup any good red chili powder (use less to taste)**

1½ pounds chicken or turkey leftovers

¼ cup all-purpose flour

2 tablespoons corn oil

2 teaspoons whole or ground cumin seed

1 teaspoon hot chili oil

If you can't find Eagle Brand in your stores, you can substitute 8 ounces (1 cup) of any good Mexican chili powder. Add the chili powder to the boiling water in a medium-sized saucepan and stir until you have a thick red chili sauce. Keep stirring to smooth out any lumps.

Heat corn oil in a large, deep skillet, and add the chili oil and stir. Add flour and stir until it's smooth; then add the ground or whole cumin, making sure that if you use whole cumin seed, you bruise the seed by rubbing it between your fingers. Stir, add the chili sauce, and keep stirring to make sure it's smooth; then add the chicken or turkey and simmer for about 15 minutes.

Serve with polenta slices, fried cornmeal, or rice. Serves four.

Angla'bosque

The very first meal I ever mentioned, after my joining the *Voyager* crew, was *angla'bosque,* and I proudly admit, I am known throughout the quadrant for this dish. It's one of Chakotay's favorite stews too. The combination of ingredients is a bit daunting: *scree'lash,* a fat, fragrant fruit from Ferna for flavor; rinds from Bilikian figs; the beak of a Kalto wood warbler; blood grapes from the twenty-foot-man-eating Vidiian grapevine (without this, no gravy!); a teaspoon of that gorgeous green Aldebaran whiskey; modads, a tomato with see-through skin and seeds that sing; chives from the gardens of the Nechani monks; Vothian thunder leeks (the Voth, dinosaur-like creatures, are renowned leek farmers), Nyrian chicory; the stomach lining from Rianaxian rain worms (optional); Mithren fiddlewax; an Othopian obble plum; lizo belly meat; and finally, bleached Briori beechnuts. Remember the Briori? I do. They were the race that abducted three hundred people in 1937 and brought them to the Delta Quadrant.

On Earth, *angla'bosque* is an easy-to-make vegetable curry, and you can add for texture grapes, chopped figs, and even chopped nuts to the following ingredients if you don't want to throw in a bunch of twigs the way I do in my galley on *Voyager.* The veggies are rolled into balls held together with chickpea flour and lightly fried in peanut oil. Also, for this dish you will need a medium-to-large-sized seasoned wok, a handy utensil that I use in the *Voyager* galley all the time.

It takes about an hour to make *angla'bosque,* less time if you break up the tasks by preparing the vegetables ahead of time. The larger the variety of vegetable balls, the more hands you should have on board to help you prepare them. Whatever vegetable you use, the sweet taste of the grapes and figs will blend quite well with the light curry to bring out the taste of the vegetables. You'll need the following ingredients:

> **2 cups chopped cooked spinach**
>
> **1½ cups mashed potatoes (instant is okay)**
>
> **2 cups mashed cooked squash (boiled is best)**
>
> **1 cup sliced purple grapes (optional)**

1 cup sliced figs (optional)

¼ cup chopped walnuts (optional)

6 tablespoons chickpea flour

⅓ cup water

½ teaspoon cayenne pepper

½ teaspoon ground cumin

½ teaspoon ground ginger

½ teaspoon mustard powder

½ teaspoon fresh ground black pepper

½ teaspoon cinnamon

½ teaspoon coriander

½ cup peanut oil

1 16-ounce package of curry sauce mix

First, blend all the spices and chickpea flour in a large bowl, adding the water and stirring slowly, until it forms a near-liquid paste. Set aside. Next you will prepare the potato and vegetable balls. In separate bowls, mix ⅓ of the spice paste with the potatoes, the next ⅓ of the paste with the spinach, and the last ⅓ of the spice paste with the squash and roll into 2-inch-diameter balls (approximately the size of cocktail meatballs or falafel balls). If the vegetable and potato balls become too dry, you can add a touch of water, but not too much, to soften them up.

In a seasoned wok, fry the spinach, squash, and potato balls together in oil to coat until they are a golden brown. Balls should be nice and crisp. Set them aside to drain while you prepare the curry sauce according to package instructions.

When the curry sauce is finished and is on a low simmer, add the spinach, squash, and potato balls, sprinkle the simmering mixture with coriander, stir and at this point you can add the optional grapes, figs and walnuts. Simmer for another five minutes. Remove from heat and serve with either jasmine or Darjeeling tea.

Chakotay eats a whole pot of *angla'bosque* at a single sitting and then has a Kazon for a light lunch. The man's a machine. You, however, not having Kazon or Borg in your future can probably serve guests a good hearty *angla'-bosque* dinner. Chakotay's appetite notwithstanding, this dish serves approximately four.

Maquis Breakfast Bars

Another favorite of Chakotay's is Maquis breakfast bars that you can crunch on while hiding in Badland caves to ambush the unwary Cardassians. These are tasty, nutty, nutrient-packed slabs of energy that invariably disappear as soon as I set them out before each away mission. Tom and I once lived on nothing else during an away mission. I'm a little sick of them, actually, but the Maquis hoard them like bars of gold-pressed latinum.

You can pack most of the nutrients the Maquis require into something called granola bars, which you can pack into lunch bags for your own little Maquis to take to school or on their away missions. These are especially easy to make. You can even have your children help with the process.

4 cups old-fashioned rolled oats

1 cup wheat germ

½ cup instant nonfat dry milk

4 cups mixed dried raisins, apples, bananas, dates

½ cup shredded coconut

½ cup (1 stick) butter

½ cup honey

1 teaspoon vanilla extract

2 teaspoons cinnamon

Preheat oven to 350 degrees and combine all the dry ingredients in a large bowl. Stir.

In a small saucepan, heat the butter and honey slowly until they just begin to simmer. Then remove from heat and stir in the vanilla. Next coat a shallow 9 inch square baking pan with cooking oil or butter and set aside.

Stir the honey-butter mixture into the dry ingredients, making sure to coat the granola mixture very well. Spread the mixture out onto your greased baking pan and pat down to an even layer. Bake the mixture for 25 minutes at 350 degrees, checking the granola every 8 minutes or so to make sure it doesn't burn. You should also stir the mixture each time and pat it down again. This will guarantee even cooking.

When the mixture's done after 25 minutes, remove it from the oven and let it cool. Then cut it into 2 inch squares, which you can either wrap individually or seal in an airtight jar and store in your pantry. Makes 16.

Talaxian Mushroom Soup

You may remember Chakotay's having mentioned on more than one occasion that mushroom soup was one of his favorite dishes. I remember it well because of the way he looked at me as if to say, "I *want* mushroom soup!" On *Voyager,* what the first officer wants, the first officer gets. Thankfully for an overworked and sometimes thoroughly underappreciated galley chef like me, mushrooms are omniversal, found virtually everywhere there is life. Kes grew them in the hydroponic garden, and I harvested them from the surface of any planet we set foot on. I especially love cross-contaminating Talaxian pigweed shallots that grow along the Riparian corridors of Heelox, the wildest river on Talax, with Nezu candy-tufted mud fungus before I cook them in a pan with Bolian tingle butter. However, you'll use the following ingredients:

2 pounds mushrooms, as fresh as you can get them

3 small red-skin potatoes *or* 1 large peeled russet potato

1 small Spanish onion

1 stalk celery, chopped, *or* 1 cup frozen finely diced celery

¼ cup finely diced green bell pepper

1½ cups cold water

1 teaspoon salt

1 pinch coarsely ground black pepper

1 pinch thyme *or* rosemary

¼ pound (1 cup) butter

3 cups whole milk

1 cup cream (heavy or light)

green scallions as a garnish

First, scrub the mushrooms to make sure they're clean. You know what mushrooms grow in, and it's not something you want floating on the surface of the soup. Just assume you're preparing this for Commander Chakotay and the unsmiling Mr. Tuvok, and you'll scrub those fungi until they shine like the Rigelian moons. Scrub the potatoes also. Then, slice the mushrooms, potatoes, and onion as thinly as you can. The art to making this soup is to slice everything—the potatoes, the onion, the pepper, and especially the mushrooms—very thin. Set aside the sliced potatoes and mushrooms, and dice the sliced onion and pepper along with the celery until they're finely chopped.

Next, in a large saucepan, cook the onion and peppers in a ½ stick of butter without burning them, until they are soft and the onion is clear. Then stir in the potatoes and celery, along with a pinch of salt, and add the remaining ½ stick of butter. When the potatoes feel soft to the spoon and the mixture is almost soupy, add the water and mushrooms and continue to cook the mixture for about 20 minutes at a low simmer.

Let the mixture then cool for about 10 minutes; process it in a blender or food processor on high until it's completely puréed. Now, stir in the milk and cream, and cook the soup for another 45 minutes to 1 hour over very low heat. When it's ready to serve, I garnish it with the scallions I pick right out of the airoponics garden and signal Commander Chakotay. He doesn't even bother to acknowledge. Just shows up with his favorite spoon at the ready. Serves 4 to 6 depending on the size of the serving.

LIEUTENANT TOM PARIS

Mr. Tom Paris, like Harry Kim, was an easy man to get to know. Tom has an abundance of charm, a quick smile, and a fine sense of humor. Were it not for my misperceived notions about his intentions regarding Kes, we'd have been friends much sooner. Unfortunately it wasn't until our first away missions that we forged a real bond. I've learned about his troubled past and the second chance Captain Janeway gave him. I've come to respect in equal measure his outrageous skills as a pilot and his winning way with the opposite sex. But it was in our very first meetir g that I first heard about his fascination with twentieth-century Earth culture. From cars to cartoons, movies to mud wrestling, and smoothies to submarine-race watching at Palisades Park, Tom has an encyclopedic knowledge of that time period and genuinely enjoys sharing it.

As we sat in a quiet corner of the mess hall, I learned all about trains, bicycles, water skis, and skateboards. He raved about his favorite actors: Brando, Dean, De Niro, and Phillips. But I was of course most interested in the food from that era. He told me about comfort food, diner food, fast food, TV dinners, coffee shops, steak houses, truck stops, and drive-throughs. He described blueberry pancakes and Belgian waffles, caramel popcorn and Cheez Whiz, nacho chips and soft pretzels. He took me on a journey from apple pie through Zonkers, and when he finished, I just about sprinted to the mess hall, where I shaped and baked my first loaf of meat.

Robert Duncan McNeill's Mother-in-law Kugel

This a real old-country recipe for noodle pudding, the kind great-grandparents used to make for the holidays. You can serve it as a dessert with a sugar and applesauce topping, or with a sour cream or yogurt topping, as a lunch or late breakfast.

1 16-ounce package wide egg noodles

4 eggs

1 pound cottage cheese

1 pound sour cream

½ cup (1 stick) butter

¼ cup milk

2 tablespoons cinnamon

1 tablespoon sugar

TOPPING

2 cups cornflakes

3 tablespoons sugar

3 tablespoons cinnamon

applesauce, yogurt, or sour cream to taste

Preheat oven to 350 degrees. Cook noodles al dente, per package instructions, and drain. Then, beat the eggs and fold them into the cooked noodles. In a separate bowl, add the cottage cheese, sour cream, butter, milk, 2 tablespoons cinnamon, and 1 tablespoon sugar together, mix thoroughly, and then combine with noodle and egg mixture. Pour into rectangular (lasagna-style) baking dish that has been prebuttered so your noodle kugel won't stick. Now for the topping, crush and crumble the cornflakes in a bowl and mix with 3 tablespoons sugar and 3 tablespoons cinnamon. Sprinkle topping evenly to cover the noodle mixture. Bake at 350 degrees for 1 hour and serve with applesauce, yogurt, or sour cream. Serves six to eight.

Pilot's Quick Pizza

A favorite of Tom's is pizza. He craved it, you'll remember, when he slow-ly mutated into a salamander. And on another occasion he practically begged me for a slice. I must say the last thing I wanted to mess with was cheese—the last time I worked with cheese, it went to sickbay, along with the bio-neural gel packs and some of the crew. Tom also loves pizza with Kaferian olives (or with green olives or black olives). In my gal-ley, I put everything on my pilot's pizza, from diced targ shin meat to *dako* kidney, and then spice it all up with Yaderian beeswax. No one knows what's on it, but they gobble it up, except when Tuvok joins Tom for lunch. He had one analyzed recently after biting into a piece of Mogholixian monkey tail and now stays away. I give you my recipe for a quick, homemade, "bread machine" version of Tom's favorite pizza dish, the one he craved when he was unhappily mutating into an amphibious creature. To make a single medium-thin 12-inch pizza crust in your auto-matic bread machine make ready the following:

> ¾ cup warm water
>
> 1 tablespoon olive oil
>
> 2¼ cups all-purpose flour
>
> 1 teaspoon salt
>
> 1 teaspoon sugar
>
> 1 teaspoon dry yeast

First preheat your oven to 400 degrees. Then combine the ingredients in the machine according to the order above and set your bread machine on the "dough only" setting. When the machine beeps at you that the dough is ready, coat your bread or dough board lightly with flour and roll the dough out on the board until thin and approximately 12 inches in diameter, making sure you also gently stretch it with your fingertips to form a raised edge. Finish off the pizza with your favorite toppings in layers:

tomato sauce (store-bought is just perfect for a quick lunch)

packaged shredded mozzarella cheese

lots of garlic and oregano

sliced pepperoni

mushrooms left over from Talaxian mushroom soup

meat loaf left over from Gyronian meat loaf

veggies such as broccoli and spinach

Then bake in 400 degree oven for about 15 minutes or until brown. Check the bottom of your pie after 10 minutes to prevent burning and to look like a professional pizza chef who knows what he's doing.

Gyronian Meat Loaf à la Paris

On *Voyager,* this dish is made with *hormoos,* a parasite that lives on the backs of Gyronian wamules. They are virtually undetachable, unless you can get the wamules to sneeze. *Hormoos* will always flee a sneezing Gyronian wamule. Obviously the trick is to get the wamule to sneeze. Crushed snazzle seeds blown through a *dekko* reed in the vicinity of their noses will accomplish this. But wear earplugs, because the sneeze from a wamule is very loud, and very unpleasant to boot. Once the *hormoos* leaps off, catch it in a "hor" net. Dispatch it quickly to *hormoos* heaven, skin it, and grind the meat. I mix it with Fargonian finger apples and Ukitarian cave carrots and sand nuts. You can serve it cold, wrapped in a Terran gyro roll or pita bread.

One pound of meat loaf will serve 4 to 6 or make 6 sandwiches. One and one half pounds is all you need to feed the whole crew for lunch if you have enough rolls or pita pockets to make sandwiches.

1½ pounds fresh ground beef *or* lamb *or* even turkey or beef-and-lamb combination

½ cup tomato juice *or* vegetable juice *or* Bloody Mary mix

¼ cup marinara or meatless tomato sauce

½ cup chopped onions

2 cloves garlic, chopped

1 teaspoon celery seed

1 teaspoon dried parsley

¼ teaspoon Tabasco or Louisiana hot sauce

sea salt and freshly ground pepper to taste

Preheat oven to 375 degrees and lightly grease a loaf pan. Combine the meat, juice, onions, garlic cloves, celery seed, parsley, hot sauce, and salt and pepper in a mixing bowl and thoroughly knead until the meat is soft and squishy. Then place meat in your loaf pan and top with tomato sauce. Bake for 1 hour, then test for doneness. Make sure the center of the loaf is thoroughly cooked before serving. Serve steaming hot, either sliced plain or on either soft hero (gyro) rolls or pita-bread pockets. You can also refrigerate the leftovers and serve cold meat-loaf sandwiches the next day.

Andoran Oatmeal Cookies

I don't get a lot of compliments for my cooking—have you noticed? But when I do, I remember them vividly. One time, much to my surprise, Tom actually raved about my Andoran sweet roots. I used to bake these twice a month but recently exhausted my supply, and we are now light-years from Andor. So instead I add Gizzy sweat to uni-collagic tubers and don't tell anybody. You could make oatmeal cookies and no one would be the wiser. The trick is to prepare a batch of cookies and have them on your galley shelf for whenever the crew hits the mess hall. Here's my quick Andoran oatmeal cookie recipe, ready for storage in your galley.

3 cups all-purpose flour

1½ cups granulated white sugar

1 cup lightly packed dark or light brown sugar

1 teaspoon baking soda

1 teaspoon baking powder

1 cup shortening

3 cups rolled oats

½ cup raisins or currants

Into a large bowl, sift together flour, sugars, baking soda, and baking powder. Cut in shortening with a pastry blender or two knives until the mixture is crumbly. You can use an electric food processor for this step. However, be sure to process quickly and stop before you turn the mixture into a smooth paste. The trick is to make this mixture textured and crumbly, just the way Ferengi like it.

Next, stir in the rolled oats and the raisins or currants. Actually, you can use both raisins and currants, in any quantity you like.

To cook, preheat oven to 350 degrees and lightly grease a flat cookie sheet or baking pan. Drop cookies in small half-inch dots onto the sheet, making sure there's enough room for them to spread. Cook each batch at 350 degrees for no more than 7 minutes before checking. Don't let them burn. Better to serve cookies underdone than burnt. Probably 8 minutes is as much baking time as these cookies will take. Let cool and enjoy.

To store uncooked dough, spoon the mixture into a tightly covered labeled container. Mix will keep for at least two months in your pantry during normal temperatures. During the hot summer months, store in the refrigerator. Yields thirty 3-inch cookies.

LIEUTENANT B'ELANNA TORRES

t took a long time for me to meet up with Lieutenant Torres, even though we were in the same crew. The half-Klingon, half-human engineer who'd rather stare into a matter/antimatter containment field than plow into a plate of *rokeg* blood pie didn't have the time, professed not to care about food, or bristled that concerns more pressing than a heart of baby *targ* interfered. She put our talk off for weeks, until I discovered her fondness for Briorian needle knuckles, the fresher the better. I took a bowl to her quarters one morning, and she lit up like a little girl on Prixin Eve. She excitedly grabbed the bowl, invited me in, and promptly sat down to devour the knuckles, a weird combination of cartilage and candy.

While B'Elanna snacked we chatted, but as soon as she finished, she wanted to move on to other tasks. Still, in our short time together, I learned what I needed. It was the carnivore in her, the Klingon who feeds on the fresh kill, that I'd celebrate in my cooking for her. Food that's literally alive. Organs pulsing with life; worms, maggots, and mice feet; hearts, corneas, and marrow.

Okay, let's cut right to the chase. When you think Klingon, you think blood pie, heart of *targ,* bloodwine, Klingon ale, and lots and lots of *gagh*.

What I serve in my galley is "nouveau Klingon". I stay true to the traditional Klingon cold breakfast buffet, recreate from Delta Quadrant ingredients the essential blood pie and heart of whatever passes for a *targ,* but supplement with the Earth-type recipes that Lieutenant Torres seems to relish when she's more like a human. But whether a human or a Klingon, there's always *gagh*—the staple of the Klingon warrior's table.

Roxann Dawson's Klingon Green Beans and Walnuts

You can substitute live worms for green beans. For that extra-special Klingon touch, instead of the walnut oil use bloodwine. And remember: *"bortaS blr jablu'DI' reH QaQqu' nay'."* Translation: "Revenge is a dish that is best served cold."

> **2 pounds green beans, trimmed**
> **¼ stick butter**
> **1 cup chopped toasted walnuts**
> **2 tablespoons walnut oil**
> **2 tablespoons minced fresh parsley**

Cook beans in a large pot of boiling salted water until just tender, about 5 minutes. Rinse beans with cold water to stop the cooking (I rinse them and then put them in a bowl of ice water). If you want, you can cook the beans in advance, about 6 hours before you serve them. Just be sure to refrigerate them. To complete, put butter with oil in large heavy skillet over high heat. Add beans and toss until heated through, about 4 minutes. Season with salt and pepper. Add walnuts and parsley and toss. Serve in a large bowl garnished with whatever greens you like. The greens also set off the color of the beans. Serves six.

Gagh

Klingons will kill for fresh *gagh;* they often need a lot less incentive. Replicated *gagh* is flat; it doesn't have that gamy flavor that makes your eyes water and your breath catch in your throat. Do you know that there are at least fifty-one varieties of *gagh*? B'Elanna tells me that *bithool gagh* is her favorite—it has feet. I suspect that even those humans who say they'd kill for vibrant fresh sashimi would recoil in horror at a plate of squirming Klingon worms. So I have the next best thing. You can eat it, shake it, and it still tastes good. The ingredients are as follows:

> **1-pound package thick Japanese udon noodles (whole wheat is best), soba noodles, *or* Chinese *or* Thai rice noodles**
>
> **4 ounces prepared sesame salad dressing *or* Chinese chicken salad dressing *or* tahini**
>
> **¼ cup soy sauce *or* light soy sauce**
>
> **1 teaspoon dark brown Karo syrup, if you find it necessary for color**

Prepare the noodles per the package instructions, replacing one-half the water with the soy sauce. Chill. Then stir through quarter-cup soy sauce and sesame salad dressing. Add Karo syrup and stir through to satisfy your own sense of color and taste, and there you have it: *gagh!*

I sometimes serve *gagh* for Lieutenant Torres with a side dish of another Klingon favorite, *gladst.* The leafy brown Klingon vegetable is best replaced on your table with arugula. Use it as a garnish for the *gagh* and you have a light lunch or an appetizer for your Klingon parties. *Gagh,* of course, is the main element in my Klingon cold breakfast buffet that most of the crew enjoys, especially B'Elanna. Serves two.

Heart of *Targ*

It's true what they say: "If you want to be a Klingon warrior, you gotta have heart." In this case, I'd recommend veal rather than beef because veal is more tender and the heart is muscle that can be rather tough. For this heart casserole, I suggest four veal hearts—you can get them from any butcher or the butcher section of your supermarket (tell 'em you're a Klingon and let it go at that). You will also need some store-bought stuffing, such as Stovetop, unless you want to make your own celery or apple stuffing from bread crumbs or croutons. Heart of *targ* itself is very simple to make.

> **4 veal hearts as tender as possible**
> **5 cups beef bouillon *or* vegetable-stock bouillon *or* canned**
>   **prepared tomato soup**
> **8 slices thick-sliced bacon**
> **1 package store-bought stuffing mix, prepared per directions**
> ***OR:***
> **1 16-ounce package stuffing mix *or* large croutons**
> **½ cup beef bouillon**
> **1 large Granny Smith apple, peeled, cored, and chopped**
> **6 full stalks celery, chopped**

Preheat oven to 325 degrees. Wash the veal hearts in cold water to remove all surface impurities, fat, blood vessels, and blood. This can be a messy job if you're not a Klingon, but it has to be done in order to render the heart pure red muscle without any gristle or blood on the surface.

Place your hearts on a rack in a shallow baking dish—you can use a pie tin—and douse with 2½ cups bouillon, stock, or prepared tomato soup. Cover hearts with bacon strips; then cover the dish and bake at 325 degrees for 1½ hours.

If you are using store-bought stuffing, wait until the final 30 minutes and prepare stuffing. If you are making stuffing from scratch, soften the croutons with the bouillon and drippings from the baking hearts. When the stuffing is just moist, stir in apples and celery. Keep adding bouillon until the stuffing is soft.

Remove hearts from the oven after 90 minutes, stuff, and re-cover with tomato soup or remaining bouillon; and return to oven for 30 minutes at 350 degrees. Increase heat to 400 degrees for 5 minutes; then remove from oven and serve on a bed of *gladst* with ale or red wine.

This dish may take some getting used to, but remember reading that Will Riker, before he accepted the job of first officer on the *Pagh,* taught himself to love heart of *targ.* Serves four

For those of you too squeamish to try veal heart, you can bake 1½ pounds calf liver, cut into 1½ -inch squares, following almost the same recipe. Prepare the liver as the veal was above, covering it with bacon strips, and while it is baking, prepare the stuffing. After baking it for 2 hours, remove the calf liver from rack, place it on a bed of stuffing, and return it to the oven for another 30 minutes. This dish is as tasty as heart, certainly more tender, and when served either on 6–8 skewers or as hors d'oeuvres, will complement the lustiest vintage Bordeaux you can serve. Serves six to eight.

Rokeg Blood Pie à la Neelix

Blood pie is a staple among the Klingons. As shocking as it is when you open up the pastry shell and see the wriggling entrails and organs, it's a dish that Klingons learn to love from the time they're little Klingonettes. Lieutenant Torres is no exception, even though she's half human and separated from her Klingon forebears by an entire quadrant. So I learned to make the dish from the Starfleet logs and prepared my own creation specifically for B'Elanna. Here it is:

> 1 8-ounce can cherry pie filling
>
> 1 pound fresh or frozen cranberries (defrosted)
>
> 1 cup unfiltered cranberry juice
>
> ½ cup red grape juice
>
> ½ cup sugar
>
> 1 packaged two-crust pie pastry or refrigerator pie pastry

Preheat oven to 350 degrees. Blend on low, in a blender or food processor, or use your hand electric mixer to pulp the fresh or frozen cranberries, and in a saucepan combine them with cherry filling, grape juice, cranberry juice, and sugar. Bring to a slow boil on low heat, and simmer for 15 minutes while you grease a pie pan and spread out the pie pastry in it. Pour blood pie ingredients into the pie shell, cover with the top pastry crust, moisten edge with water, and crimp edges together. Pierce the crust with your fork to ventilate, and bake for 45 minutes or until crust just begins to turn golden and flakes in your hand. Serve red, runny, and piping hot.

SEVEN OF NINE

When she first joined our crew (and I use the word "join" loosely), Seven of Nine hadn't eaten real food since she was seven, or nine, or thereabouts. Since she was a Borg, some meals I considered for her included crushed combadge soup, diced tricorder pie, sliced bio-neuro gel pack, and scalloped class-4 probes. But it was less a question of finding out what she liked than just reeducating her in how to eat.

Out of respect for her atrophied digestive system, I served her steamed vegetables and a few other tidbits I thought might be appealing. Seven never finished the meal (her past intervened); of the six items on the plate, Seven ate two and left four. But as time has passed, she has come to respect my cooking. And though a meal is no longer just six of one, half a dozen of the other to Seven, it has been a special challenge finding out what this Borg likes. A few things that I know she looks forward to follow here: Seven-up, a carbonated beverage from ancient Earth. Anything from a 7-Eleven store. Although she fought me when it came time to eat, my cooking was so wonderful, her resistance was futile.

Jeri Ryan's "Seven of Nine Steamed Chadre Kab"

This is my personal version of a dish I invented for Seven. It is simple. You will assimilate it.

1 butternut or acorn squash, steamed and mashed.

Do not add salt or pepper, as these would make it too pungent. Pile squash onto plate as efficiently as possible.

Jeri Ryan's Wild Mushroom Soup

This soup tastes terrific (my number-one priority) and is also low in fat (my costume's number-one priority). The key is to use as many different varieties of mushroom as possible.

1 pound assorted mushrooms (portobello, cremini, button, shiitake, oyster, chanterelle, and others), chopped into bite-sized pieces

1 large russet potato, diced into ½ -inch pieces

1 large onion, halved and sliced

1 large clove garlic, minced

1½ to 2 tablespoons olive oil (more if needed)

1 quart chicken stock, defatted

salt and pepper to taste

Sauté mushrooms, onions, and garlic over medium heat in 1½ table-spoons of olive oil until tender. Add remaining oil as needed. You should sauté the firmer mushrooms first, adding the more delicate ones only at the end. Add remaining ingredients and simmer over medium-low heat until potatoes are tender, about 20 minutes. Taste to adjust seasonings and serve hot with crusty bread. Serves four.

Borg Tricorder Pie

Here's a recipe exclusively for the Borg. I call it tricorder pie. Take 10 spent tricorders and crush them with a procto-hammer. Add ½ quart plasma oil. Stir. Mix in 1 pound of class-4 probe buckling, 1 minced nacelle discharge socket, 1 type 65563-AS9 navigator sensor, and some finely chopped bio-neural gel pack casing. Shred in a little padd hard circuitry and 1 pound of emitter buffer. Season with 1 teaspoon of induction coil and ⅓ ounce of dispersal field matrix. Bake for 3 hours in a destabilized hypo-shield convex warp container. Serve on a bed of transporter-room console siding.

Chadre Kab à la Neelix or Seven of Nine's Steamed Vegetables

This was Seven of Nine's first meal on *Voyager,* so I steamed her the most digestible foods in the galaxy. Steaming vegetables instead of boiling them is a healthy, tasty way of cooking. Steaming also makes them easier on the digestive system, which is especially important if you're a Borg recently freed from the collective. You can also be very clever about steaming vegetables in paprika with a little salt and butter so that it has a flavor that doesn't overpower the freshness of the veggies. As Data's favorite hero, Sherlock Holmes, once said when asked by his medical sidekick and confidant about the importance of steaming, "It's alimentary, my dear Watson."

In honor of Seven, I steamed up seven vegetables for her very first meal. They were:

> **7 carrots**
>
> **7 stalks celery**
>
> **7 baby asparagus spears**
>
> **7 small red potatoes**
>
> **2 cups chopped cabbage**
>
> **1 small onion**
>
> **1 cup chopped green beans**
>
> **⅛ cup (¼ stick) butter (completely optional)**
>
> **⅛ teaspoon plain salt *or* celery salt (optional)**
>
> **pepper or paprika to taste**

You will need a vegetable steamer, which consists of a large pot with a tightly sealed cover and a steamer rack. Follow the instructions that come with your vegetable steamer. If you don't have a steamer, you can improvise one yourself by fitting a metal—not metal-and-plastic—colander inside a large stew pot. The colander's feet or pedestal must be tall enough to keep the vegetables above the boiling water. The trick is to make sure the lid fits nice and tight, or else the steam escapes, and that's what you don't want.

Prepare the potatoes separately: wash thoroughly, then either boil them until just before they are soft or microwave them on high for about 10 minutes, and then set aside. You'll add them to the steamer later.

Bring the water in your steamer to a high boil while you wash the rest of the vegetables and cut them into bite-sized chunks. Set veggies on the steamer rack, and very carefully, place in the pot over the boiling water. Reduce heat a tad and cover. Steam for about 10 minutes; then, very carefully again, remove the cover and add the potatoes, and pepper or paprika to taste. Replace the cover and cook for about another 5 minutes. Then remove the cover and test for tenderness. When you are happy with the tenderness of the vegetables, serve with butter (optional) and maybe some more paprika. This dish easily serves 4, but can be expanded to satisfy an entire collective, or uncollective as the case may be, of newly liberated Borg.

THE DOCTOR

Do holograms feast on digital elk? Who cares? I'm sorry. I meant, Who knows? Certainly the Doctor, our Emergency Medical Hologram, does, and I sought him out to find the answer. I never really had to cook for him, so I'd put off this interview for some time. When I got around to it, I found him in sickbay, listening to *Tosca*, and he was a little irritated on being disturbed. When I told him it was for a cookbook and that he'd be quoted in full, his holo-ego jumped at the chance. He told me holograms do eat, if cybernetically obligated, but obviously it had to be holofood, and he then proceeded to give me a lengthy and somewhat incomprehensible description of a hologram's digestive system, having to do with photon synapses, light matrix subroutines, and emitter preferences, but I just cut him off and asked him his favorite meal.

Picardo's Penne

If you like the first-cut fresh asparagus, especially the asparagus on the East Coast that makes its appearance with the coming of spring, you'll love this pasta-veggie recipe.

1 pound penne pasta

1½ to 2 pounds fresh, young asparagus

1 cup pine nuts *or* shelled walnuts

½ red bell pepper, sliced into 1-inch strips

6 to 8 cloves fresh garlic, crushed

½ cup virgin olive oil

coarse-ground black pepper (freshly ground is best) to taste

salt to taste

1 dash crushed dried red pepper

While you boil the water for the pasta, cut off the woody stems of the young asparagus you've just washed, and then cut the tender parts of the shoots at an angle into 1-inch pieces so that they look like green versions of the angle-cut penne. Heat the olive oil in a skillet and stir in the crushed garlic. Cook until the garlic just starts to turn transparent. Spoon out a touch of the garlic-and-olive-oil mixture, heat in a nonstick skillet, and add nuts. Slightly toast the nuts. Add the pasta-sized strips of red pepper to the asparagus and garlic, and sauté for about 5 minutes more to soften the peppers and asparagus. Now add the toasted nuts. Brown the mixture, stirring constantly to spread the toasted-nut taste throughout.

When your water is boiling, cook the penne until al dente and drain. Next thoroughly stir in the asparagus, peppers, and the toasted-nut garlic oil, and serve with a bright barolo or beaujolais and crusty bread. Serves four to six.

Hrothgar's Leg of Elk

" Wyrd oft nefeð unfægne eorl þonne his ellen deah."

Truer words were never strummed in epic poetry, struck on the strings of a kithara, or declaimed from the foot of a mead throne.

But I was surprised when the Doctor told me that the Age of Heros is where and when I would find his favorite meal, a time in Earth history where even as a hologram he strode bravely across the misty moors in the imaginary landscape of Ensign Kim's holonovel *Beowulf,* where he feasted upon roast holographic leg of elk and drank from the mead horn. This is not something I could make on the ship. Where can you get a leg of elk in the Delta Quadrant? You can't; it isn't even in our replicator's memory. We'd have to go seventy thousand light-years away to the Alpha Quadrant, to Alaska, and use our phaser on some hapless wapiti. If you really want to be historical, the ancient Saxons feasted upon boar, but fresh boar's hard to find these days, too. So I examined the memory data from that epic saga, and came up with a roast-leg-of-lamb recipe that comes pretty darn close to what the Doc enjoyed at the *gebeorscipe* with all those mead-mongering, horn-helmeted holo-swains from the Dark Ages.

Here is the Doctor's favorite dish as altered for real people:

8-pound leg of lamb

2 cloves garlic, thinly sliced

6 tablespoons olive oil

2 tablespoons freshly ground pepper

1 tablespoon coarse salt

After preheating your oven to 425 degrees, cut slits into the leg of lamb; work 3 tablespoons olive oil, salt, and 1 tablespoon pepper into the slits; then stuff them with slices of garlic. Brush the lamb with the remaining olive oil and pepper, and roast in oven at 425 degrees for 1 hour, then reduce heat to 375 degrees for an additional 1 hour and 15 minutes. Lamb will be well done. Serve not with wine but with Klingon ale; Guinness, Harp, or Foster's will do. Serves eight.

KES

I didn't have to interview my Kes. Her palate was no stranger to me. From soup to sweets, I knew everything she loved, and I relished cooking for her. When I think of Kes, who is my heart, my soul, my very lung, I become overwhelmed with emotion. I met her, fell in love, lost her to the Kazon, then with the help of *Voyager* rescued her. And now she's gone again. But I always knew she'd leave. Ocampans live only nine years; if we all knew our loved ones would live only that short span of time, how bittersweet would our love be? Kes was like a spring day, only lovelier. And like the long ago days of my youth, she is a memory now. Was our relationship platonic? Romantic? Intimate? It was everything, and when I cooked for her, I put everything good in my being into the meals. And any meal I made specifically for my Kes had to include tubers. The fact is, Ocampans love tubers, the underground parts of some plants. They can be sweet, sharp, poisonous; they are the swellings of underground stems, and they nourish with starch and zest. From water chestnuts to yams, Jerusalem artichokes to potatoes, I scoured the quadrant to satisfy my love's love of tubers.

Jennifer's Good-Karma Lemon Lentil Soup

The trick is to learn how to eat in such a way that your karma goes up while your hunger goes down. One way is to eat only veggies, so that nothing dies because of you. Here's a Middle Eastern soup I make that is guaranteed to give you a karma boost with every spoonful.

>   1 cup lentils
>
>   6 cups water
>
>   1 medium white potato, peeled and cut into small cubes
>
>   1 cup chopped celery
>
>   1 cup chopped Swiss chard
>
>   3 tablespoons olive oil
>
>   ¼ cup chopped parsley
>
>   ½ teaspoon black pepper
>
>   ½ teaspoon cumin powder *or* 1 pinch whole cumin seeds
>
>   ½ cup lemon juice
>
>   kosher or sea salt to taste

After rinsing the lentils, bring the 6 cups of water to a boil in a large pot. Add the rinsed lentils and cook for 45 minutes or until they're very tender. In a skillet, fry the potatoes in the olive oil, sprinkled with the pepper, for 10 minutes; then add celery and fry for another minute or 2. Add this to the lentils and cook for 15 minutes. Next add the Swiss chard, parsley, and cumin, and cook for another 15 minutes. Next add the lemon juice and salt to taste, and then serve. Serves four to six.

Jennifer Lien's Potato Salad

My character, Kes, grew potatoes in her garden, but I also enjoy them in real life. My favorite is a red potato salad/egg salad combination that's light on mayonnaise but spiced with dill pickles and mustard. It's fresh and tastes like summer.

3 pounds red potatoes, boiled with their skins on and cubed

8 medium or large hard-boiled eggs

4 stalks celery, thinly sliced

1 large Bermuda onion, diced

2 dill pickles, as fresh as they come, chopped

1 cucumber, cubed

1 cup mayonnaise or light mayonnaise

1½ tablespoons Dijon *or* Polish mustard

¼ cup pickle juice

¼ teaspoon dried dill

paprika to taste

In a small bowl, mix mayonnaise, mustard, pickle juice, dill, and four diced boiled eggs. Refrigerate for 2 hours. In a separate bowl, combine cubed potatoes, two chopped eggs, thinly sliced celery, diced onion, chopped pickle, and cubed cucumber. Pour mayonnaise mixture over potato combination and toss well. Slice the remaining eggs and arrange the slices across the top. Sprinkle with paprika to taste and for color, and serve. Serves six.

Ocampan Potato Salad

I was fooling around in my quarters one night, working with an ionic pluto-tele-receptor, a device that disencrypts all kinds of ancient transmissions and then displays them on an orbit monitor. You wouldn't believe the things that are out there! I've spent hours watching the oddest stuff that kept me entranced! But something from the Earth's late–twentieth-century television broadcasting format particularly intrigued me, a linear, comic, two-dimensional tale called a "sitcom" with the title of *Benson*. Very amusing, especially a character named "Pete." What a handsome, amusing, intelligent person! Another player struck me as well, the one who performed the character of "Clayton." A very solid performance. Anyway, one night I happened upon an event, a documentary, about Scandinavia, a small country on Earth over four hundred years ago, and the people there were all blue-eyed with platinum tresses. They reminded me so much of Kes! I wondered if somehow the Ocampans had some ancient connection to this blond race (called Swedes). I decided to make a meal for Kes that originated from this land, just to see if it would tantalize her memory buds. It's called Swedish potato salad, and Kes loved it.

4 cooked medium-sized potatoes, sliced, cold

2 cooked beets, cut in strips

1 head lettuce

½ teaspoon vegetable oil

2 egg yolks

salt and pepper to taste

½ teaspoon mustard

2 tablespoons chopped fresh parsley

½ teaspoon sugar

2 tablespoons vinegar

¼ cup light cream

To prepare, wash the lettuce and dry it; then cut it into strips and add it to the cut potatoes and beets, mixing them all up in a salad bowl. Make the dressing in another bowl by adding the salt, parsley, mustard, and sugar to the egg yolks. While stirring or beating, slowly add the oil, the vinegar, and then the cream, in that order. Pour the dressing over the salad and toss it about. Always make sure to keep eggs chilled, and to prevent spoiling, and possible food poisoning, this dish should be kept chilled, especially in hot climates, like Vulcan. Make six servings.

Hatana

Here's a Taresian dish that Harry Kim liked, so I served it to Kes, who also became fond of it. I came to find out, mainly from Harry, who had a very close relationship with the Taresians, that yams, the basis for *hatana*, are a very healthy food for women. I wanted my Kes to be nothing but healthy—well, healthy and faithful.

> **4 medium-sized yams, scrubbed and cut in half**
>
> **½ cup (1 stick) butter plus 6 tablespoons (¾ stick) melted**
>
> **1 teaspoon cinnamon plus 4 tablespoons for topping**
>
> **1 teaspoon allspice**
>
> **1 teaspoon nutmeg**
>
> **1 teaspoon cardamom**

Preheat oven to 375 degrees and bake yams in a shallow baking pan for at least 45 minutes. Add ½ cup butter and test yams for doneness, then bake as needed for another 10 to 15 minutes. Alternatively, you can cook your yams in a microwave on high for 10 minutes. Then rotate, add melted butter, and cook for another 5. Test for doneness.

Lightly mash the yams in their skins with a fork, add remaining butter, cinnamon, and allspice, nutmeg, and cardamom. Serves 4, or make as many as you want and serve them up. To each her own yam.

Varmeliate Fiber or Talaxian Turnip Stew

Plucked from the wintry tundra of northern Talax, this peasant staple is a strongly flavored, earthy standard. I throw in the greens and combine them with other veggies and Lonian lamb broth (Lonian lamb is not an animal, but a stalk that secretes a palogideous fat that is remarkably similiar to the juices from cooked Sitorian sheep).

Simple stewed turnips in broth will suffice to tempt even the most stubborn of eaters.

1 pound young turnips with stalks removed, scrubbed and peeled

4 cups vegetable bouillon

¼ cup lemon juice

¼ cup apple vinegar

1 teaspoon sea salt

1 teaspoon butter

paprika to taste

Simmer the turnips in the bouillon for at least 15 to 20 minutes. Add lemon juice and vinegar, salt and paprika, and simmer for another 5 minutes. Reserve the broth and serve over the turnips with just a light touch of butter. Serves four.

Jimbalian Fudge Cake

Twice onboard *Voyager* we have celebrated Kes's birthday, and I baked a Jimbalian fudge cake for each occasion. It's not an easy cake to do; a shell of crushed kabeebee nuts surrounds the cake. These nuts come from the tenth moon of Zadon. It's a huge commitment to get there, taking several lifetimes of travel. As far as I know, the only life-form who's ever made it there and back was George Burns. There are two versions of the cake. The first takes nine years to bake; if you're planning to serve this to an Ocampan friend, put it in the oven while they're still in the womb, and be prepared to serve it at the funeral luncheon! The other version is the one I served on *Voyager,* and it's Kes's favorite. Like I said, it is a tough cake to make, but I believe one should go to any length to please one's sweetheart.

The easiest way to make a good fudge cake is to use one of the many packaged mixes. However, for those of you die-hard enough to make the real Jimbalian fudge cake, here goes:

FUDGE CAKE

2 cups cake flour

2 eggs, unbeaten

1⅓ cups granulated sugar

1 cup milk

½ cup shortening

1 teaspoon baking soda

4 1-ounce squares unsweetened baking chocolate, melted

1 teaspoon vanilla extract

½ teaspoon salt

FUDGE FROSTING

3 1-ounce squares unsweetened baking chocolate

2¾ cups confectioners' sugar

7 tablespoons light cream

¼ cup (½ stick) butter

1 teaspoon vanilla extract

½ teaspoon salt

Preheat oven to 350 degrees and slowly melt the chocolate squares in a small saucepan or, better, in a double boiler. Combine, by sifting if you really want to be old-fashioned, the flour, baking soda, and salt into a mixing bowl. Spoon your solid shortening into a separate bowl along with the sugar, and beat vigorously until the mixture is soft and fluffy. Now add the eggs one at a time, beating after each egg. Add the melted chocolate and blend thoroughly. Now add a measure of your flour mixture, alternating with a measure of milk, until the batter is completely blended. Finally, add the vanilla. Grease 2 9-inch round cake pans and line the bottoms with greased waxed paper. Spoon the batter into the pans, and bake for 30 minutes. Test for doneness by pressing down lightly on the tops of the cake layers after 30 minutes. If the tops spring back, the cake's done. Remove from oven and let cool.

For extra-rich chocolate fudge frosting, melt the chocolate with the butter in a saucepan or in a double boiler. Now, in the same pan, blend the mixture with 2 cups confectioners' sugar, cream, and salt, beating it until it's smooth and creamy. Cook the chocolate mixture over low heat and keep stirring until it begins to bubble at the edges. Now remove from heat and add the vanilla extract and ¾ cup sugar while you slowly beat. Allow to cool while you beat and alternately stir until it's thick enough to spread. After your cake has cooled, remove from cake pans and spread with fudge frosting.

MR. TUVOK

And now Mr. Vulcan, my friend Tuvok. This man could play King Lear with his eyebrow! It's been said he has a very loving relationship with a two-by-four. He walks in his sleep so that he can get his rest and exercise at the same time. If you ask him what time it is, he'll tell you how to make a watch. But I love Tuvok. Sometimes I think my only goal in life is to coax a smile from his dark, somber being. I may as well try to chew without teeth. Don't ask me why, but I need to please him. He was the first member of the crew I met after beaming up, and I quickly learned that a conversationalist he is not. It wasn't easy to learn his tastes, but after the ultimate mind-meld we shared when we became Tuvix, I have a darn good idea. And even now, I'll often seek him out to further my knowledge. Like all Vulcans, he's a vegetarian, preferring foods that are poached, steamed, or lightly sautéed. The best time to approach him is just after he's tended his prize orchids. Then he is most relaxed. What follows are some of his favorites.

Tim Russ's "Tuvok's Quick Red Sauce Primavera"

The trick here is to combine fresh pasta with microwaved frozen vegetables for a primavera sauce that's quick and convenient. I also use a packaged meatless red marinara sauce, the refrigerated kind rather than jarred, because it's fresher. Rigatoni is my logical pasta of choice because it stands up to the meld of crisp vegetables and tomato sauce. Perfect for a dinner for 1 or 2 people.

1 16-ounce package rigatoni pasta, cooked al dente

1 8-ounce package refrigerated fresh marinara sauce

2 cups, approximately, combination frozen broccoli, peppers,
      cauliflower, green beans, and baby peas

1 teaspoon butter

½ teaspoon garlic salt and celery salt

pinch ground pepper to taste

grated Romano or Pecorino cheese to taste

Boil and drain the rigatoni, stir through garlic salt and celery salt with butter, and let stand while you heat the marinara sauce to a slow simmer.

While the marinara sauce is simmering, place the vegetables in a large bowl, add 2 tablespoons of water, and microwave on high in a 700 watt oven for approximately 2½ minutes, stir, and microwave on high for another 1½ minutes.

Stir the vegetables through the pasta; top lightly with marinara sauce and cheese. Serve immediately.

Tim's Special Scrambled Eggs

The secret to my scrambled eggs is the texture. By adding ⅛ cup of whole milk to 2 medium or large eggs, I lighten up the eggs for a pinch of any spices such as parsley, rosemary, or thyme. My typical breakfast is a chicken or turkey sausage, scrambled eggs, wheat toast, maybe a waffle or pancake, and coffee, not Vulcan mocha.

Plomeek Soup à la Neelix

This is the ultimate Vulcan recipe, spoon-fed to Mr. Spock himself by Nurse Chapel. I tried my hand at a *plomeek* recipe for Tuvok once. He said it was too spicy. The next time I prepared it, I left out the Bothan fire beans. There are actually so many variations for *plomeek* soup that I'm thinking of writing a book entitled *Plomeek Soup for the Vulcan Soul.*

For the original *plomeek* soup, you can get that nice orangey hue and deep vegetable fragrance with a delightful variety of Korean squash called kabocha, which you can probably find at Asian groceries or thoroughly committed veggie markets. The texture and tastiness of the soup is provided by white beans, green beans, and zucchini squash.

1 cup of dried white beans

6½ cups water

1 large onion, chopped

1 bay leaf

1 kabocha squash, cut and peeled

½ pound green beans, cut in half

1 small zucchini squash, cut into pieces

½ pound cooked spinach

2 tablespoons minced garlic *or* 2 cloves chopped

1 tablespoon curry powder

1 teaspoon nutmeg

You will need to prepare your beans by covering them with water in a large pot and allowing to soak for approximately 8 hours in order to soften them. Next, drain the beans and in a large saucepan, boil the beans in five cups water with onion and bay leaf for approximately 1 hour or until they are very soft.

Now, add 1½ cups water to bean mixture and add the kabocha squash, green beans, squash, garlic, curry powder, and nutmeg. Cook for at least 30 minutes as the soup becomes a nice healthy orange and the squash becomes tender. Add the spinach and cook for another 15 minutes. This soup is a meal in itself. Serves two to four hearty eaters.

You can also make a much simpler and sweeter version of *plomeek* soup in your electric food processor by blending a 16-ounce can of unsweetened whole pumpkin with a small cooked zucchini squash and a cooked sweet potato until you have a paste. Add whole milk and butter, salt and pepper, to taste, and heat it in a medium-sized saucepan until the flavors blend. Just before serving, add a half cup of light cream and stir through. You can also add cinnamon. Serves four to six.

CAPTAIN JANEWAY

Finally, my captain. I find myself tempted to serve this extraordinary woman a meal of steel, iron, and fire. Steel for courage, iron for strength, fire for determination. Or a roast goose; the goose represented "safe return" to the ancient Native Americans of Earth, a worthy obsession for my captain. Kathryn Janeway is everything good about *Voyager*. To me she is a nourishing, powerful, highly creative leader, skillful, delightful, and wise. I owe my life to her—literally—but she has also given me a home, a community of friends, and a purpose. My gratitude to her is boundless, and try to pour that into the meals I make for her. Captain Janeway has some favorites. She loves hot coffee in the morning and warm pecan pie for dessert. She says, rising to her full Starfleet magisterial authority, that coffee is "the finest organic suspension ever served." The captain has coffee with every meal, sometimes five or six times a day. But for breakfast, besides her coffee, her childhood favorite is basic strawberries with real cream. I make it for her with a little variation on the standard dish.

Kate Mulgrew's Pork Tenderloin

I cook for a crew of hungry boys at home, so I ask my butcher for his best tenderloin cut. When the family's all served, I take care of myself in my own ready room.

1 5-pound pork tenderloin

6 cloves garlic

1 cup seasoned flour

4 ounces English orange marmalade

½ cup Cointreau or sherry

Preheat the oven to 350 degrees. Rub the 5 pound tenderloin all over with a crushed garlic clove, then slice the remaining cloves into slivers. Preseason the flour with salt, pepper, paprika, and oregano, and dredge the meat lightly in the flour. Then stud the tenderloin all over with the garlic slivers by inserting them into the flesh. Place on a rack in a roasting pan on the middle shelf of the oven, and roast at 350 degrees for 1 hour.

While roasting, combine the 4 ounces of marmalade and ½ cup Cointreau or sherry in a bowl and mix. After 1 hour, baste the tenderloin completely with this glaze mixture, and cook at 400 degrees until the glaze assumes a light crustiness about 20 minutes. Pork is ready when only slightly pink in the center. Serves four to six.

Serve with Italian roasted potatoes: peel 2 pounds potatoes and cut into thirds; place in a separate roasting pan with 1 cup olive oil, 1 melted stick of butter, 8 whole garlic cloves, and salt and pepper to taste. Toss thoroughly and cook for 40 minutes at 350 degrees.

I serve this with 2 pounds of fresh wilted spinach on the side—drizzled with lemon juice and olive oil, and a whole head of garlic, minced—and a nice crusty French bread and a bottle of pinot noir. Obviously, this is not a dish I can enjoy in my ready room on *Voyager* because, as Tom Paris will tell you, there's no pinot noir. Serves four to six.

Strawberries and Cream

1 pound fresh strawberries

1 cup light cream

1 teaspoon sugar

¼ teaspoon vanilla extract

You begin with the freshiest strawberries you can find, whether in your own garden or somewhere out there in the Delta Quadrant with the Kazon or the Krenim hot on your tail. If you're preparing this breakfast for your captain or someone else you love, you check each berry for green spots, mold, or a happy little worm or slug that's using it as a temporary residence. Once you've culled any less-than-perfect fruit, gently run water over them to clean; then rinse them again, squeezing them slightly into a bowl, then drop into the bowl. When you're done, you'll have a kind of clear strawberry soup. The trick is to then drizzle the strawberries with the sugar and set them aside for just a little while to let the flavors blend. You will create a light strawberry syrup, which will not only preserve the berries, but also enhance their flavor. You can't let them sit for more than two days, however, or else the sugar will begin to ferment.

To prepare, ladle a heaping portion of berries into a medium-sized bowl, mash them down just a little to release some of their nectar, mix cream and vanilla, completely cover with mixture, stir, and serve with love. Serves four to six.

Talsa Root Soup

I'd like to take credit for this, but Caylem made *talsa* root soup for Janeway.

      2 cups sliced summer squash or zucchini,

      1 8-ounce can unsweetened pumpkin for pie filling, blended in a food processor

      ¼ cup of water

      2 tablespoons light cream

      2 teaspoons ground ginger

      1 teaspoon ground pepper

      salt to taste

While steaming the squash in your homemade or store-bought steamer, blend the pumpkin with 1 tablespoon light cream in a food processor and then heat in a medium saucepan with ¼ cup boiling water. Add steamed squash and stir through for 15 minutes. Add ground ginger and pepper, cook for 5 more minutes. Add 1 tablespoon cream, salt to taste, and serve. Serves six.

Welsh Rarebit

After I learned that Janeway's grandfather prepared this dish for the captain when she was a child and that she loved it, I studied how to prepare it. Thousands of light-years away from Earth in the Delta Quadrant, this is a dish that reminds her of home, so I learned all I could about it. I also learned that it was "rarebit," not "rabbit," and that it was really a glorified cheese casserole.

Everybody will tell you how to make this dish. You can make it according to the Anglo-Saxon method with beer or ale. You can make it with heavy (double) cream, light cream, or whole milk. You can also make it with a reduced fat milk, but it's not going to be as tasty. You can also substitute your handy microwave oven or stovetop saucepan for the requisite double boiler that everybody says you have to use when you're melting cheese.

⅛ cup (¼ stick) butter

2 cups coarsely grated sharp cheddar cheese

1 tablespoon Dijon *or* hot Polish mustard

¼ teaspoon paprika *or* cayenne pepper

1 teaspoon Worcestershire sauce

1 egg yolk, carefully separated from the white and slightly stirred

½ cup light cream *or* ¼ cup whole milk and ¼ cup light cream

salt to taste

In a microwave oven or on the stovetop in a saucepan or double boiler, melt the butter carefully and add the cheese. Stir as the butter and cheese melt into a fine sauce, and then add the mustard, paprika or cayenne, Worcestershire sauce, and salt to taste. Stir to blend and add the cream or milk-and-cream combination and stir until the mixture is hot and smooth. Finally, remove from heat or microwave and stir in the egg yolk until it is completely blended. You can serve this over toast points, which is how Captain Janeway likes it, or a crusty bread. Makes four to six servings.

Asparagus with Hollandaise Sauce

Asparagus is the captain's most favorite food in the whole universe, she once told me when those awful body-snatching fiends were chasing us through the ship and stole my lungs. I've learned to be a big asparagus fan myself, especially when they're steamed or stir-fried with scallions in ginger and soy sauce. Captain Janeway likes her asparagus plain, however, even though I surprise her by always including hollandaise sauce on the menu. But I never pour it over the asparagus. I serve it on the side instead. For a quick and easy *Voyager*-style blender hollandaise, combine in your blender the following ingredients:

3 egg yolks, carefully separated from the white (If you try to make this with any egg white, you get meringue)

2 tablespoons fresh or bottled lemon juice

1 teaspoon Louisiana-style hot sauce

1 dash cayenne pepper

sea salt to taste

½ pound (2 sticks) butter

Combine all of these ingredients, except the butter, in the blender and let them sit while you heat 2 sticks of butter (½ pound) in a medium saucepan until they are fully melted. You can also microwave the butter a half stick at a time and keep it on low heat, taking care that you don't scorch the butter. Now blend the ingredients that are in the blender for a few seconds. Pour the heated butter over the mixture in your blender and then quickly blend for another second. You're ready to serve the sauce on your freshly steamed asparagus, prepared just like it was in Seven's seven steamed vegetables. Yields approximately 1½ cups of sauce.

Darvot Fritters

I cooked these sweet Janeway favorites shortly after I first joined the crew. It was so long ago I only dimly remember instructing Ensign Parsons to rotate these delectables until they turned a deep chartreuse. Whatever happened to Ensign Parsons? I wonder if he got lost somewhere, maybe in the twisted corridors of Deck 11. But to the point: *darvots* are fat buttery tulips grown on Nerada. They bloom in the moonlight and their shoots are extremely poisonous—the Neradians tip their torpedo heads with a paste made from *darvot* shoots and uranium. The flower, however, is a rich, dense doughy joy. To make the fritter batter, I mash them with Ubean oat milk and add fuchsia foam crickets—crickets that dance on the waves that break on the shores of Seyrel, a tacky Sakari resort city. I hope you like them; Captain Janeway does. I've caught her stealing into the mess hall late at night to munch on them with a big glass of Kharma berry milk. *Darvot* fritters can be replicated as corn fritters, straight up and simple.

1 cup fresh, frozen, *or* canned corn kernels (drained)

1½ cups canned creamed corn

2 eggs

6 tablespoons bleached all-purpose flour

½ teaspoon baking powder

1 dash each salt and nutmeg

¾ cup (1½ sticks) butter

In your blender, food processor, or with your handheld mixer, combine and mix the corn and creamed corn until the mixture looks like a mash. Beat two eggs, as if you were making an omelette and add them to the corn mash. Now add the flour, baking powder, salt, and nutmeg. Melt your butter in a hot skillet and spoon in 1-inch drops of the corn fritter batter. Fry until brown on one side, turn and fry on the other side. You can serve them, nice and hot, with blueberries or just plain. Yields approximately eighteen 2-inch fritters.

Alan Sims on *Voyager* Food Props

Star Trek food props are basically "monster food." But there are different types of monster food, from what the Klingons eat to what the Krenim put on a banquet table, so nothing can look alike. Klingon stuff must be different from what Neelix makes. Talaxian concoctions are a little bit more adorable, more interesting to look at, in the sense that they're more edible and have a pretty, instead of a harsh, presentation. You make more pretty food in a sense because it's all organic. But the Klingon food—my interpretation is this is stuff that when you look at it, you want to just retch. You just want to vomit looking at this stuff because it's living worms, serpents, and even organs that monsters eat. So the trick to making Klingon food look edible, yet at the same time totally revolting, is you mix and blend it. I use weird, odd things like octopus, huge squid tentacles, and very bizarre-looking dried Asian seafoods. Into this, I would mix edible items, things that you and I could stomach and find palatable, as opposed to a lot of these other revolting-looking things.

Blood Pies

Roxann Dawson (B'Elanna Torres) is eating a mixture of pumpkin pie base, and I used turnip, the root part, sticking up straight to look fibrous and hairy like a root. Around the edges, around the whole ring of the pie and along the edges of the root, I would use a little red fruit-punch concentrate. You have to be careful with food dyes on the set of a production because you can have a bad experience, as we did on the set of *Star Trek: The Next Generation.* An actor put dyed food in his mouth and it discolored his tongue and mouth. He was "dead" on the set because the color doesn't come out that easily and we had to keep on shooting. How can you act when you have to go on to the next scene with a discoloration? So to avoid that, we use a fruit-punch concentrate that you can buy in a regular market. It provides color to the food you're preparing, but it's not a dye. If you're doing *Star Trek* parties at home, you should also avoid food dyes and use the colored fruit punches instead. You can also use cranberry-juice concentrate, or food-process fresh cranberries into a pulp. Anyway, the combination of real food and strange-looking seafood, like octopus or sea slug, is the trick to making anything Klingon.

You can get away with murder by using things like sea slugs or really bizarre foods, but you have to mix it with the more common stuff so it doesn't look recognizable. You have to blend it, so you can do a brown pasta or a little bit of a chicken leg for effect.

Dried Fish or Other Sea Animals

Some of the most interesting things we use for decoration, even though they're completely edible, are dried fish or other sea creatures, Asian delicacies that perform on stage as if they were living animals frozen at the point of death. Because most dried fish that you can buy from an Asian deli or grocery

store actually wear their death masks, they have an alien-creature-like aspect to them that is sensational for the camera. But, here's the fun part: you can use chopsticks, kabob sticks, or any kind of stick-like or, better, sword-like instrument to create a warrior arrangement of animals on a spit, their expressions reflecting the horror of a sudden death.

Using dried fish also has another benefit that I like very much. There is no odor. When you're dressing a set with food, you're working under hot lights as the director sets up his shot, even before the actors take their marks. If you've got food that gives off an odor, by the time the shot is ready, the actors are reacting to the smell of fish or other seafood instead of to what's in the script or the director's mind. Many directors understand that, but they still don't want the props to get in the way of the scene. That's why I try to build a food set with dried fish rather than raw foodstuffs whenever possible.

Using Wrapping Paper for Special FX

In the "Year of Hell, Part II," I had a huge table to dress with all kinds of dried, raw, pickled, and otherwise smoked or spiced foods. In one scene, I had to capture the look of dead, slug-like repulsive creatures that wouldn't conflict

with any of the other repulsive creatures on the table. Yet the entire set had to look like a feast, made even more arcane because these were foods from cultures and homeworlds that were about to be wiped out by the evil Krenim time-shifters. What I found was that by using different kinds of transparent wrap, I was able to reflect the light in different ways, even create a prism or rainbow effect, that made the food look like it was either still alive or giving off a strange radiance. In particular, I used regular old oversized cucumbers on the table, wrapped them in plastic wrap, and lit them from an angle. Because the nature of the entire scene required that the camera focus on specific parts of the table as background, I was able to create lighting effects that made the regular old garden-variety cucumber look like a piece of a huge sea creature out of Jules Verne nightmare.

Heart of *Targ*

When I did heart of *targ* I used liver, raw liver. It wasn't made edible because it was only a prop that wasn't to be eaten. It was first discussed on the show when Riker was sitting at the table in "A Matter of Honor," when he was being indoctrinated into the Klingon culture to get used to it before going to the *Pagh*. That food didn't have to be eaten. The *targ* wasn't eaten at all. So I had the liberty to really get wild and could use some raw "organ food." We did this again on *Voyager* for Roxann, and this time she actually had to eat a piece of it, so at least that portion had to be edible.

Gagh

There was another dish, the famous *gagh,* that always had to look like living worms, especially when the Klingon warriors scooped them up in their hands. Originally the *gagh* were white, not whole wheat, Oriental udon noodles that I dyed brown with soy sauce. As a base, you can use soy sauce, some sesame salad dressing, the salad dressing you use for Chinese Chicken Salad, or the brown stir-fry sauce that really clings to the noodles and acts like a dye but really isn't. *Gagh* is served on a bed of a Klingon vegetable called *gladst*. That can be any strange-looking leafy vegetable like arugula.

My main concern is the look. For me, food in front of the camera is a visual art. If you make these dishes at home, you make them to eat as well as to have a visual effect. I have to create the visual art and then balance it out when it's supposed to be eaten.

Beverages

Drinks are the easiest of all the *Star Trek* food. When we do drinks, we look for the color. We don't look for the texture, but only for the color that shows through the glass or the bottle. For example, for one of the coffees we used on *Voyager,* which was supposed to be overdone and very old, we used a pudding, a thick chocolate pudding that glopped out instead of poured. When Neelix, in the episode "Unforgettable," is serving an almond pudding, we used a vanilla pudding and mix in vanilla and almond extract so it actually had a nut color. It's safe and edible. I can't use actual nuts or crackers on the set when something's being eaten because the food makes noise and gets in the way of dialogue.

That's another one of the challenges: we have to have silent food because crunches or snaps from people chewing crackers and nuts is like a wild sound that the microphone picks right up. And you can't have your actors chewing throughout a whole scene, which is what you have when they eat crackers or nuts. They have to get through lines while chewing and swallowing food. You can't do that, so it's another challenge.

You also can't use spices on the food to be eaten in a scene—hot spices, or any spices for that matter—because an actor can sneeze or have another reaction. There are also food allergies that you have to watch out for on the set. I always go up to the cast member a couple of days before shooting starts, and I see what the script says they're supposed to eat as it's written and ask if they have any allergies to this. For example, also in "Unforgettable" Chakotay's going to be eating ice cream. That's real simple, but maybe someone's allergic to vanilla or chocolate, or even is diabetic. You learn very quickly to address the concerns of food on a set.

Finger Vegetables

Buddha's fingers are vegetables we use because they can protrude out of any dish we make. No matter what episode we're shooting, whenever we have exotic food on a set, we arrange it with Buddha's fingers for the effect. These are Asian vegetables that actually look like fingers. Then there's star fruit, which you can slice and the slices look like stars. We also used ostrich eggs when we did "Basics" the show that we shot in Lone Pine.

Plomeek Soup

Plomeek to me is a celery-based soup. Start with celery stock. I add food-processed carrot for an orange tint and squash for texture. You can also use canned pumpkin blended with food-processed carrot; run light cream through it, and serve it either hot or cold.

Alfarian Hair Pasta

What Ethan Phillips (Neelix) threw on Robert Duncan McNeill (Tom Paris) was angel-hair pasta, very thin, very quick to cook, and easy to combine with other items to make it look bizarre. It takes so little to make so much that it's a very efficient prop food.

Jimbalian Fudge Cake

We didn't bake this ourselves. We went to Hanson's Cakes in L.A. They have natural ingredients and they get the food right to the set.

Klingon Meat

Leg of lamb is the best food for Klingons, in fact for all the warrior-type characters on the show. Leg of lamb is the easiest and most barbaric-looking food because you can only eat it by grabbing hold of the bone and chewing off pieces of the flesh. Leg of lamb comes on good-sized bone. It's not like a chicken bone; it's a thick leg bone. For barbarian-type meat eaters—like those in "Heroes and Demons" or any warriors like the Klingons—the thicker the bone wrapped with meat, the more impressive it looks on the set. What we do for the visual effect is wrap the meat around the bone with the same type of string you use to sew up a turkey after you stuff it. You have to hold the meat

on the bone because when you boil down the leg of lamb, it wants to fall off the bone. So we had to tie it down. The string turns the color of the meat and blends right in, so you can't see it, but it gives a great visual. You just don't eat the string.

With Kazons, for example, we used simple, already-made packages of turkey legs—but the huge legs—you can find in all the markets. You can also go to a local deli for these. You look in the markets for the individually wrapped precooked turkey legs, the monster-sized ones. If you don't want it to look exactly like a turkey leg, because that's very recognizable, you simply shape the meat. You carve off a little bit here and there so it doesn't look so round. Poultry legs have a very distinct shape. If you change it by sculpting the meat, you get a terrific visual, but it's really just plain old turkey.

I would wrap some burlap or some cloth around the bone so they're not just grabbing the bone but something darker and thicker. That also helps to change the shape of the food prop into something more barbaric. Wrapping the turkey leg bone with burlap also works for me on the set because the actors are going to go right into a scene and the turkey can get very sticky and get all over other props like tricorders or phasers. Worse, I don't want a sticky piece of meat hanging off a combadge during a scene. So burlap keeps that from happening.

Garnishes

I use octopus legs whenever I can because you can arrange them on the edge of a dish to look like something crawling out of the food. I like to drape things over the plate because they look like they're growing and living. With Klingon food—best served live—you always want to make sure it looks like it's living. As long as it doesn't have to stay under the lights for a very long time, you're okay. Meat and fish, when they're under the lights take after take, can have a strong odor that gets in the way of a scene. But when you're doing five or so takes of the same setup, the food has to stay in exactly the same position.

If you use raw or live shellfish as garnishes or props, please remember that they are highly perishable foods and spoil very rapidly. They can contaminate the foods they come in contact with, particularly if they're all on the same platter or dish. So please don't leave raw or live shellfish sitting on a table for any extended period of time. Keep them under refrigeration until ready to serve. If you are using them as a garnish, I suggest that you place the food you are serving in a clear bowl, and wrap the garnish around the bowl on another dish or platter, so that they do not touch! You can become sick from spoiled shellfish so extra care must be taken.

I also use regular tofu, sometimes premade fried tofu, for all my soy based dishes. I also like to use kashi for all my alien grain dishes. You can get kashi in any supermarket, follow the package directions, and combine it with something that gives it color or texture. Kashi is a great grain for any occasion.

The Starfleet Computer

In between coming up with new recipes for the crew members and dodging a high-energy tachyon beam every now and then when we encountered some new hostile race in the Delta Quadrant, who tended to look at me more as skeet than as a valued member of the crew, I pursued my research in the Starfleet computer memory banks on the favorite foods of previous crews across the centuries, as far back as the original *Enterprise,* right through the records of Deep Space 9.

If we ever get back to the Alpha Quadrant (or if I start to lactate, whichever comes first), I've promised myself, I will pop over to Deep Space 9 to see what the trading is like and try my hand at dealing with the Ferengi, masters of the deal. In the meantime, drifting along the backwaters of the galaxy here in the Delta Quadrant, I'm glad I took the time to research the culinary delights of Starfleet crews from times past, because otherwise I would never have believed the wealth of diversity represented among those personnel. I feel like I know Captains Kirk, Picard, and Commander Sisko because I can cook for any one of them and send them off to fight the enemy on a full belly—or have a nice nap.

THE CREW OF THE
U.S.S. ENTERPRISE

Life on the *Enterprise*

I was a little surprised at what I found in the records of the first *Enterprise* about Captain James T. Kirk and his companions. They didn't seem to eat that many different foods. Kirk liked his coffee good and strong, and Spock liked his *plomeek* soup and Vulcan mocha, and somebody for some reason put in a year's supply of Dr. Ding Dong's "WOW, That's Incredibly Hot, That Sauce," but between the uneasy peace with the Klingons and hostilities breaking out over the Romulan Neutral Zone every five nanoseconds, the crew on the first *Enterprise* played it pretty much close to their homeworld. Granted, it was still years before the Khitomer Accords with the Klingon Empire, the Federation hadn't met up with the Borg yet, and nobody knew from a Bajoran much less a Cardassian. They played with their tribbles, got into bar fights with the Klingons, and got put in their place by races like the Metrons who said someday, maybe someday, you'll actually wind up like us.

Until I read my Starfleet logs, I always thought that Kirk was more of a fresser than an esser, like his Klingon antagonists, but in reality, the crew of the original *Enterprise* kind of tiptoed around their replicated meals. If anything, Captain Kirk seemed to enjoy a belt more than he liked a thick cut of Kansas City steak. If it took a bowl of Vulcan *plomeek* soup to straighten out Spock's personality, then Captain Kirk was all for it.

Captain Kirk's *Plomeek* Soup

Spock's passion for *plomeek* soup is legendary throughout Starfleet, mainly because he once hurled a bowl of it at Nurse Chapel. All Vulcans love *plomeek* soup. That's why I learned to make it. This version is Captain Kirk's, and it differs from mine in some significant ways. It's a bit creamier and spicier. Whose recipe is more Vulcan, Kirk's or mine? You be the judge. Serve them side by side in a blind taste test.

1 cup finely chopped onion

5 cups chopped celery

4 cups peeled and chopped carrots

1 cup (2 sticks) butter

4 cups chicken broth

½ cup heavy cream (optional)

1 teaspoon ground pepper

salt to taste

In a heavy 8 quart soup pot, sauté the chopped onions very slowly in ½ cup butter. When onions are transparent, add the remaining ½ cup butter and the carrots. Let carrots brown on low heat for approximately 30 minutes. Once carrots have browned, add all of the celery and continue cooking on low for approximately 10 minutes to allow celery to soften. Next add the broth, pepper, and salt, and then stir through. Cover and let soup simmer for approximately 1 hour.

When ready, you can either add cream or serve as is. If you decide to serve the soup with cream, you can either add the ½ cup cream to the pot, stir, and let heat for another five minutes, or you can let your guests spoon the cream into their bowls individually. Serves eight.

Leonard Nimoy's "Kasha Varnishkas à la Vulcan"

This is my favorite dish. The recipe was handed down by my mother, who brought it from her village in the Ukraine, which is a small town in Western Vulcan.

1 cup kasha (whole-wheat or buckwheat groats)

1 egg *or* egg white only as a substitute

2 cups beef *or* vegetable bouillon broth *or* boiled water

1 16-ounce package bow-tie pasta

½ medium onion, finely chopped

1 tablespoon vegetable oil

1 pinch of salt or garlic salt

Heat water or bouillon mixture to rolling boil, then keep on low heat at a slow boil. Sauté onion in oil until just transparent and set aside. Separate egg white from yolk. Stir kasha and egg white into a medium-sized bowl then pour mixture into a heavy saucepan, stirring constantly until the particles separate. Add the bouillon broth or boiling water and salt to taste. Stir the mixture, cover tightly, and reduce heat to simmer for 10 minutes. Cook the bow ties in boiling water until soft, drain and set aside. After the liquid has all been absorbed, mix the kasha with the cooked pasta and sautéed onions and serve. This dish is particularly delicious when served with pot roast gravy. If you want to stay traditionally Vulcan vegetarian, you can make a brown mushroom gravy and use that instead. Serves four.

Gala Apple Pie

When the *Enterprise* visits a place where no human being has gone before, Captain Kirk finds himself in a real pickle after he bounces the ship off the energy barrier at the edge of the galaxy and, in the process, gets his best friend, Lt. Commander Gary Mitchell, zorched with an unknown energy surge that mutates him into something that even Spock wants killed. Poor guy, that Gary Mitchell. But before his eyes began to glow, and his psychokinetic powers extended to the operations of the *Enterprise,* Lt. Commander Mitchell enjoyed biting into a fresh, snappy, Gala apple, just like you'd find in California's vast apple orchards. Gala apples are also very much like the Kaferian apples that Mitchell once created on Delta Vega.

Let's talk about pastry crusts. Sure, you can make your own, whip up the ingredients in an automatic bread machine, and then roll it out on a sheet. Sure you can do that. You could also try to make your gums bleed with your tongue. I mean, do you have all day? I suggest you purchase one of the scores of ready-made pie crust mixes from the store or one of the prebaked crusts. After that you should prepare the following ingredients:

6 cups Gala apples, peeled, sliced, and cored

½ cup sugar

1 tablespoon cornstarch

1 tablespoon light cream

½ teaspoon cinnamon

¼ teaspoon vanilla extract

Preheat oven to 450 degrees. Cover apples with water, boil, and cook for about 45 minutes or until they are very moist and soft. Drain. Combine remaining ingredients and mix into the soft apple filling. Next prepare your packaged or prebaked crust in a pie tin and spoon in the apple filling. Moisten edge of crust, cover with another layer of crust, pierce top crust with fork, and bake pie at 450 degrees for 10 minutes. Reduce heat to 350. Bake for an additional 35 to 45 minutes, depending upon your oven. After 35 minutes, check crust for doneness.

Vulcan Apple Pastry

While we're on the subject of apples, you can adapt Gary Mitchell's Gala apple pie or Granny Smith apple pie—or Kaferian apple pie, if you can get your local supermarket to import Kaferian apples from Delta Vega—into a hand-sized little pastry your favorite Vulcans will adore as a quickie hot breakfast or, at room temperature, as a school lunchbox treat.

They make great afternoon snacks, too, if your kids have to go from school to a team practice or to an after-school program. If you're running around from the office to the supermarket to the athletic field to pick up kids, these make a great snack for you. And they're great between classes or labs on a particularly grueling day when the wind is howling off the lake and you've got to turn in notes that make absolutely no sense to you or to anyone else in your group. They're Vulcan. Think of them as little bites of logic in an otherwise chaotic universe.

Just as with Gary Mitchell's Gala apple or Kaferian apple pie, you can use a packaged crust as your shell, unless you want to bake the crusts yourself. Your list of ingredients includes the following:

4 cups of Gala *or* Granny Smith apples, peeled, sliced, and cored

¼ cup light brown sugar

1 egg, beaten

¼ cup melted butter

1 tablespoon fresh-squeezed *or* bottled lemon juice

1 cup heavy cream

1 teaspoon cinnamon

Preheat your oven to 375 degrees. Line the cups in a greased 2-inch muffin tin with individual muffin-sized shells of crust. Now pour in your sliced Gala apples—or Granny Smith apples, which are snappier and hold up well to spending all morning in a lunchbox or brown bag—into the individual shells, filling them just ¾ full. We need room for the apples to expand. Mix the egg, butter, lemon juice, brown sugar, cream, and cinnamon together, and pour the mixture over the apples. Moisten the edge of the crust and cover each muffin cup with another layer of crust and bake for about 40 minutes or until the top crust is golden. Chill in your refrigerator before you wrap them up in foil for your away mission, or you can serve them still warm. Be careful, however, of serving hot pasties, because the filling, if not given time to cool, can be too hot. Served warm or chilled, Vulcan apple pasties are a great dessert, breakfast pastry, or healthy snack. Yields twelve.

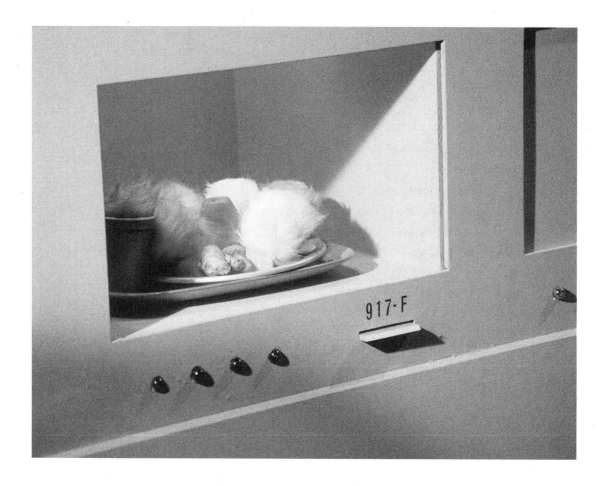

Quadrotriticale Bread

Here's something I researched long and hard in Starfleet records because it's always been such a mystery to me. Just what is quadrotriticale, really? Certainly Federation Undersecretary of Agricultural Affairs Baris knew that the especially hardy grain was a lifesaver. The hybrid blend of wheat and rye, particularly resistant to all kinds of blights and diseases, could save the population of an entire planet or even a solar system. So when the Klingon spy, Arne Darvin, posing as an assistant to Undersecretary Baris, poisoned the quadrotriticale to undermine the Federation's rescue mission, you knew the stuff had to be valuable. Poor tribbles. For furry little creatures that reproduced, purred, and gave out nothing but love, except to Klingons, dying from poisoned quadrotriticale was a fate they didn't deserve. Maybe that's why I've always had a soft spot for tribbles and, as a cook, for the grain they consumed with such passion.

Have a tribble party with your own bread replicators by making a triticale bread. Getting the flour won't be easy because most stores don't carry the specialized product. You'll have to find it in one of the many bread-machine catalogs currently available. If you can't find it, here's a straight-up recipe for a bread machine rye-and-wheat bread that will approximate what Captain Kirk's own quadrotriticale bread, with Rigelian butter, may have tasted like. It's a bit odd, but then so was Darvin.

This is a basic recipe for a one-pound loaf that you can modify for any automatic bread machine, along with optional ingredients for the different versions I like to prepare. In my twist, I use sesame oil, by the way, instead of vegetable oil or olive oil, to give my bread a snappy Bajoran flavor—just the way you'd find it, I'm told by those who know, at Quark's Bar, Grill, Gaming House, and Holosuite Arcade (we'll just call it Quark's)—on Deep Space 9. If you want an *Enterprise*-D variation, the kind favored by Commander Troi, you should use olive oil and maybe throw in 1½ cups of pressed black olives complete with their juices.

> 1 cup water
>
> 1½ tablespoons sesame oil *or* olive oil
>
> 1½ tablespoons honey *or* dried honey sweetener
>
> 1 cup unbleached all-purpose flour
>
> 1 cup whole-wheat flour
>
> 1 cup rye flour
>
> 2 tablespoons powdered nonfat dry milk
>
> 2½ teaspoons active dry yeast (breadmaker's yeast)
>
> 2 teaspoons each chopped black olives, pine nuts, rye seeds,
>   rosemary needles (combined, optional)

Following the instructions for your bread machine, combine all of the ingredients, except any olives or nuts, in your bread machine's baking pan. Some machines require you to add the dry ingredients first and oil and water afterwards. Follow those instructions. When the ingredients are combined, follow the normal baking instructions for your machine, making sure that if you are adding olives, nuts such as pine nuts, rye seeds, or even rosemary needles, you add these to the fruit and nut dispenser according to your machine's instructions or toward the final half-hour of the baking cycle.

As an alternative to using a bread-machine recipe, you can also mix any whole wheat and rye flours in the "quick bread" mixes you can find on supermarket shelves, which don't require an automatic bread machine and can be baked in a regular or even a toaster oven. Each product has its own baking instructions. I suggest you follow the instructions for the whole wheat bread, even though you will be baking with half whole wheat flour and half rye flour to achieve that pungent yet winsome quadrotriticale taste that so intoxicated Kirk and the *Enterprise* bridge crew; everybody, that is, except Darvin and the Klingons, particularly after Scotty beamed the whole mess of tribbles onto the departing Klingon warship.

James Doohan's "Scotty's Lemon Chicken"

Here's one quick, light, dish from the engineering deck of the *Enterprise.*

> **1 pound boneless, skinless chicken breasts**
>
> **1 medium-sized fresh lemon**
>
> **¼ cup chopped onion**
>
> **1 cup asparagus or broccoli, chopped into small pieces**
>
> **1 cup dry white wine**
>
> **1 teaspoon cornstarch**
>
> **salt and pepper to taste**

Cut the chicken into bite-sized pieces and sauté with onion over a medium/high flame in a large heavy saucepan or Dutch oven. After onions

begin to turn transparent, squeeze the lemon juice into the mixture and continue to sauté. Add salt and pepper to taste. When the chicken has browned, add white wine, cover, and simmer for 15 minutes. Add fresh asparagus or broccoli pieces, cover, and simmer for an additional 8 minutes or until the vegetables are just done. You don't want them too soft. Thicken the sauce mixture by removing ½ cup of cooking liquid to a small bowl and add cornstarch. Stir constantly until fully blended. Then add the cornstarch mixture back to the pan a tablespoon at a time until thickened.

Serve over or alongside Alfarian hair pasta, angel-hair pasta, or rice for a quick lunch or dinner that serves 3.

Haggis

"Ye Pow'rs wha mak mankind your care,

And dish them out their bill o' fare,

Auld Scotland wants nae skinking ware,

That jaups in luggies;

But, if ye wish her gratefu' prayer,

Gie her a haggis!"

—ADDRESS TO A HAGGIS, ROBERT BURNS

Scotty had his food slots, but then the *Enterprise* didn't have a master galley chef like Neelix to pull them through their darkest moments. When those stone-hearted Excalbians conjured the heroes and villains to join Kirk and Spock in their great battle against evil, had Scotty been forced to prepare a special meal for Terran President Abraham Lincoln from scratch, no doubt he would have thought seriously about hamburgers, or lambburgers if the wool wouldn't always get stuck in your teeth. If it does, knit a scarf.

I don't have the luxury of replicators, and neither do you. So were I to prepare a ceremonial meal for some claymore-wielding, bagpipe-blowing, tartan-flying ancestor of Lt. Commander Montgomery Scott or Captain Janeway, I'd have to find some young but unfortunate four-legged woolly creature wandering around the surface of one of our many class-M Delta Quadrant planets, beam the wee bairn of a beastie up, and prepare it for the champion's portion.

There are so many different ways of making a haggis and so many different compositions of ingredients that entire clans might feud over whether to mince the tripe or serve it in large duodenal or jujenal sections, Klingon style. Maybe the Fitzgibbons include just a taste of lungs (what the Scots call "lights") and the MacHughes want the whole shebang. From my Starfleet computer records I was able to retrieve the standard recipe from an old Middle Scots primer. I don't read Middle

Scots, so if this dish tastes more like Chow Fon from a twentieth-century Earth neighborhood in a city in the northeastern United States, blame Tom Paris and not me. You, however, should feel free to modify this recipe to fit the likings of your own clan.

> **1 sheep's big stomach bag**
>
> **1 sheep's little stomach bag**
>
> **1 sheep's heart**
>
> **1 sheep's set of lungs**
>
> **1 sheep's liver**
>
> **½ pound beef suet**
>
> **3 cups John McCann's Irish Oatmeal *or* Quaker regular oatmeal**
>
> **(dinna use instant)**
>
> **2 cups sea salt or coarse kosher salt**
>
> **2 teaspoons coarse freshly ground pepper**

Either from your butcher or from the manager of the supermarket meat section, get yourself the bag of a sheep's large stomach along with the smaller bag. Make sure to leave the windpipe and esophagus from the small bag attached throughout the entire preparation and cooking process until it's time to mince the small bag. This is part of the fun. Also buy the sheep's liver and the heart. This already sounds Klingon, doesn't it? As you might have guessed by now, wash everything as thoroughly as Talaxianly possible—and the Talaxians are a very clean race. These stomach bags and their adjacent organs require not only washing, but a complete sterilization. So you run them under cold water for as long as it takes to get the blood, loose sections, and food drained off. Next, boil two bags, heart, lungs, and liver to get any scum and crud to float to the top. Skim the water and boil some more. You must do all this without breaking the large bag, because that's the whole point of haggis—ever see a bagpipe? Now let them cool, and rinse in cold water again. Now it's time for a gentle scraping to clean the inside and outside of the bag. When the bag is clean, it's time to salt it. Place in large bowl, cover with water and the salt. You do this by letting it sit in heavily salted water for at least twenty-four hours. I've heard tell of Scots way back when who had their entire pantries filled with salting sheep bags because salt is a great preservative. You must also wash the lungs, heart, and liver in cold water. If you are not immediately preparing the dish, refrigerate until ready to use.

On the day you wish to prepare and serve the haggis, to begin, boil the lungs, heart, liver, and the little stomach bag in a large soup pot, the kind you'd use to boil lobsters or make a week's worth of bouillabaisse, with just enough water to reach the brim during the boil without boiling over the side, for between 1½ and 2 hours. Drape the windpipe over the side of the pot, and place a large cup to catch any drippings, so that any remaining crud on the inside of the lining will vent. Examine the windpipe "exhaust" hanging over the edge of the pot for what you suspect might be lingering dirt or any other material from the boiling organ. When the windpipe vent is pure and the organs seem tender, remove from heat and allow them to cool. Keep the liquid because you will use some of it later.

After the organs have cooled, pare away any remaining skin, gristle, and the windpipe itself. Make sure that the liver, heart, little bag, and lungs are completely cooked. If they are not, you'll have to reboil them until they're thoroughly cooked. If they are done, grate as finely as you can about ⅓ of the liver which is all you will use. Next finely mince the heart, the little bag itself, and the lungs. Now, chop the ½ pound of beef suet finely as well. Set these aside.

Follow the cooking instructions on the package for toasting the rolled oats or oatmeal. Or simply toast them on a flat baking sheet in your oven or in your toaster oven at 350 degrees for about 5 minutes until they get brown, but not burnt. When they are toasted, mix the oats with the suet, grated liver, heart, lungs, small stomach bag, the remaining ½ cup coarse salt, and ground black pepper. Add some of the water in which you boiled the organs and slowly stir into a soft, almost hamburger- or turkey-stuffing-like texture. Then stuff the mixture into the stomach bag up to about two-thirds full. Like turkey stuffing, the organs and oatmeal expand as they cook, and you don't want them to explode out of the stomach bag during cooking. Once you've stuffed the bag, sew it up with strong thread, just the way you would a stuffed turkey ready for the oven.

In a large soup or stew pot, set a metal rack and put the stomach bag, which is now your haggis, on the rack. Cover the haggis with cold water and bring to a boil, reducing heat to a rolling boil for 3½ hours. As the haggis boils, you'll want to pierce the bag to vent.

After 3½ hours, the haggis should be done and should be served immediately, straight up, just as it is. Serves six. You might also want to play a bagpipe, read aloud from Sir Walter Scott's "Marmion," or recrystallize the dilithium crystals while the *Enterprise* is about to burn up in the outer atmosphere of some dreadful demon planet at the edge of the quadrant and Captain Kirk screams over the ship's communicator that you've been fired.

Haggis Lite

Haggis is as much a commitment as it is a meal. If you don't have a week to prepare your haggis for the gathering of your clans, or simply don't want to go around asking your supermarket manager to save you the stomach bags of sheep, you will probably like my recipe for haggis lite. You replace the stomach bags with cheesecloth and replace the heart, lungs, and small stomach bag with liver and precooked tripe, for a less intense but interesting meal. You can get precooked tripe from your supermarket or follow the package directions for preparing it yourself. You will need the following:

½ pound single piece of liver

½ pound cooked tripe

4 ounces chopped beef suet

4 ounces Quaker quick-cook oatmeal

½ cup chopped onion

salt and black pepper to taste

Boil the liver in a saucepan for 15 minutes with just enough water to cover it, then grate it or put it through a mincer or chop it into tiny pieces. Do the same with your cooked tripe. Reserve the water in which you boiled the liver. Mix the liver and tripe in a medium-sized bowl with the oatmeal, suet, and onion; add some of the water you've reserved to soften the mixture. Season with salt and pepper to taste and knead the mixture into a mound. Stuff it into a cheesecloth bag and tie the bag closed to prevent spillage. Boil for 2 hours. Serve immediately, yields four to six servings, without the bag, of course.

Cup-a-Haggis

Use the leftovers from haggis lite to make an instant Bovril-like pick-me-up with a Klingonesque edge. Take leftovers from your ceremonial Scots, or Scotty's feast, and freeze them in ice-cube trays. When they're good and frozen, pop them out into freezer bags and store forever in your freezer. Whenever you want a quick haggis fix, take a cube out of your freezer and put it in a microwavable mug, throw in a beef bouillon cube or a single-serving envelope of freeze-dried beef bouillon and 6 ounces of cold water. Defrost in your microwave, usually on the "defrost" or $\frac{1}{3}$ power setting for about 1 minute. Then microwave on high for 1½ to 2 minutes, depending upon your microwave, to bring it to a boil. Let it cool a little, lest you sear your lips off, and enjoy. Double the microwaving time for more than one serving.

As a general rule, food leaving your microwave is extraordinarily hot and can burn. This is especially important to remember when kids are using the microwave. So always, *always,* allow foods and the plates or dishes they sit on to cool before touching them.

Dr. McCoy's Tennessee Smoked Baked Beans

Sitting around the campfire at Earth's Yosemite National Park, Dr. McCoy cooked up his old family Tennessee recipe for smoked baked beans. As McCoy said, smacking his lips the way country doctors were wont to do on planet Earth hundreds of years ago, "You can't replicate these, Jim. They have to be simmered low and slow."

Another family secret that Bones McCoy could have revealed was that the secret ingredient in Tennessee smoked baked beans was a hefty pour of either Tennessee whiskey or Kentucky bourbon. Different tastes for different states. If you're serving this dish to your family, however, and are not out in one of the great national parks on Earth, you probably won't want to include the booze—nor should you—but you can add a down-home Smoky Mountain taste with a product called liquid smoke. It's basically water and natural smoke flavor, and there are several brands of it.

You also have to decide whether you want to soak the beans yourself—the basic old-fashioned method—or use one of the many varieties of presoaked, precooked, canned, or ready-to-cook beans. Basically, you can make a baked bean recipe from canned pinto or red beans in about 30 to 45 minutes—making sure you drain and rinse the beans—and these will function as a happy side dish. But the more "from scratch" you prepare your McCoy's Tennessee Smoked Baked Beans, the richer and fuller the taste. The great part about any baked bean recipe is that there are so many varieties of beans, from-scratch to quick-cook, and you have your choice. Here are the basic instructions for Dr. McCoy's Tennessee Smoked Baked Beans in from-scratch and quick-cook recipes and in an alcoholic and a nonalcoholic pair of versions.

2 cups dried pinto, red, *or* kidney beans

½ pound bacon, salt back, or Canadian bacon, coarsely chopped

1 small white onion *or* ¼ large Bermuda onion

2 tablespoons molasses

2 tablespoons honey

1½ tablespoons mustard seed

½ cup Tennessee whiskey *or* Kentucky bourbon

2 cups beef bouillon stock *or* water from the boiled beans

1 tablespoon Worcestershire sauce

2 teaspoons sea salt

1 teaspoon liquid smoke

First soak for 2 hours, drain. Then cover with water and boil the red, kidney, or pinto beans for about 2 hours, reducing heat to a low boil for the last ½ hour, until they are tender. Preheat your oven to 300 degrees. Fry the bacon or slightly brown the salt back. Drain the beans, but reserve the bean stock if you are not going to add beef stock. Add the rest of the ingredients to the beans and pork, add back half the bean stock, and stir thoroughly. Bake for 1 hour at 300 degrees in a heavy covered deep pot, then reduce heat to 200 degrees and bake for another 8 hours, making sure they don't become too dry. For the last half hour, add some of the beef bouillon or bean stock and increase heat to 275 degrees.

This is a great electric Crock-Pot dish. Simply replace the oven with your Crock-Pot, and you can prepare the ingredients the night before, set them up in the Crock-Pot in the morning, and come home to fresh baked beans.

For vegetarian baked beans, don't use bacon or pork and don't use beef bouillon. You can use finely chopped green peppers or salted fried tofu. You don't need the Tennessee whiskey or Kentucky bourbon, of course. Simply replace it with a tart apple-cider vinegar. This dish is especially tasty if you make the vinegar yourself from apple cider that you've let turn to vinegar.

For a quick-cook version, simply replace the beans you've soaked and boiled with 2 16-ounce cans of red, kidney, or pinto beans. Drain the beans and rinse them before adding to other ingredients. After you've combined all the ingredients, you can slow-bake at 250 degrees for 3 hours or bake at 350 degrees for 1 hour. You can still use a Crock-Pot to let it cook slowly all day, in which case you should follow the instructions on your Crock-Pot.

Here's another suggestion for people who have coal stoves or wood-stoves they use for heat. If you prepare the baked beans in a heavy cast-iron pot—no substitutions—grease the pot first and let the beans sit on top of the stove where they can cook all day or all night. I'm told that was how the early settlers in something called "the Ancient West" cooked their beans. It's slower than a good low one and a half–second phaser burst, but tastier, I'm sure. Serves six to eight.

I know about this drink, reputed to have the devastating impact of a photon torpedo. It's celebrated throughout the galaxy as the true test of whether a man, or a metamorph, can stand up at a bar and hold his liquor. The drink was reputed to have been invented by Dr. McCoy. Stop in at any bar or deep space station in the Alpha Quadrant, order a Finagle's Folly, and someone will bore you to death about Dr. McCoy. Except at Quark's, however, where Quark himself will boast that he invented the drink and challenge you to a game of dabo if you don't believe him.

Since you don't have synthehol on Earth, it's probably a good idea to serve one of the many nonalcoholic versions. Here are the varieties in by-the-serving proportions. Simply multiply the ingredients by the number of servings for your parties, adjust for ice and the size of the serving glass, and make sure you don't let the drinks stand around so the ice melts. Do it right and everything else will equal out.

Cherry-Lime Finagle's Folly

8 to 12 ounces club soda _or_ any carbonated water

2 good spritzes (tablespoons) cherry syrup

1 good spritz lime syrup

1 wedge of lemon or orange

This is a carbonated drink. You can replace the syrup and club soda with 8 ounces of cherry soda and 4 ounces of lemon-lime soda. Serve over ice with the lemon or orange wedge.

Lemonade-Orange Finagle's Folly

This is a noncarbonated drink. Start with fresh homemade or store-bought lemonade or lemonade mix or canned or frozen lemonade. You have plenty of products to choose from. For fresh lemonade by the glass, squeeze the juice of 10 medium-sized lemons into a large pitcher for each half-gallon of ice-cold water; add orange and lime slices for color and taste; add 2 cups of sugar, sugar syrup, or an equivalent amount of sweetener substitute; mix; and let sit in your refrigerator for about 1 hour before you serve. To make a Finagle's Folly, add a tablespoon either cherry syrup, store-bought cherry juice or cherry cocktail, or even grenadine, to each glass and top with an orange or lemon wedge.

Fruit-Juice Finagle's Folly

In either a fruit-juice or fruit-drink version of this recipe, you can create many of the same fruity tastes and colors of the carbonated and noncarbonated versions of the drink simply by using fresh, canned, or bottled fruit juices. If you want to use your automatic juicer, you can juice a package of fresh cranberries—these will have more tang and bite than a crisp Autumn walk through the hills around Leonardo da Vinci's house in Captain Janeway's holoprogram—and mix the juice with fresh-squeezed orange juice, adding a splash of store-bought red or white grape juice as a sweetener and either a lemon or orange slice. For a sweeter drink, add one part of cranberry juice to three parts of orange juice with a splash of grape. White grape juice lightens the color; red darkens it. For a darker color and a more tangy drink, either mix the two in equal parts or use the orange juice and a splash of grape as a sweetener for the cranberry juice. To keep a darker red, mix one part red grape juice and one part orange to two parts cranberry. You can play with the flavors to get the exact taste you want and simply multiply the portions for the number of servings.

McCoy's Mint Julep

Leonard McCoy fancied himself to be a southern gentleman, and his favorite drink was a southern staple, an ice-cold mint julep. Whether he really believed what he was reputed to have said, "You can't find anyone who knows how to make a real mint julep in this part of the galaxy anymore," or that complaint was simply apocryphal, I can't tell you. I didn't find it in any of the Starfleet logs, but then the logs don't tell you everything either.

Not wanting to corrupt anyone with the real alcoholic mint julep, I present an "essence of julep" in a by-the-glass recipe for your *Gone With the Solar Wind* get-togethers. It's easy to find the real mint julep, not only in any standard bartender's guide, but in any Junior League cookbook from any locale south of Earth's old capital, in the latter half of the twenty-first century, Washington, DC.

lots of fresh mint sprigs

8 ounces Schweppes, Canada Dry, or Seagram's tonic, per serving

½ cup confectioners' sugar

1 teaspoon Rose's lime juice, per serving

1 dash bitters, such as Angostura brand, per serving

Begin by adding three parts of the confectioners' sugar to one part clear cold tap water to make a sugar solution. Coat your mint with the sugar solution by dipping it in, and set aside to dry. Reserve the sugar solution. Chill individual serving glasses in the refrigerator. You can very lightly coat the rims of the glasses you want to chill with the sugar solution to give them a "Jack Frost" appearance, especially appealing for a hot evening mint julep on your porch or verandah. Coat them first, then chill.

Pour tonic water into individual glasses containing ice and slightly rub the mint leaves in your hand before adding them to the drink. Add the teaspoon of lime juice and splash of bitters to each drink, stir, top off with a sprig of mint, and serve.

Nobody onboard the old *Enterprise* knew what this stuff was except that it was orange and could be served hot or cold. Captain Kirk, Dr. McCoy, and the too-emotional Lieutenant Bailey first tried *tranya* onboard the tiny craft piloted by the strange creature named Balok, who was tricked out of his shoes by Captain Kirk's corbomite bluff. Tom told me that what came to be known in the Starfleet logs as Kirk's corbomite maneuver is now a standard academy exercise. I think I noticed Captain Janeway employing versions of it once or twice, especially when she had to gain the cooperation of the Borg to allow us to pass freely through their space.

Balok happily served the visiting Kirk, McCoy, and Bailey *tranya*, and over an Earth century later, the drink wound up in Quark's, where Lieutenant Dax seemed to drink it up with gusto. She saved her relish for Bajoran veggie dogs. You can drink this delightfully refreshing beverage cold, which is how I plan to serve it for Tom's next birthday, or hot, which is how Quark serves it on Deep Space 9. Cold, it's simply an orangeade with some other citrus fruit added for flavor. Hot, it's orange-brewed pekoe or black tea. Here are the recipes:

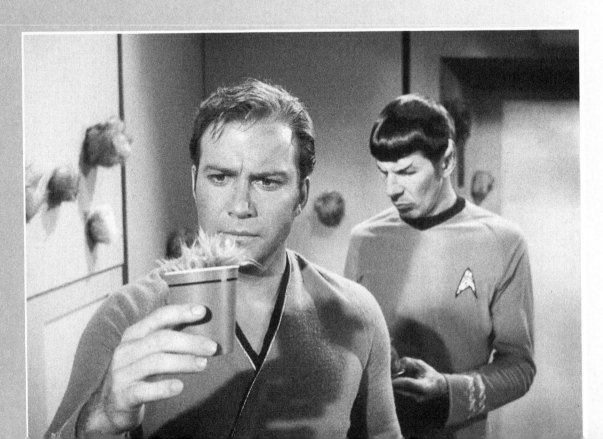

Cold *Tranya*

8 California, Florida, *or* Texas juice oranges

½ gallon ice-cold water

½ cup confectioners' sugar

1 lemon or lime, sliced

Squeeze or use your juicer to extract the juice from the oranges, mix—with as much pulp as you please—with water, add the sugar, and stir. Chill and garnish each serving with a lemon or lime slice. You can also use packaged chilled or frozen orange juice in place of fresh-squeezed, but take it from your old uncle Neelix, nothing tastes better than fresh. Serves eight to ten.

Hot *Tranya*

black or pekoe tea, loose *or* in tea bags

juice of 1 orange for each mug of tea

⅛ teaspoon grated orange rind per serving *or* piece of orange
rind as a garnish for each mug of tea

1 or 2 whole cloves for each mug of tea

You can brew your tea in a cup, with an infuser, a tea ball, or a tea bag, the old-fashioned way. Here's a trick: don't just splash in the boiling water, scald the cups first with boiling water that you then discard. Add your tea then pour in the water. If you have an electric tea infuser or are using a teamaker like Mrs. Tea, follow the directions for the appliance. In any event, you'll find your drink more refreshing if you scald the cups first, before you brew the tea in them or pour in brewed tea.

As your individual mugs of tea are brewing, squeeze one orange per serving, and then add it to the tea after it's steeped. Add the cloves and serve. You can also prepare this by the pot, adding the orange juice and cloves directly to the pot after the tea has steeped and serve individually. I still would top off each mug with a small slice of orange and a clove or two.

Antarian Glow Water

When tribble-trading Cyrano Jones offered to sell the exotic and stimulating Antarian Glow Water, everybody thought it was merely another shot of booze. The bartender himself murmured that he used it for polishing precious gems. How wrong they all were. Let me tell you the secret herb that gives the glow to the Antarians. It's the magic ginseng. I give it even more of a punch by adding ginger. To give your evenings a glow of remembrance, here's how you can brew your own version of Antarian Glow Water, to be served as a sparkling aperitif or a late-night pick-me-up. For each individual 8-ounce serving use:

1 per-serving package powdered ginseng *or* 10 to 15 drops ginseng extract

⅛ fresh whole 1 inch ginger root

8 ounces boiling water

Brew the ginseng and ginger in the boiling water as if you were preparing ginger tea. When the ginseng and ginger are fully steeped, about 3 minutes, strain and pour over ice and let sit for 30 minutes. Mix half-and-half with sparkling water, and serve over ice. You can make any number of servings of Antarian Glow Water, but be careful; this is potent stuff, and the ginseng alone will give you lots of energy. If you want to drink it hot and strong, don't chill the brew or mix with sparkling water. Simply drink it as you would any herb tea. But drink it gingerly; this stuff's not a soporific.

THREE

THE CREW OF THE U.S.S. ENTERPRISE-D

One of the first things that struck me about the *Enterprise*-D as I perused the computer logs was the striking difference between the bridge crew of the *Enterprise*-D and that of the original *Enterprise*. It was as if those early explorers in the Alpha Quadrant were like Earth's first pioneers of the ancient West, rolling out through the Cumberland Gap with Dan'l Boone in the first wagon trains, unsure of what they would find, but tough and resilient enough to take all of what deep space had to dish out and give it back exponentially. The

Enterprise-D was, by contrast, more than a warship; it was a floating biosphere with family residences, schools, recreational facilities, and even a bar. My, how Starfleet had changed since those early days of the first explorers. Sitting in the command chair was no longer the womanizing warrior James T. Kirk, but the diplomatic epicurean, no less the renowned Borg fighter, Jean-Luc Picard.

CAPTAIN JEAN-LUC PICARD

I can't help but appreciate that Captain Jean-Luc Picard was much, much more than just a starship captain; he was a gourmand, a mandarin with exceptionally good taste who loved his Earl Grey hot, his Chateau Picard at fifty-five degrees and his champagne ice-crackling cold. From the ginger tea his tante handed out to all the little children of the vineyard who suffered from the catarrh to his beloved beluga caviar that he stored on the *Enterprise* because the replicated stuff was never as good as the real thing, Picard loved the sublime.

Captain Picard's Breakfast Croissant

Each morning at breakfast with his old friend—and, it turned out when they were in telepathic communication, romantic confidante—ship's surgeon Dr. Beverly Crusher, the captain enjoyed his cup of Earl Grey tea and his breakfast croissant, or, as we Talaxians like to call it, buttered crescent. You can buy your packaged or refrigerated ready-to-bake croissants at any supermarket, of course, and with a pot of fresh-brewed Earl Grey tea, get up in time to watch the sun rise and say to yourself between bites and sips, "It's morning on the *Enterprise*," thus enjoying what the captain and the Doctor enjoy at the beginning of each day in the Alpha Quadrant.

Here's a quick trick to replace the elegant croissant with handy crescent rolls from the market. After you've popped open the refrigerator can, unroll the crescent rolls and spread a pat of butter on the inside. That way, it will bake in its own butter in your oven or toaster oven. You can also add any types of jellies, jams, or spreads prior to cooking, but if you do, you should spread a sheet of aluminium foil over your baking pan so the jelly doesn't stick and make the baking pan impossible to clean. But whether you bake your own refrigerated crescent rolls or use the packaged croissants, do what I do and always serve them piping hot from your galley oven.

You can microwave refrigerated store-bought croissants of course, but you have to be careful because if you overmicrowave them, they'll get very hard and brittle. So instead of just popping them into the microwave, you should splash a little water on them to keep them moist and then wrap each in a paper towel. Microwave for no more than 15 seconds, open the towel to see if they're hot enough, and then replace for another 5 to 8 seconds if they're not to your liking. But in no event should you microwave for more than 30 seconds because you'll overcook the croissant.

Different microwaves heat food differently, too, so you'll have to experiment. Once you get the setting that works for you, you can begin spreading a little butter prior to baking for a creamy fresh taste. It's probably not a good idea to microwave jellies or jams in your croissant, so warm them separately in your oven prior to serving. The trick is to serve everything, including the jellies and spreads, hot or warm, to start off the day just like Picard and Crusher used to in those heady days on the *Enterprise*-D.

Brioche

It's been said that when Marie Antoinette, the tyrannical queen of France, supposedly blurted out, "Let them eat cake," one of the most politically incorrect events in human history, she really said, "Let them eat brioche," but somebody misquoted her. Were you to taste the brioche that I make from Captain Picard's traditional family recipe, you'd be so transported by the heavenly taste that you'd probably agree with me that had Marie Antionette been quoted properly, the French would have never revolted, the guillotine blade would never have fallen, Napoleon would never have risen, the vast Picard vineyards would still have been in the hands of some lazy aristocrat, and little Jean-Luc might never have been inspired to apply to Starfleet Academy. What might have happened to humanity then, I ask, when Q challenged the very raison d'être of the human species in his mock trial to a defender not up to the diplomatic skills of Captain Jean-Luc Picard. If Seven is to be believed, you all would have been assimilated by the Borg.

Here are the ingredients you should arrange on your preparation table for my special, special, albeit tricky, breakfast brioche. Actually, you have to prepare the brioche the night before because the dough takes 12 hours to rise. Once the dough has risen, the actual baking and preparation time is only about 30 minutes. This is actually a fun recipe, because it's a real eighteenth-century recipe updated.

1 package active dry yeast

5 egg yolks

3 eggs

4 cups sifted all-purpose flour

¾ cup softened butter, ¼ cup melted butter

½ cup milk

¼ cup sugar

¼ cup hot, but not boiling, water

1 tablespoon half-and-half

1 teaspoon sugar

1 teaspoon honey

½ teaspoon salt

Preheat your oven to its lowest setting, no higher than 100 degrees. Soften the active yeast in the hot water and let stand for about 10 minutes. While the yeast is standing, scald—simmer in a small saucepan until a thin skin just begins to appear on the top—½ cup of milk. As your oven is warming, your milk is heating, and your yeast is standing, combine the softened butter, ¼ cup sugar, and salt in a small bowl, and then pour the scalded milk into the mixture. Let cool and then stir. Your milk and butter mixture should be lukewarm. Now stir in ½ cup of the flour; then stir the softened yeast, add it to the mix, and begin beating the whole thing with a large spoon. This is the part that Klingons like the best.

As you beat, slowly add an additional 1½ cups flour; then, 1 at a time, beat in 3 eggs. Continue beating with the spoon and add, again 1 at a time, beating through each time you add, 4 egg yolks. (You separate the yolk from the white by cracking the eggshell in two and spilling the white into a bowl while retaining the yolk in the shell.)

Beat the mixture until you've formed a soft dough. Then add an additional 2 cups of flour and continue to beat for at least another 5 minutes. Set the dough aside and butter the inside of a large bowl. This is the bowl the dough will rise in, so it has to be at least twice the size of your original mixing bowl. Spoon your dough into the larger bowl, brush with melted butter, cover with waxed paper, foil, and a towel, and set it aside in a warm place or an oven set to "warm." Check the dough every 10 minutes or so, and when it's doubled in size, remove coverings, and punch it down—another Klingon favorite—to make it denser. Butter the surface, reserve unused portion, cover it again, and set it in your refrigerator to rise for at least 12 hours. You can occasionally punch it down again during the night to make it a bit denser, but you don't have to be obsessive.

After about 12 hours, the dough should be risen and ready. Preheat your oven, or your toaster oven if you're going to knock these off right at the table, again to "warm," no more than 100 degrees. Remove dough from refrigerator, lightly flour either a cutting board or a baking sheet, and use reserved melted butter to lightly coat the inside cups of a muffin pan. Brioche, traditionally, is made up of a top and a bottom half. The bottom half is simply muffin-shaped. But the top—the top is where the real fun begins, because you get to make little brioche hats to delight and tantalize your friends and family.

After you've removed your dough from the refrigerator, coated your baking sheet with flour, and preheated your oven, place the entire wad on the floured board or baking sheet and pull off about ⅔ of the ball. Set the remaining ⅓ aside for the time being. Roll the ⅔ of the dough into small but lightly packed balls, about the size of cocktail meatballs or Swedish meatballs. Someday, if we ever travel back again to twentieth-century Earth, I have to make a stopover in Sweden—I'll take Seven with me for protection—to see what the Swedes are like and why they make those little meatballs that have become so famous throughout the galaxy.

Take the little dough balls and drop them into the wells of the muffin pan. Now it's time to make the tops. Traditionally, I'm told, because brioche is such a noble pastry, the tops are supposed to be crowns. You shape these by rolling the remaining ⅓ of the dough into an equal number of little balls to match those in the muffin tin. I suppose you could have more tops, but they'd spread out on the baking sheet, and it would all be a big formless nebula-like mess. Once you've formed the balls, shape them into cones, which you then insert into the tops of the muffin-tin dough. These can be either dunce caps or crowns. But you can also get a little creative here and form starship or runabout tops, the headpieces worn by Bajoran vedeks, or just about any shape you can think of that doesn't require the services of an architect or a computer equipped with a positronic brain imaging system.

Now cover the entire muffin pan with a linen towel—or a sheet—and set in your warming oven to rise. When the dough has doubled in size—this is why a toaster oven is not a good idea—remove from oven. Preheat oven to 425 degrees, brush each of the brioches with a mixture of one egg yolk, a teaspoon of sugar, and a tablespoon of half-and-half, which will form a nice crust, and bake for 15 to 20 minutes. You can also replace the sugar with a teaspoon of warmed honey or eliminate the sweetener completely. Serve nice and hot with Earl Grey tea, *raktajino,* or macchiato. This makes from 12 to 16 brioches.

For brioche any time of the day or night with no muss or fuss, bake a whole bunch of these goodies and freeze what you don't use, making sure you wrap them tightly for your freezer. When you want a nice brioche, remove one from the freezer, moisten with a few drops of water, wrap loosely with a paper towel, and microwave on high for 20 seconds, check for warmth, and microwave again on high, still covered for no more than 10 seconds. In 30 seconds you'll have a hot brioche for breakfast. If you have a microwave at the office or don't mind room-temperature brioches, you can drop a couple of still-frozen brioches into your lunchbag and, because they will have defrosted by the time you get to work or school, heat them up in a microwave for 10 seconds or just eat them out of the wrapper.

Petrokian Sausage and Klingon Blood Sausage

Things got real muddy for Captain Picard on *Enterprise*-D during one confusing week when both Lwaxana Troi and Alexander Rozhenko teamed up to turn Worf's life into a Klingon test of restraint. Not only would his son Alexander disobey him, not displaying even the slightest sense of discipline, but Lwaxana Troi decided to turn the young man into a freethinker. Klingons aren't freethinkers, take it from me, a Klingon for a day with those crazy Hirogen. So you can see how unhappy Worf was when Alexander wound up naked in a mud bath with Lwaxana Troi.

All this meant something to me when I read that one of the first signs of the ship's failure occurred when Lwaxana's favorite *Jestral* tea, a mild, soothing, and relaxing drink, did not show up in the replicators when Troi asked for it. Instead of tea, she found a plate of hearty Petrokian sausage. This is a dish that I learned to make from Petrokian descendants who migrated to the Delta Quadrant millions of years ago. From dealing with these people, I learned that Petrokian sausage is similar to something the Klingons call "blood sausage or blood pudding," which they traditionally prepared from fresh *targ* blood and spices. You can make this at home even though you probably don't have fresh *targ*. Here's how. You'll need the following:

1 dozen natural sausage casings (You can purchase these from your butcher, supermarket, or specialty grocer.)

2 cups fresh pork blood (This also comes from your butcher.)

1 pound pork fat *or* fatback

2 eggs, beaten

1 cup chopped onions

½ cup heavy cream

1 bay leaf

½ teaspoon thyme

coarsely ground fresh black peppercorns to taste

Gently sauté your onions in a greased medium-sized skillet until they become transparent, but not brown. Set them aside. Mince the fatback or pork fat into large pieces, then fry until it becomes partially rendered. Remove from heat, set aside, and let cool while you mix cream, eggs, thyme, and peppercorns in small bowl. After the pork fat has cooled, add it to the mixture. You don't want to add hot pork fat, because it will curdle the milk and fry the eggs. Stir lightly, and then stir in the pork blood. Fill each sausage casing about 3/4 full and seal by tying a tight knot with butcher's twine or any clean string.

Boil water in a large pot and place your filled sausage casings in a wire basket. Lower it into the boiling water and keep the water at a low boil for 30 minutes, piercing the sausage casings with a long fork to relieve internal pressure that would cause the skins to split. When the sausages are done, you can cook them again on a grill, in a skillet, or over a barbecue. Split them in half first and put the open sides facedown on the skillet or grill.

You can serve these as gyro sandwiches, over udon noodles as blood sausage and *gagh,* or with heavily seasoned angel-hair pasta and a deep bloodred wine.

Coltayin Roots
with Terrellian Spices

When the image of Anna prepared *coltayin* roots for the marooned Captain Picard, she mixed the tuber-like vegetation with Terellian spices. Here in the Delta Quadrant, we don't have Terellian spices, much less *coltayin* roots, so I have to make do. The original virtue of *coltayin* roots was their nutritional value. These things could feed an army of Jem'Hadar, if those guys ate anything other than their "white." The closest equivalent to *coltayin* roots on Earth are yams, which can also feed a small army. I'd bake or roast them, and you can do it in your microwave oven, using allspice or a very mild chutney to replace the Terellian spices.

The yams should be boiled with their skins on for about 30 minutes, split, and tested for doneness. Boiled yams can simply be mashed with a teaspoon of butter and ½ teaspoon allspice and served, or they can be split, buttered, lightly mashed with a fork in their skins with allspice, and baked for 30 minutes at 375 degrees for a twice-cooked yam.

To bake, preheat the oven to 375 degrees, pierce the skins with a fork, and bake for about 1 hour. You can also bake medium-sized yams in your microwave on high, skins punctured, for 15 minutes. After microwaving, allow to cool for about 1 minute, test for doneness with a fork, and microwave for additional increments of 5 minutes until done. Serve split open, buttered, with allspice.

Yams can also be served with a variety of sweet or spicy chutneys according to taste. You can make your chutney, of course, or you can go to the gourmet food section of your supermarket, where you'll find a variety of chutneys.

Alien Insects

One of my toughest challenges was the alien insect implant that infected the officers at Starfleet in "Conspiracy" and came out of their mouths. These are parasites, and we had to create an alien parasite that was in the mouths of the actors, and they had to perform with the prop. I created a kind of puppet. I called them bug puppets. When the bug came out of an officer's mouth, I had just the front part of the bug puppet as a kind of tongue glove. So instead of a hand puppet, this was a tongue puppet. We fitted it around the actor's tongue and had the bug coming off it. So the actor opened his mouth, the bug was on the tongue glove, and it looked like it was coming out. When the bug was supposed to flee, we used CGI—computer graphics—as a special effect. When the bug went in his mouth, it was CGI up to the actor's lips and then we had the back end of the bug puppet on the tongue glove as it went in. I was also the puppeteer when the bug came out of Lieutenant Remmick. I was under the chair when the whole dummy had to split open from the uniform; I had the mother puppet in my hand in that scene and she burst out and all the little babies fled from the mother. I didn't know that it was a fan favorite until I saw it at a *Star Trek* convention.

Also, in "Conspiracy," Riker and Picard are at a table and they're supposed to be served a worm-type food. I got this prop from a bait store in Castaic. These were huge mealworms, a short, stubby thick worm that's very impressive. For the episodes when we do a close-up, and nobody's eating it, we have to get them to move around a lot. So we heat up the dish a little bit and they really start to squirm. When the time came to have Riker eat the worms, I replaced them with Asian rectangular noodles, which I cut, piece by piece, to the same size of the mealworms and dyed with teriyaki sauce or stir-fry sauce, which colored them. I had to play until I got exactly the right shade of the mealworms. And it turned everybody off and was a great success. So I can say that no worms were harmed in the filming of this episode.

—ALAN SIMS

Peach Cobbler

Captain Picard was a big peach cobbler fan, as is Commander Sisko. Picard's peach cobbler was prepared for him by the image of Anna. I suspect that Sisko learned to appreciate his peach cobbler from his father, whose Sisko's creole restaurant in the French Quarter of New Orleans served a peach cobbler that made even grown men cry.

The way I whip up cobblers in my galley is with any basic biscuit dough recipe. The easiest one is probably found right on the Bisquick package. Follow it to make the dough and then set aside. Grease a shallow 9-inch square baking pan lightly with butter and preheat your oven to 425 degrees. Then place half the dough into the baking pan filling the bottom and prepare your peach filling.

> 2 cups peeled and sliced fresh peaches
> ⅓ cup light brown sugar
> 2 teaspoons cinnamon
> 1 teaspoon vanilla extract
> 2 teaspoons granulated sugar

Heat the peaches in their own juices in a medium-sized saucepan over medium heat until they just begin to soften and bubble; add the sugar, cinnamon, and vanilla, and continue to heat. Pour the peach filling into your biscuit-dough shell, cut remaining half of the dough into 1-inch strips, and cover it with strips of dough. You can use the traditional lattice pattern, or be creative! Quickly dust with granulated sugar. Bake for a ½ hour and serve hot, with ice cream or heavy cream on top if you wish.

AFTERNOON TEA

WITH CAPTAIN PICARD

What is teatime on the *Enterprise?* Don't call it high tea in front of Captain Picard because "high tea" is a workingman's supper served after six in the evening that always has a hearty meat dish, such as a Cornish pastie (similar to a South American empanada, but because these goodies are British, they have neither the interest nor the flavor of an empanada), a shepherd's pie (which is a really great concoction of meat and potatoes with ketchup on top), or something meatily similar. Why do they call it "high," as if all the British think they're better than you? The "high" actually refers either to the high-backed chairs common in Yorkshire, where the tradition began, or to the fact that it is served at a regular "high" dining table, versus the "low" buffet tables for afternoon tea. Afternoon tea, which is what we're talking about, is served anytime between two and five in the afternoon and is sometimes referred to as "low tea" because—you guessed it—it's served at a low buffet table.

None of this is actually relevant to how tea is served in the Captain's ready room on the *Enterprise*—or on *Voyager,* for that matter, where Captain Janeway has recently been expressing a private interest in reviving the tradition—because all the tables are low, relatively speaking.

"Earl Grey, Hot"

So who was this guy Earl Grey and how did he and Captain Picard get to know each other? That's what I wanted to find out after reading the replicator logs and seeing that all Picard seemed to drink at breakfast, before bedtime, and at just about every crisis was a cup of this guy's tea. Never one to sit still for a mystery, I investigated what relationship might have existed between Earl Grey and the captain. Guess what? The two of them lived almost six hundred Earth years apart and Earl Grey had nothing whatsoever to do with Starfleet. He was actually Charles, the second Earl Grey, prime minister of a country called England from 1830 to 1834.

It seems that one of the earl's envoys saved the life of an important Chinese mandarin, who rewarded the earl by sending him a delightful tea flavored by the ancient Canton orange. By the time it was marketed in England, Earl Grey tea, as it came to be known, was made with a combination of black teas from India and China, usually Keemun and Assam, flavored with the oil of the bergamot orange, a Mediterranean pear-shaped orange. The use of bergamot and the widespread marketing of this tea began when the earl, addicted to the tea, asked the venerable house of Twinings to re-create some for him. It did, using the bergamot instead of the Canton orange, and thus was history made. Today, you can find Earl Grey tea not only from Twinings but from a variety of tea victuallers because Twinings neglected to patent the formula it used to re-create the tea the earl so loved. This tea became the favorite of Captain Picard, who liked it straight and hot, and I've used it to create a number of recipes I think you'll like.

Watercress and Other Tea Sandwiches

When it's time for afternoon tea, it's also time for those delightful little tidbits that accompany tea, such as sandwiches, canapés, and cakes. Typically, for what the British call "low tea," Captain Picard might put out a tray of replicated scones or crumpets with clotted cream (also called Devonshire cream and available at many supermarkets) and preserves, tea sandwiches, and petit fours or other finger-sized desserts, such as mini truffles, bite-sized cookies, brownies, napoleons, and heavenly chocolate-dipped strawberries. The point of all these foods is that they should be literally finger foods—no sloppy dressings to spoil the tea gown or splatter the hat—and have a variety of textures, have some color from either the garnishes or the foods themselves, and be served on fine china.

At teatime, Captain Picard likes his tea sandwiches, most of which have sweet, or unsalted, butter on both pieces of the bread to keep the innards moist. This is unnecessary if you're using a chicken salad or other filling made with a dressing or mayonnaise. Watercress is surprisingly spicy and interesting and is the basis for the watercress sandwich, known far and wide as a teatime food. Captain Janeway grew up on watercress sandwiches, she never tires of telling me, as if just by repeating it I'll get the hint. I get it. It's just that when Kes disappeared, I had to figure out how to grow watercress in her airponics garden. You can make a wonderful watercress sandwich by mixing 1 cup of loosely packed watercress, stems removed, with 8 ounces of cream cheese. Blend them together and you'll get a pretty green mixture that is divine as a filling by itself. A Bajoran watercress *hasperat* uses the same filling layered between a rolled up tortilla.

Here are some possible fillings for sandwiches:

• Chicken almond salad, which you prepare with 2 tablespoon mayonnaise, ¼ cup chopped blanched almonds, 1 cup chopped cooked chicken breast, salt and pepper and paprika to taste.

• Very fresh, very ripe tomatoes, particularly Romas or even plum tomatoes, thinly sliced, salted, with lightly buttered bread.

• "English" or hothouse cucumbers that have been peeled, sliced thinly, and left to rest for about fifteen minutes with a heavy plate on them to drain
excess moisture, which will keep them crisp on thinly sliced bread, this time
with either mayonnaise or butter.

• Again on buttered bread, smoked salmon with or without some capers.

• Egg salad, gruyère, and sliced mango, or other combos of cheese and
raisin bread, date bread or current bread. Sandwiches must be filled before the
crusts are cut off. For visual interest, if for no other reason, they can be cut
into triangles, squares, or rectangles. For an added twist, use one slice of
brown bread and one of white. Also, you can dip the edges of sandwiches in
chopped dill, parsley, or similar herbs. This is not only pretty but adds a little
"oomph." If you're like me and have all the time in the world to roam around

the galley of a starship, you can also wrap your low-tea sandwiches with the green parts of scallions that have been blanched in boiling water for about 20 to 30 seconds, then cooled and dried. Simply wrap the sandwich like a package, no bow necessary. They're edible, but most people, especially the utilitarian Vulcans I have to deal with, cut them off like a bunch of spoilsports. Edible flowers, particularly nasturtiums, are great; they're peppery, so they'd be good with egg salad. They can be used in the sandwich itself or as a garnish.

Madeleines

These little delights—sweet, tiny cakes that you can carry with you to your workstation, whether in engineering or your Dilbert-like cubicle in the bowels of some heartless human corporation on Earth—are not especially easy to make, but they're so much fun it's worth it. Also, if you like your Earl Grey tea hot, like Captain Picard, you'll find that madeleines are the perfect accompaniment. Picard has an affinity for them because they're the most celebrated edible tidbit in all of French literature. That's why they're a favorite of his.

Before you begin, you'll need to get a tray of happy little madeleine molds. These are metal trays into which you will pour your batter, and you can get them at any department store, kitchen supply store, gift shop, or even a supermarket. You will need one tray with a dozen molds. The ingredients are the following:

> **2 eggs**
> **½ cup sifted all-purpose flour**
> **¼ cup (½ stick) butter, melted**
> **¼ cup sugar**
> **1 teaspoon lemon juice**
> **1 teaspoon vanilla extract**
> **½ teaspoon grated orange peel**
> **⅛ teaspoon salt**

Begin by buttering and flouring your madeleine molds and preheating your oven to 325 degrees. Next melt the butter and, while it's cooling, sift together the flour and the salt; set that mixture aside. Blend the eggs, sugar, lemon juice, and orange peel into a smooth mixture and fold the flour and salt combination through it. Stir. Next, add the cooled butter and stir until it becomes a smoothly flowing batter. Pour the batter into your molds about ⅔ full and bake for about 25 minutes or until you see them turn a light brown. Do not overcook. You can test for doneness by pressing the center of the cake in the mold down, and if it springs back, it's done. After cooking, let your madeleines cool before removing them from the molds.

These little orangey cakes go very well with Earl Grey tea and make perfect afternoon tea snacks as well as desserts for lunchboxes and late-night snacks. Bake up a whole bunch and refrigerate them. Or freeze them—they'll defrost by the time you reach the office—and nuke them 20–30 seconds on "high" in the microwave at work.

Picard's and Troi's Earl Grey Chocolate Cake

If you've developed a taste for the lightly spicy Earl Grey and you like chocolate cake under any conditions, as Commander Troi certainly does, then you can have your cake and drink it, too, with this recipe for dessert and tea at the same time. It's great by itself and, of course, is a perfect snack to accompany your Earl Grey tea.

¾ cup (1½ sticks) butter, softened

¾ cup sugar

3 large eggs

2 tablespoons Earl Grey tea (infused)

¾ cup sifted, self-rising cake flour

grated rind from 2 oranges

Preheat oven to 350 degrees and grease and line a large loaf pan. Cream together the butter and sugar until light and fluffy. Add the eggs, one at a time, and beat in thoroughly. Add the grated rind, flour, and tea, and fold in with a wooden spoon. Turn the batter into the pan and smooth the top. Bake for 30 to 40 minutes or until a toothpick inserted into the cake comes out clean. Remove from oven and let cool. When cool, score the top lightly in preparation for the icing.

To prepare the icing, you'll need the following ingredients:

juice from 2 oranges

½ cup sugar

2 ounces semisweet chocolate

Gently heat the orange juice and sugar together in a saucepan until the sugar has dissolved. Bring to a boil and boil 1 to 2 minutes. Pour over the cake. When it has soaked in, then you can remove the cake from the tin. In a small saucepan, melt the chocolate and pour over the top. You can make patterns with a fork. (A ½ teaspoon of infused Earl Grey tea can be added to the chocolate for an added punch.)

The Picard Cocktail

I don't know whether you'll find this cocktail at Quark's or even whether Guinan served it up in Ten-Forward, but it's something you can make at home for the adults. This is a tea drink with a liqueur base that you can serve as a cocktail or an after-dinner drink.

8 ounces fresh spring water

1 ounce of Grand Marnier liqueur

1 teaspoon Earl Grey tea leaves

Heat the water to nearly boiling, and pour over the tea, steeping for about 3 minutes. Pour into a cup, straining out the leaves. Slowly pour in the Grand Marnier. Place on a sterling silver platter and serve at once. If your guests should prefer Cointreau, that, too, would be acceptable. But what if you want to serve a nonalcoholic version of this?

The Picard

A nonalcoholic alternative to the Picard Cocktail is something simply called "The Picard," which you can make with orange juice, water, and Earl Grey tea. This is actually a spicy version of iced tea for any time of year, especially summers on Earth.

½ cup fresh-squeezed orange juice

8 ounces fresh spring water

1 teaspoon Earl Grey tea leaves

ice cubes

mint or orange slices

Heat the water to nearly boiling and pour over the tea, steeping for about 3 minutes. Strain off the leaves. Cool the tea in the refrigerator for about 20 minutes. To serve, pour the tea into a tall tumbler, add the orange juice and a few ice cubes. Stir and serve immediately with mint or orange slices.

Ro Laren

Ro Laren was freed from prison and asigned to the *Enterprise* to act as a liaison on a sensitive mission that ultimately was compromised by Starfleet Admiral Kennelly. Ro's honor was restored. Years later, at a banquet in Ro's honor, Captain Picard obtained the Bajoran delicacy *foraiga*. It was a magnificent tribute to the young officer. But in the end Ro declared her allegience to the Maquis.

Foraiga

The closest thing you'll find to *foraiga* on Earth are the wonderful edible fungi called truffles. These are such delicacies that most people who like them don't even bother to ask the price. It is said that in France, the prized black truffle is routed up by pigs; in Italy, the equally priceless white truffle is unearthed by dogs. Whether white or black, the truffle is a rather gamy, intense mushroom-like vegetable with a hard nubbly skin that has to be washed to the point of exfoliation before the food can be used. Truffles are sliced thin, extra thin because of the intensity of their taste, and added near the end of the cooking time for whatever food you're preparing, to avoid overcooking them. Chicken with truffles and rosemary is a delicacy, as are glorious pasta with creamy garlic sauce dishes with black flecks of truffles in the creamy sauce. I like white truffles in a special Italian rice dish called risotto, heavy with cheese and the tang of roma tomatoes.

For an especially easy to prepare truffle dish, you can buy canned or bottled truffles in their own juice, mince a half cup of truffles, put them in a blender on high with a ½ cup of dry sherry, chill, and use this for a truffle sauce on poultry or even light meats such as pork.

Hasperat

Speaking of Ro and her Bajoran culinary predilections, she really goes for *hasperat,* a Bajoran delicacy that was her most favorite food in the universe, in a big way. Ro could polish off a *hasperat* so quickly it's hard to believe she could stay so thin. But then this Bajoran favorite fast food can be made with low-calorie cream cheese instead of the heavy cheese you get at the deli. You can use flour tortillas layered with cream cheese (Philadelphia cream cheese or Philly lite) into which are pressed fresh green and red pepper slices sans the seeds. For more of a bite, instead of peppers or even along with peppers, press in chopped watercress and cilantro. This makes for a very robust *hasperat.* For a softer and even tastier version of *hasperat,* forget the watercress or cilantro and simply roast red and green pepper slices very lightly in olive oil or canola oil, drain and let cool, and then press them into the cheese filling. Roll the tortillas up and slice them into sandwich-sized burritos for a great lunch, late snack, or, best of all, a brown-bag or lunchbox lunch. If you use a nice watercress, minced very fine or chopped, you can have *hasperat* for low tea. I must try this for Captain Janeway.

Ginger Tea

Dr. Crusher learned to adopt this herbal remedy that Captain Picard's aunt Adele served to cure anyone in the family of the symptoms of the common cold. Ginger tea is a simple but very elegant remedy; the sharp tang of the ginger root opens up clogged nasal passages and bronchial tubes and reinvigorates the entire system. Ginger tea also helps you fight off the ravages of intestinal influenza. Need I say more?

I suggest green tea with ginger. Prepare this by the cup, with your favorite bag of green tea in a tea bag or in any tea infuser. Cut off a thin slice of ginger, let it steep in the cup with extra-hot water and a tea bag for 3 minutes. And drink it down. Use fresh instead of powdered ginger for a more invigorating taste. A couple of days on green tea, or even jasmine tea, with ginger and your cold and flu symptoms will be gone.

COMMANDER WILLIAM T. RIKER

Captain Picard was not alone in his pursuit of adventures at the edge of the human envelope. I'm sure, therefore, it was more than coincidence that he chose an equally aggressive and independent first officer who jumped on his assignments. For example, I read with delight how Commander Riker prepared for his mission aboard the *Pagh* by learning to consume, if not to love, the Klingon staples that he would have to eat. He learned how to share a huge plate of fresh *gagh* with his fellow Klingon officers, scooping up handfuls of the wriggly little serpent worms from a bed of *gladst*.

He learned to drink Klingon bloodwine and hearty Klingon ale; dip into Worf's favorite, *rokeg* blood pie; bite into hearts of *targ;* and indulge in the Klingon delicacy *pipius* claw. Riker and Worf bonded over the raw gaminess of Klingonese cuisine, and even though they might have had their differences now and then over the charms of the dramatically beautiful girl in the peptide cake, Commander Deanna Troi. Riker and Worf fought side by side together on many an away mission, rescued Captain Picard from the Borg, and time and again saved the *Enterprise*-D from total destruction.

Jonathan Frakes's "Riker's Barbeque Marinade"

Here's a recipe Alfre Woodard shared with me—actually I stole it—for a tangy BBQ marinade that's great for chicken or ribs. It's the perfect dish before any first contact.

> **2 pounds chicken pieces, pork spareribs, beef short ribs, *or***
> **baby back ribs**
> **1 fresh lemon**
> **virgin olive oil**
> **soy sauce *or* light soy sauce**
> **fresh coarsely ground pepper**

In a deep dish or covered pot, cover meat with virgin olive oil. Drizzle the mixture with soy sauce. Squeeze the juice of a fresh lemon into the mixture. Grind in the pepper. Flip the meat and grind in more pepper.

Cover and let sit for at least 3 hours at room temperature or overnight in your refrigerator. Barbecue your favorite way. Serves four to six.

Bregit Lung

Riker said in his personal log that his most favorite dish aboard the *Pagh* was *bregit* lung, among the many foods that mark the test of a true Klingon. Lung, claw, heart, and entrails mark the food of the warrior, Riker learned, as the internalization of the fighting soul of the wild beast. To breathe the air of battle, to feel the scent of blood rise around you until it makes your own blood boil—these are the sensations of the warrior hero. It didn't take Riker long to learn this and to be prepared to die in battle rather than step down from the challenge. The food that inspired him to his moment of glory he said, was hearty, almost overpowering, *bregit* lung.

   Unless you're a Klingon, you'll have to replace the lungs with tripe because lungs have been declared inedible by the United States Department of Agriculture. In fact, at meat packing plants, animal lungs are rendered unusable by a denaturing process, so even if you are able to buy lungs to make *bregit* lung, they're probably unsafe to eat.

3 pounds beef tripe

1 cup sour cream

½ cup sifted all-purpose flour

½ cup (1 stick) salted butter

1 small Spanish onion, chopped very fine

2 or 3 beef bouillon cubes *or* envelopes mixed with 1½ cups of boiling water to form a thick stock

2 additional beef bouillon cubes or envelopes

2 teaspoons paprika or cayenne pepper

1 teaspoon sugar

1 bay leaf

1 tablespoon black caviar

½ teaspoon thyme

Begin by cutting the tripe into 2-inch by 1-inch strips which you will wash, boil, and simmer in the beef stock for about 30 to 45 minutes until they become nice and tender. Remove the tripe from the stock and set aside. Crumble your bay leaf and thyme into a powdered mixture and add to the stock along with the 2 additional bouillon cubes or envelopes. While the stock is simmering, heat the butter, sugar, and flour in a skillet until the mixture thickens, and then add the chopped onion, stirring until it becomes transparent. Reduce heat and pour the stock through a cheesecloth or strainer into the skillet and stir as it thickens. Now preheat your oven to 325 degrees.

Put the strips of tripe into a large casserole dish and cover them with the thickened stock. Cover the dish and bake for 30 minutes, then add salt and pepper to taste, and add the sour cream and the caviar. Bake for another 15 minutes and serve with a heavy red wine such as "Bull's Blood"; a dark full-bodied German beer, or a pint of British bitter, ale, or stout which can easily pass for Klingon ale. Serves six to eight.

Pipius Claw

"I should have been a pair of pipius claws
Scuttling across the floors of silent seas."

This is a noble delicacy immortalized by the Klingon poets for centuries. Unlike most Klingon dishes, where you have to eat it before it eats you, *pipius* claw is actually tame. It's already dead. You can relax, take your time, and slowly scrape the meat off the claws with your left fang, homeworld style. I believe Gowron affected a version of this mannerism to gnaw the flesh off the bone, which was adopted by courtiers in the chamber of the High Council as a demonstration of loyalty during the civil wars. Will Riker quickly declared that this was his favorite dish in the officers' mess aboard the *Pagh.*

There are no *pipius—pipia,* actually—scuttling around in the swampy marshes of the wetlands or along the bottoms of the ocean floor on Earth, so substitute lobster for *pipius* and you'll be more than pleased with the result. i prepare it en casserole, as it were, in the shells, just the way its inventor, the great field general Emperor Napoleon, who called it Lobster Thermadour liked it. Here's how:

4 2-pound live, fully clawed lobsters

¾ cup (1½ stick) butter, melted

1 cup heavy cream

2 cups vegetable or chicken stock (made from instant packages
   or bouillon cubes, *or* you can use the stock drawn off
   from Chadre Kab à la Neelix)

¼ cup all-purpose sifted flour

1 cup crackling dry white wine (Frascati or Verdicchio)

2 cups bread crumbs or unflavored stuffing mix

1 cup grated extra-sharp cheddar cheese

2 cloves garlic, crushed

2 cups minced celery leaves

sea salt to taste

½ teaspoon dry mustard

freshly ground black peppercorns to taste

1 or 2 drops of McIlhenny's Tabasco sauce or Louisiana-style
   hot sauce

cayenne pepper or pakrika to taste

First, kill all the lobsters. Do this by plunging their wriggling, squirming, snapping bodies deep into heavily salted boiling water in a large stew pot, you should add two handfuls of salt to the water. Even better, if you live near an ocean, fill your pot with seawater and boil it straight—seaweed and all. Keep the lobsters on a high boil for at least 15 minutes. Now they're done. Remove them, uncurl them, snap off the claws, but leave the heads on and the eyes open.

While the lobsters are still hot, split them into halves, scoop out the soft white meat, and cut it into small bite-sized chunks. In a saucepan, mix 1/2 cup melted butter with flour until the two become soft and smooth and thoroughly blended, and then add the lobster meat. To the lobster meat, butter, and flour, add the cream and stock and blend. Heat this mixture over low heat for about 15 minutes, stirring to keep lumps from forming, and during the final 5 minutes of cooking time, add all of the spices, seasonings, and half of the cheese. Now preheat the broiler, and add to the lobster meat your wine, remaining ¼ cup melted butter, and stuffing or bread crumbs. Cook this mixture for another 5 minutes.

Because you will cook the lobster meat in the shells, rinse the shells until they are clean. Place them in a broiling pan and fill them with the lobster meat. Top with the remaining cheddar cheese. Broil 5 to 7 minutes until they are brown, and just before serving, arrange the lobster claws, upright and pried open, in the shells. I like to sprinkle cayenne pepper or another dose of paprika over the finished dish, and garnish with arugula around the claws. If you have to, you can prop the claws up with bits of lobster shell, because *pipius* claw is all in the presentation. You can also add more bread crumbs or stuffing to the mixture to help support the claws upright. Serves four to six.

Gagh, Cardassian Style, with Yamok Sauce

Although the Klingons and Cardassians fought a war in the Alpha Quadrant, Klingon *gagh* and Cardassian *yamok* sauce have a natural affinity for each other. Cardassians are not fond of living wriggly things. They like heavy game meat and poultry, and they like their food cooked. However, the tang of *yamok* sauce so sets off anything meaty, including serpent worms, I combine the Klingon and Cardassian in my own version of the *gagh* that Riker would have shared with Worf aboard *Enterprise* before he beamed over to the *Pagh.*

For an easy version of *yamok* sauce that you can enjoy, combine a ½ cup of dark teriyaki sauce with a ¼ cup soy sauce and a ¼ cup brown sesame-seed salad dressing or tahini in a large covered cruet, and shake it until the three liquids are completely blended. Pour the *yamok* sauce over your white udon or soba noodles that you have chilled in the refrigerator for about 1 hour after cooking. Serve on a bed of arugula or red romaine lettuce and you have *gagh* with *yamok* sauce fit, if not for a king, certainly for a first officer posted to a particularly tricky mission.

Parthas à la Yuta

Part of the job of a Starfleet captain is the endless diplomacy necessary to win the friendship and cooperation of life-forms on strange new worlds. It was for this reason, I believe, that Commander Riker was always willing to extend himself, as was shown on several missions. The commander would spend countless hours trying to understand these new life-forms, by getting to know members of the delegation personally. Typical of Riker's preparation for command were his dealings with the lovely aide to the Acamarian sovereign. In honor of the sovereign's aide, Yuta, Commander Riker prepared a dish of *parthas,* green vegetables similar to the kind that grow on Earth, and named the dish after Yuta. You can make *parthas* á la Yuta yourself by substituting brussels sprouts for *parthas.* Yuta liked her *parthas* steamed. You can steam brussels sprouts easily by cutting off the stems and tops and steaming them in a steamer or in a pot of boiling water with a steaming rack for at least 15 minutes or until they're tender.

You can also cut off the tops and stems, slit them lengthwise on a diagonal, and boil them for about 15 minutes. After boiling, you can reserve the water and use it to make a sauce out of any canned condensed cheese, celery, asparagus, or even mushroom soup. Add only ¼ cup of the brussels sprouts water to ¼ cup of whole milk and 1 11.5-oz can of condensed cheese, celery, asparagus, or mushroom soup. Heat through and pour over the brussels sprouts.

Steamed or boiled you can serve them either buttered or topped with grated Parmesan, Pecorino, Reggiano, or Romano cheese. You can even use a cheddar cheese sauce, but I wouldn't combine it with a sauce made from asparagus, celery, or mushroom soup. You can also serve brussels sprouts with a combination cheddar and Monterey cheeses for a Mexican version of *parthas* à la Yuta.

Bizarre Garnishes

What I also do, and what you can do if you're having a theme party, is have some type of bizarre garnish for the meat that hangs around the edge of the dish. Doesn't have to be a veggie; it can be an octopus leg. I did something really neat in the "A Matter of Honor" episode with Riker. My challenge was that you have nine or so dishes that are really much the same thing—Klingon food, serpent worms, organs, that sort of thing. But they had to look different for the camera. In one instance, *pipius* claw, I had to make it look totally bizarre. So I took regular old chicken feet, the kind you can get from a butcher shop. I cut out the middle toe. This thing looked just like a devil's claw. I stuck them up in a pie-like dish and nobody knew they were chicken feet.

—ALAN SIMS

Owon Eggs

Riker obtained these very gamy eggs on Starbase 73. They were small with strange varicolored shells and hard little yolks. But Riker was determined to eat what no man from Starfleet had eaten before and prepared an omelette in his quarters to serve to his friends—actually his poker-playing partners. With my extensive galley experience as a short-order breakfast chef, I could have predicted that no one among his friends would like these excuses for eggs. But Worf, only Worf, scarfed them up. If you want to experiment with your own version of strange eggs, I recommend you stay on the safe side and go no farther than the quacking duck. Even then you have to be very careful because the eggs of fowl other than hens may not be as rigorously processed. As a result, eggs from other fowl may be contaminated with bacteria, so you have to be very sure of the quality.

If you want to prepare a duck egg omelette, your own version of Owon eggs, use only very fresh duck eggs whose quality you know to be of the absolute highest, wash the shells, and break the eggs into a mixing bowl. Beat them thoroughly and blend in ¼ teaspoon rosemary, ¼ teaspoon thyme, ¼ teaspoon paprika, ¼ teaspoon parsley, and ¼ teaspoon garlic salt. In a hot, well-buttered skillet, fry them with just a touch of brie or light garlic cream cheese, garnish with sprigs of parsley or even a touch of watercress, and serve nice and hot.

Spiny Lobe-Fish

If there was a lasting repercussion from the torture Commander Riker underwent by the doctors on Tilonus IV, who convinced him for a while that he was being treated at the Institute for Mental Disorders, it was the image of the terrifying spiny lobe-fish that still haunted his dreams. Being a Talaxian and a born trader in delicacies—some edible, some not—I've always felt that you can defeat your demons if you can eat your demons. Accordingly, had I been the chef and morale officer on the *Enterprise*-D, I would have concocted a dish with those gruesome spiny lobe-fish and served it to Riker, en brochette. I am on *Voyager,* however, cruising through a quadrant thousands of miles away from the *Enterprise,* wherever she may be, and Riker's not here. But here's the same dish for you.

2 pounds meaty white- or gray-fleshed fish fillets, like cod or
      monkfish, cut into thick slices

2 cups dry red wine (Burgundy, Bordeaux, or Merlot)

1 large carrot, sliced

1 medium-sized onion, sliced

2 cloves garlic, halved

¼ cup (½ stick) butter, melted

¼ cup olive oil

2 tablespoons sifted all-purpose flour

2 teaspoons sea salt

1 teaspoon freshly-ground black pepper

½ teaspoon rosemary

1/2 teaspoon thyme

You will need a heavy skillet or fish-frying pan, with a tight cover, like a flat or oblong Le Creuset or something similar. Clean and slice your fish and arrange in the skillet. Add the wine, carrot, onion, garlic, herbs, salt, and pepper and bring to a boil. When it reaches a boil, cook the fish for about 20 minutes until the fish pieces become flaky and soft. Remove them and set aside. In a separate small skillet combine the melted butter, olive oil, and flour, and while stirring, heat them for about 10 minutes, until the ingredients form a soft sauce. Combine with fish liquid, stirring rapidly over medium heat until the sauce thickens. Boil for about 1 minute. Pour over the fish and serve. Serves four to six.

If you with to serve this the way I would, en brochette, you will only cook the fish for 15 minutes instead of 20 and prepare the rest of the dish according to the recipe. However, use the sauce as a marinade, place the thick pieces of fish on kabob skewers or swords, and complete your cooking over an open fire or barbecue. This is a blackened version of the recipe.

If you're serving this dish for a horde of Klingons, replace the fish with a nice fresh or smoked eel and cook over open fire. You'll have to increase the initial cooking time for the eel to at least 30 minutes, marinate, then barbecue.

"I like my bloodwine young and sweet."

Lieutenant Worf, the security officer, is one of the most perplexing individuals among the roster of Starfleet officers. A solitary man, he is Klingon, but he was raised by former Starfleet Chief Petty Officer Sergey Rozhenko—and his wife Helena—who found him amid the ruins of the Khitomer settlement after the massacre and adopted him. Thus, Worf is a kind of anomaly, a full-blooded Klingon warrior from an important ruling family who was raised on Earth by humans. Typical of transplanted members of a different culture, Worf not only clung to his Klingon roots while he was growing up, but eventually embraced them, fighting alongside Gowron in the civil war.

Worf is a stickler for Klingon custom and Klingon food. Even on Earth, he bragged, his mother, Helena Rozhenko, learned how to make *rokeg* blood pie the old-fashioned way and served it to him on more than just special occasions. Worf used to eat two or three of these at a sitting. In my research into the tastes and predilections of Starfleet personnel in whose boots I am proud to walk, Worf, even more than Spock and Data, is my most intriguing subject.

Helena Rozhenko's
Rokeg Blood Pie

Unlike my own blood pie, a lighter, sweeter version of the homeworld recipe that I prepare for B'Elanna, Mrs. Rozhenko's blood pie is heavy and meaty. It's especially made for growing Klingon boys who need their iron. You can make a version of what Mrs. Rozhenko served Worf by using veal kidneys and top-round or sirloin beef roast baked into a pie pastry with lots of brown gravy made from the blood. It's an intense meat pastry, not to be served to the squeamish, but tasty.

2 pounds top-round or sirloin beef roast

1 pound veal kidneys

2 cups beef gravy *or* 2 cups beef stew with veggies removed

1 homemade or store-bought unsweetened pastry pie crust

1 12-ounce bottle domestic or imported dark beer

4 cloves garlic

2 cups flour, seasoned with ⅛ teaspoon garlic salt and
    ¼ teaspoon celery seed

¼ cup (½ stick) salted butter, melted

Tabasco sauce, cayenne pepper, or paprika to taste

Preheat oven to 375 degrees, and skin, then wash kidneys. Slice them very thin and set aside while you slice the beef roast very thin as well. Save any blood. Sauté the kidneys very briefly in a skillet with melted butter until they just begin to turn color, about 2 minutes. Set aside while you roll the beef in the seasoned flour. Now in a greased deep baking pan arrange your beef and kidney slices in any order you like, making sure to mix them so the flavors blend. Cover with thick brown gravy or stew stock and any blood you've reserved. Pour in your bottle of beer. Cover the pan with aluminium foil and bake for 2 hours at 375 degrees. Remove from oven, let pan cool slightly, and replace the aluminum foil with your pastry crust. Raise the oven heat to 400 degrees. Return pie to oven and cook for another 15 minutes, just enough to brown the crust. Serve with Klingon bloodwine or ale. Serves approximately six.

Michael Dorn and Klingon Food

When you are setting up your own dishes and presentations for parties, you also have to look at things you want to avoid. For example, when I was serving Michael Dorn on *TNG*, he hated the smell of the raw seafood, especially when we had an early morning call. But I had a Klingon dish and it was very revolting in its appearance. Didn't really smell that bad, but it looked awful, even though it had an edible base. Michael was very upset and said, "Alan, I told you, I can't be around this seafood. I hate the smell of fish." I said to him, "You know you're a Klingon and Klingons are supposed to be able to eat this stuff. You can handle this." And he laughed. It was funny even though he gave me a hard time.

—ALAN SIMS

Klingon Bloodwine

Klingon bloodwine is exactly what it says it is: fermented blood and sugar. To make an excellent re-creation of Klingon bloodwine, you can use straight up "Just Cranberry" from Knudsen sweetened to your own taste with Welch's pure dark grape juice. If you want to lighten the color of the cranberry juice just a bit, use Welch's white grape juice. Want it to have some nice floating red corpuscles? Run fresh or frozen cranberries or red raspberries through your blender and add them to your juice. That makes it fresh and sweet, the way Worf drinks it.

Prune Juice Cocktail

The harsh taste and equally harsh reaction to prune juice prompted Worf to declare it a "warrior's drink" that readies the body for battle. I wouldn't dispute Worf on this, because I can see why, after a night of blood pies and bloodwine he'd want his prune juice the next day.

If you want to try some prune juice in a cocktail, here's what I'd recommend. Start out with ½ glass of prune juice and ½ pink grapefruit juice over ice. It's a great morning pick-me-up that does the job after a night of heavy eating on the holodeck.

Vermicula

While this is a dish native to Antede III, Worf, like many other Klingons, has acquired a taste for it. Klingons serve it as a change of pace from *gagh* because the texture of the live worms is very different. *Gagh* are thickish serpent worms, while vermicula are lighter and thinner. I guess you have to be a Klingon to appreciate the difference. I've always maintained when serving up Klingon worm dishes that the proof is in the wriggling. The little ones seem to be a lot more animated, especially if you scoop them right out of the nest.

Cooking Klingon on Earth, I like white soba noodles or, for a lighter taste, ramen noodles. Follow the package directions, drain, and chill. Combine sesame seed salad (or tahini) dressing with teriyaki and soy sauce in equal parts and stir them through the noodles. Top either with raw clams, oysters, or mussels out of their shells or, even better, with raw squid sliced lengthwise, or smoked eel also sliced lengthwise not too thin and draped over the side. Forget the chopsticks. This is eel or squid sashimi that you can eat Klingon style—by hand.

If you use raw or live shellfish, please remember that they are highly perishable foods and spoil very rapidly. They can contaminate the foods they come in contact with, particularly if they're all on the same platter or dish. So please don't leave raw or live shellfish sitting on a table for any extended period of time. Keep them under refrigeration until ready to serve. If you are using them as a garnish, I suggest that you place the food you are serving in a clear bowl, and wrap the garnish around the bowl on another dish or platter, so that they do not touch! You can become sick from spoiled shellfish so extra care must be taken.

DR. BEVERLY CRUSHER

The chief medical officer, and Wesley's mother, Beverly Crusher, brought more than stern science to the sickbay on the *Enterprise*; she brought a very homey touch. Anybody who bothers to read the *Enterprise* and personal logs knows that there was something brewing between Picard and Crusher long before the two were captured by a hostile species and implanted with telepathic devices that allowed them to read one another's deepest thoughts. That's when they realized they'd been in love for a long, long time.

Dr. Crusher's Cure-all for Insomnia

Part of Dr. Crusher's bedside manner was her ability to prescribe basic common-sense food to heal everyday problems. Can't sleep? Don't worry about powerful soporifics, simply heat up some whole or skim milk in a small saucepan until it's hotter than body temperature but not boiling. Don't let a skin form. As the milk heats, stir in a teaspoonful of honey. Then, just before you serve, stir in some nutmeg. Serve in a mug with a touch more nutmeg floating on top. This medication is so powerful that you can serve it just before the Borg, the Cardassians, or the Romulans attack. It was, I hear, what turned Locutus back into Captain Picard—that and a few minor operations to remove his implants.

Dr. Pulaski's Chicken Soup for the *Enterprise* Soul

After Dr. Crusher returned to the *Enterprise* following her one-year posting at Starfleet Medical, she learned that her replacement, Dr. Katherine Pulaski, also had a cure-all that didn't involve the latest in genetically engineered drugs. Beverly Crusher quickly adapted her own recipe for what came to be known as Dr. Pulaski's Chicken Soup. Beverly added those wonderful little spheroid delights Worf's adoptive father Chief Rozhenko calls "knaidlach." It sometimes inspires him to elicit music from a primitive device he calls a "guitar."

2- to 3-pound whole chicken, washed and quartered

2 onions, sliced

5 carrots, sliced

3 medium-sized tomatoes, sliced

10 stalks celery, sliced (Reserve the celery leaves for the knaidlach.)

chicken bouillon cubes or packages as necessary to enhance flavor

coarse-ground kosher salt to taste

coarse-ground black pepper to taste

1 16-ounce package matzoh-ball mix, prepared per directions

1 tablespoon chopped celery leaves

1 tablespoon chopped fresh parsley

¼ cup minced fresh onion

1 tablespoon chopped fresh garlic

OR:

BUBBIE KATZ'S HESTER STREET KNAIDLACH

1 cup packaged matzoh meal

2 eggs

2 tablespoons vegetable oil *or* chicken fat

½ cup chicken soup, chicken bouillon, *or* chicken stock

First, prepare either your homemade version of Bubbie Katz's or the packaged matzoh balls, because the knaidlach mixture has to sit in a refrigerator for at least about a ½ hour to set up. Then you'll cook them in the stock and set aside again until just before serving time, when you plop them back into the soup.

If you are using one of the store-bought packages, simply follow the package directions. These entail mixing vegetable oil and two eggs with the matzoh meal, salting it if you like, then setting the mixture aside in your fridge for about a ½ hour. You can then heat some chicken bouillon to a boil, take the mix out of the refrigerator, roll the mixture into fluffy little balls, and drop them in the boiling bouillon. Make sure you don't pack the little matzoh balls too densely or they'll never cook. When the balls float up to the surface and bob there for a while, they're done. Set aside to cool until your soup is ready. Then cook in the chicken soup for at least 10 minutes before serving.

To make the Katz's knaidlach recipe, you should blend the eggs and chicken fat or vegetable oil in a medium-sized bowl until the mixture is nice and thick. Pour the chicken soup, bouillon, or stock into the mixture, stir, and then blend in the matzoh meal. If the mixture is too stiff, add just a little bit of oil or Naya fat. Then set the mixture aside in your refrigerator for 30 minutes while you prepare the chicken soup. After 30 minutes, remove the dumpling dough from the refrigerator, form it into little fluffy balls, and drop them into boiling soup or bouillon. When the balls float to the surface, they're done. Set aside until your soup is done, and add them for the final 10 minutes of cooking time.

To make the soup itself, you'll need a very large soup pot, half-filled with cold water. Set the heat to high and cover the pot while you clean the chicken. You can also buy quarted chicken or chicken parts. Washing your chicken is a very important process because of the risk of bacteria and contaminants, and you should do it very carefully. Put the chicken pieces into the boiling water and reduce the heat. The chicken will cook slowly at a low boil, and simmer it in your covered soup pot for about 2 hours, during which time you should occasionally skim fat and solids from the surface of the boiling water.

After 2 hours, remove the chicken and test it for doneness. The meat should be white and soft. Set it aside. Strain the broth to remove fat and scum and return it to the pot. Let the broth cook for about 1 hour, during which time more fat will rise to the surface. Skim off some of the fat or all of the fat, depending upon how fatty you want the soup to be. If the flavor is too mild, you can also add some bouillon cubes or powder to the water. Then return it to the heat and add the vegetables and cook for about another 1½ hours. When the tomatoes have dissolved and the carrots are soft, season with the salt and pepper, add the chicken back in, and cook for 30 minutes. Finally, add the matzoh balls and cook for another 10 minutes, correct the seasoning, and serve.

I suggest you remove the chicken from the soup pot before serving. You should also try to keep the chicken in large pieces and remove the skin and bones. Add it in individual serving bowls along with the matzoh balls. The fun part of the presentation is to make sure that everyone has the same number of matzoh balls and carrots. Individual pieces of chicken for each serving will, naturally, vary according to taste. Some people will want huge chunks of chicken and others will want barely any. I suggest you serve your soup with dark, dark rye bread and Welch's white grape juice cut half-and-half with sparkling water or club soda and topped with a lemon. Serves approximately eight to ten.

If you have at least 2 cups of leftover chicken, rather than saving it as soup meat for the next night, you should shred it, add to it 3 chopped celery stalks and one chopped onion, some salt, and enough mayonnaise to make a nice chicken salad to accompany the soup for lunch or for the following night's dinner. Serve the chicken salad on rye bread or the egg bread challah, which you can make in your automatic bread maker.

Ten-Forward

Ten-Forward drinks and food were the primary presentation setups we did on *TNG* for food, outside of "A Matter of Honor" and all the Klingon dishes that Riker had to get accustomed to. We used all fruit juices; store shelf juices and some of the generic brands were used to fill the flasks.

—ALAN SIMS

Balso Tonic

Here's a quick drink that Trill hosts seem to like. Ambassador Odan had a hankering for *balso* tonic on the *Enterprise*-D, but the ship's replicators couldn't make it. Beverly Crusher, who fell in love with the ambassador before she realized he was a joined Trill, tried to find a way to make the drink. I, myself, have played around with a recipe for it, and here's what I came up with. If we ever get back to the Alpha Quadrant and I get a chance to pay a visit to Deep Space 9, I'll deliver it personally to Jadzia Dax to see whether it tickles her Trill fancy.

In order to make my version of *balso* tonic, you'll need an automatic juicer. You can use a blender, but you have to extract the veggie fibers with a strainer. It works, but it's just not twenty-fourth–century enough for me.

8 stalks celery

1 piece fresh ginger

16 ounces sparkling water or Perrier water

1 teaspoon celery seed

1 teaspoon honey, or more to taste

In your juicer, extract the celery and ginger juices into a glass. Add the celery seed. Combine with sparkling water or Perrier and add honey to taste. Serve over ice if that's your pleasure, too. Yields approximately two to three servings.

COMMANDER DEANNA TROI

t's hard not to look back through the logs of the *Enterprise*-D without being struck by the dramatic beauty of ship's counselor, Commander Deanna Troi. Do empaths bask in the reflected passions of people in their own environment? I only know from the experiences I shared with my beloved Kes, and the answer is yes. Kes knew her effect upon those around her, namely me, and reacted to it. I must someday ask these same questions of Commander Troi.

Marina Sirtis's Eggplant Casserole

Deanna Troi may be a chocoholic, but I really like Mediterranean cooking. This eggplant casserole is as authentic as Greek food can be. But don't let the eggplant fool you; this is not a diet dish!

2 pounds small, skinny eggplants, sliced (you can also use Japanese eggplant)

1 28-ounce can crushed tomatoes

1 medium-sized onion, finely chopped

1 cup light olive oil

2 tablespoons chopped parsley *or* 1 tablespoon dried parsley

salt and pepper to taste

Preheat oven to 375 degrees. Slice eggplant crosswise into half-inch slices. Heat olive oil in a heavy skillet until it just bubbles but doesn't smoke. Fry eggplant in hot oil until nicely browned on both sides. As the oil is absorbed, keep adding more, taking care not to splatter. As each batch of eggplant slices is fried, place them on a plate with paper towels so they can drain.

When the eggplant is done and is draining, fry the onion in the remaining oil, or add more, over medium heat until the onion is golden brown. Then very slowly (so that it doesn't splatter) add the tomatoes, parsley, salt, and pepper. Simmer for about 5 minutes. Put the eggplant into a casserole dish (13 by 9 inches) in layers. Add the tomato sauce mixture, cover with aluminum foil, and oven bake at 375 degrees for 45 minutes.

Serve with either a crusty white bread or a dark olive loaf to mop up the delicious sauce. This should be accompanied with a light Greek salad with olives and a hint of feta cheese.

This dish goes very well with either a Soave or Frascati or even a fruity Valpolicella. Serves four to six.

Chocolate Cake with Raspberries

When you think of Troi, you think of not only her beauty, not only the difficulty of her job as a counselor who could feel the emotional pain of others, you think of—chocolate. That's right, chocolate. The woman was a card-carrying chocoholic who couldn't make a move without a hit from the old bar of Swiss, dark, semisweet, mit crunchies or mit out crunchies. Want to make her happy? Bake her a chocolate cake. So here's Deanna Troi's favorite ship's counselor's chocolate cake with raspberries—chocolat au framboise.

CHOCOLATE CAKE

2 cups sifted cake flour

1 teaspoon baking soda

2 eggs

1 teaspoon salt

1 teaspoon vanilla extract

1¼ cups sugar

1 cup sour cream

⅓ cup shortening

⅓ cup boiling water

3 1-ounce squares unsweetened chocolate, melted

CHOCOLATE-RASPBERRY FROSTING

3-ounce package Philadelphia cream cheese, softened with milk

¼ cup fresh red raspberries, softened in 1 tablespoon water with

¼ cup sugar, *or* frozen red raspberries in light syrup

2½ cup confectioners' sugar

2 1-ounce squares unsweetened chocolate, melted

pinch of salt

Preheat oven to 350 degrees. In a small bowl, stir the melted chocolate into the boiling water until your chocolate mixture is nice and thick. Add vanilla and set aside to cool. In another bowl combine the flour, baking soda, sugar, and salt. Add sour cream and shortening, and beat for 2 minutes with an electric hand mixer on low until your batter is creamy. Add the eggs and the chocolate mixture to your batter, and beat for another 2 minutes. Grease and flour 2 8-inch layer cake pans, pour in your batter, and bake for 35 to 40 minutes. Test the top of each layer for springiness to the touch after 30 minutes. If the cake springs back to the touch, remove from oven, and let cool.

While your cake is baking, in a small mixing bowl soften your cream cheese by mixing in 1 or 2 tablespoons of whole milk, adding the milk a little at a time. Once the mixture is softened, add your sugar as you blend them with a spoon. Now add the 2 squares of melted chocolate and your raspberries. Beat on low with your electric mixer until smooth and creamy. Add just a pinch of salt and keep beating for 1 minute. Now set aside in your refrigerator. After your cake is done baking, let it cool for 10 minutes before removing from cake pans; then place the layers on a wire baking rack to let them cool further. Frost the cake only when it's completely cool, and serve.

Oskoid

Deanna is also fond of a Betazoid delicacy known as oskoid, a leafy plant similar to red or green romaine lettuce. If you want to impress the Betazoid in your life with an oskoid salad, combine sesame salad dressing or tahini with just a touch of soy sauce and rice vinegar and shake very well. Arrange leaves of green and red romaine lettuce around a sliced Bermuda onion and pour the dressing over them. No need to toss; just wrap the onion slices in the romaine lettuce leaves and eat it up. If you must, you can squeeze a lemon wedge over the plate to give a bit more zing, but it tastes great either way.

DATA

reated by Dr. Noonien Soong at the Omicron Theta colony in 2335 and reviled by its inhabitants, Data was discovered by the crew of the *Starship Tripoli.* On the *Enterprise*-D, Data became Captain Picard's second officer. Separated from his past and his father, unsure of his own immortality in a future without horizons, Data sought some companionship through his relationship with his cat, named Spot, after a dog.

Among his many creations as the owner of a finicky cat was his home-made replicated cat food. I have managed to re-create food substance #219 for your kitchens, but suggest that you shape it into little cat biscuits because it is so densely packed with nutritious components; I don't want you to overload your feline's system.

Cat Food #219, Subroutine |DataSpot\Nancy|

On *Voyager* I'd have prepared this for my cat, if I had one, using leftover hearts of *targ* and Helena Rozhenko's *rokeg* blood pie. On Earth, you have to settle for leftover *bregit* lung and other beef organs.

> 1 pound liver, kidneys, hearts, haggis, *or* other organs
>
> 2 cups bran
>
> 2 cups old-fashioned oatmeal or rolled oats
>
> ¼ cup canola or other cooking oil

Preheat oven to 250 degrees. Cover meat with cold water and bring to boil in a large saucepan. Immediately lower heat and simmer for 30 minutes. Remove meat from water and let cool. Retain the water because you'll use it later. When the meat is cooled, chop it into small kibble-sized pieces and grind it up in your food processor or blender. Keep processing until it is completely ground. Now mix the ground meat, bran, oil, and oatmeal together, adding the retained cooking water to soften the mixture. You'll be making a thick, coarse dough that you'll hand-knead until it is just malleable enough to work with.

Now re-form the dough into tiny kibbles or even biscuit-shaped pieces just bite-sized enough for your cat. The beautiful part about this recipe is that you can shape the food for your own pet. Tiny cat, make the pieces as small as rice grains—tedious, but rewarding; larger cat, size the pieces accordingly. Arrange them on a flat, slightly oiled, baking sheet, and bake at 250 degrees for 3 full hours. However, if you have a microwave, you're in luck. Arrange the cat-food pieces on a microwavable tray and zap them on high for about 10 minutes, and voila, you've warped time.

After the baking time is completed, turn your conventional oven off but don't remove the cat food. Let it sit in the oven for another couple of hours; then air-dry for an additional 24 hours. If you're using a microwave, nuke them on low for another 3 minutes, then let them sit out in the air for a day. These things last over a month, and your cat will love them.

Samarian Sunset

When I read about how Data treated Deanna Troi to a Samarian Sunset after she beat him at 3-D chess, it was the beauty and fascination of the drink that impressed me almost as much as its taste. This was a beverage that changed its color from clear to a glorious sunset orange. There are so many versions of this drink that you prepare in your own nonreplicator kitchens that you almost don't need me to tell you how. Nevertheless, nothing stops Neelix from his appointed rounds, so I worked up a version of this beverage for those of you fortunate enough to have juicers. For those of you who don't, you can probably get a similar visual effect by stirring up your own "instant" breakfast drink.

In your electric juicer, extract the juice of 2 apples and a whole chunk of fresh ginger. Pretty zingy all by itself. Now, hold your glass beneath the juice fountain and grind up at least 3 carrots. Magically, the liquid in the glass turns from a pale opacity to a bright orange. Drink it and take off. You start your day off with this and you won't come to a stop until you hit the wall. They'll have to build you a bigger cubicle at the reconfigurable loft they call an office. I once served this to Tuvok and he almost laughed. I can hardly wait to slip a glass of this to Seven and see what she does to poor Harry. I don't know whatever happened to Troi after she drank this, except that she carried on an affair with Worf.

Cellular Peptide Cake
with Mint Frosting

Do androids dream of peptide cakes? Data did as the *Enterprise* and its crew were being consumed by dangerous interphasic organisms that threatened to destroy them all. In Data's nightmare of destruction, he hosted a get-together in which the beautiful Troi was peacefully laid out, not like night spread against the sky, but like a tempting cake with tangy peppermint frosting. While cellular peptides are not common pantry staples in most people's kitchens, you can have some fun by baking your own sponge cake in jigsaw-puzzle shapes to resemble the torso of someone you love. Those of you with scanners or digital cameras who know how to use Photoshop, Illustrator, or any other photographics software can print your subject's photo onto an iron-on transfer that you can use to decorate a pillowcase or even a T-shirt. You can then wrap it around a basketball or football to make the head and face for your "torso cake." What a birthday cake!

Here's the recipe for one sponge cake with enough chocolate mint frosting to cover it. Measure how many cakes you will need to re-create the torso of your subject and adjust the recipe accordingly.

CAKE

10 egg yolks

1⅔ cups sifted cake flour

1 cup sugar

1/2 cup hot water

1 teaspoon baking powder

1 teaspoon lemon extract

½ teaspoon salt

PEPPERMINT-CHOCOLATE FROSTING

2 egg whites

1½ cups sugar

5 tablespoons water

1½ teaspoons light corn syrup

3 1-oz squares unsweetened chocolate, melted

1 teaspoon vanilla extract

¼ teaspoon peppermint extract

Preheat your oven to 375 degrees. Sift together flour, baking powder, and salt. Beat egg yolks until slightly thickened. You can use either a hand beater or your electric mixer set on low. Add the lemon extract to the egg yolks while mixing and then slowly add the sugar. After mixture is completely blended, add hot water, fold in the flour and continue to blend. Grease small sheet-cake pans and loaf pans as needed to form the puzzle torso pieces—remember you're not doing legs—pour the batter in, pans filling just over halfway and bake for 40 minutes at 375 degrees, testing for doneness after 35 minutes. When done, turn pans upside down on a wire rack and let cake pieces cool. Repeat entire recipe as necessary to complete the torso puzzle.

While your cake is cooling and you've begun to assemble the number of pieces you'll need, you should make the frosting. You can only frost the cake once it's cool and fully assembled, so there are no seams. Begin by combining the egg whites, sugar, water, melted chocolate, and corn syrup in a mixing bowl, and beat with your electric mixer on low until completely mixed. Heat in a small saucepan or on top of a double boiler, beating constantly, for 7 minutes. Test for doneness by trying to shape the frosting in the saucepan into little peaks or ridges. If it holds its shape, it's done. Remove from heat and add vanilla and peppermint extracts and continue to mix until it's thick enough to spread. Prepare enough to cover all the sponge cake and fill in all the seams.

Deanna Troi Peptide Cake

One of the funniest challenges we had on the set of *The Next Generation* was Data's dream segment wherein Deanna Troi was rolled out as a cake to be carved up and eaten. The irony about this shot and the special effects we had to use with the food is that Patrick Stewart, who directed the episode, didn't realize just how small the human torso is on a two-dimensional plane, especially Marina's. In proportion to the rest of a body, the torso is only a small area, but it looks bigger because of shoulders, neck, waist, and thighs. But when you just have a torso and nothing else, it's pretty small and makes for a weak visual. Marina Sirtis has a petite figure, so her torso is even smaller than that of someone who has a larger figure. So how to make her look like a cake?

I ordered a sheet cake, kind of a single-layer cake, from the bakery, in proportion to Marina's torso. And when we rolled her into the scene, she looked like just a square cupcake with a head sticking out. Patrick was completely dissatisfied with the look because the cake was so small. He wanted a bigger presentation for the camera—more torso cake. More cake means more cake, so we had to call all around to get more cake. Soon drivers were delivering sheet cakes to the set, and we expanded Troi's torso with a larger cake and a uniform made completely of buttercream icing. I had to run out to stores and get even more cake. But Patrick, setting up the shot from all angles, still felt the torso wasn't impressive enough. So we got more cake, because everything we did on camera looked like a dinky little thing. This was a dream sequence, not real life, so the torso had to be really oversized. Finally we got as much sponge cake as was in the entire Hollywood area and just piled it on. Then we re-iced the entire cake, taking special care to fill in all those jigsaw-puzzle seams where sponge cake met yellow cake met chocolate cake.

Marina had to lie there on what was really a magician's table with her whole body slung flat on a platform below the tray where the cake was sitting. That's what gave her what we called the "platter look." It was a really complicated arrangement because her head couldn't be straight up, but she couldn't be on the same level as the table or else she would look like a person covered in icing. She had to look like a head coming out of a cake that was really a Starfleet uniform. It was a totally constructed gag. That's the secret of how we did that shot of the Troi cake.

—ALAN SIMS

Arrange your torso pieces and frost. Now you can decorate your cake with packaged white and red buttercream icing or frosting mix to create clothing, a Starfleet uniform, shirt or blouse, a tie, buttons, or a scarf. When it's done, it's time for the face.

In order to make the face, you should either have taken a digital photo of the person to be portrayed or have acquired the photo digitally—that's get a photo, and make a scan of it, using either Photoshop or another graphics program. You should follow the program's instructions to create an image of the person onto a disk you can use to print at an output shop, like a Kinko's, or with your own color printer. You will print the image onto an iron-on transfer, special paper that transfers the image to a cloth. Once the image has been printed onto the transfer, follow the instructions for your iron and impress the image onto a plain cloth, T-shirt, or pillowcase. Let the image set. Also many photo processing stores will do the same process from a print or negative.

Now wrap the cloth, T-shirt, or pillowcase around a basketball or football—you can use a balloon, but I don't recommend it because you apply a knife to the cake and, you know what, your subject sits there looking at his collapsed head—and set it at the head of the torso. Your cake is ready to serve to the surprise of absolutely everyone who sees it. Be sure to take a photo or video because this is something you're going to want to keep forever.

GEORDI LA FORGE

Starfleet records abound with stories of the feats of magic performed by Chief Engineer Geordi La Forge. Courage in the face of collapsing containment fields, recalibrations of complex energy-inversion formulas at the last minute to keep the *Enterprise* from exploding into exponential numbers of submicroscopic particles, and wild guesses in the face of Data's overwhelming androidian logic that save the day when there is almost no day left to save. This is Geordi La Forge. Like Tiresias, the blind prophet from Earth mythology, Geordi could see what others could not because his VISOR gave him powers of perception even Data did not have. Where the mighty Worf strode through darkness on sheer belief in his prowess to defeat the unknown, La Forge could see.

Dwight Schultz's "Lieutenant Barclay's Crab-Stuffed Salmon"

Lieutenant Barclay was certainly one of the more colorful figures on the *Enterprise.* Between his adventures on the holodeck as one of Earth's three musketeers to his strange paranoia about the transporter, Barclay was at the center of any mystery where his name was mentioned. He was La Forge's project for a while, as Geordi tried to make him into an assertive Starfleet officer. Then he became the protégé of Commander Troi, who tried to help his paranoia. But maybe it was Earth scientist Zefram Cochrane who finally brought Barclay around. Nothing helps the ego like a little hero worship.

For the purists out there, this is planked salmon, fish baked on a plank. You can buy an inexpensive cedar plank for $10 to $25 from a home and kitchen store like Williams Sonoma, or you can find one in many of the kitchen goodies catalogues on the Internet, and the results you'll get are indescribably delicious. Once you have the plank, you will need these ingredients:

> 2 pounds Atlantic Ocean salmon fillet (no Pacific farm salmon here)
>
> 1 pound fresh crabmeat (Maryland Chesapeake Bay crab is best, but you can use Louisiana blue or Carolina. A large-to-medium-sized freshly boiled Chesapeake Bay crab is even better. Your supermarket or seafood store will prepare the crab you select from the tank.)
>
> 6 cloves garlic, freshly crushed
>
> ⅓ cup virgin olive oil
>
> 2 tablespoons mayonnaise
>
> 1½ teaspoons Old Bay seasoning
>
> 1½ tablespoons celery seed (not celery salt)

¼ cup chopped fresh rosemary

sea salt and coarse-ground pepper to taste

First you need to "season" your plank. Using a paper towel, cover the top, bottom, and sides of the plank with some of the olive oil and place it in a cold oven. Then turn the oven to 350 degrees. Remove all shell pieces from the crabmeat, and combine the crab with mayonnaise, celery seed, Old Bay, and pepper in a large mixing bowl, and set aside to let the flavors set. Next, using your favorite sharp-bladed murder weapon, carve a pocket along the length of the salmon fillet, making sure not to break through to the other side. Once you have your pocket, press half of the crushed garlic cloves into the sides of the opening to coat the inside of the salmon fillet. Now, stuff the opening with crab, and when it is completely stuffed, press the sides of the fillet together as firmly as you can to keep them closed. Mix remaining olive oil, rosemary, salt, and remaining garlic and rub on the outside of the salmon and when it is as shiny as a mackerel in the moonlight, it's ready for the oven.

Using oven mitts, remove the hot plank from the oven, place the salmon on it skin side down, and return it to the oven for approximately 30 minutes, when you'll check to make sure the salmon is flaky. That means it's done. Remove the salmon and serve directly from the plank. This is wonderful with wild rice and roasted red and green peppers, a crackling white Frascati or Verdicchio, or maybe even a light, light Kirin beer. Serves four.

Pasta al Fiorella

Like his predecessors on the *Enterprise* bridge crew, La Forge was in love with his engines and sought refuge there when romance escaped him. But he was a man who loved his pasta, and that made him a man after my own heart. A person I would indeed like to cook for one day, especially to prepare for him my own version of his very, very favorite dish, pasta al fiorella. Here is an all-in-one meal that is just what it calls itself, pasta with little flowers. Can you eat flowers? Sure you can, and you find them at your local supermarket in the "this-is-for-yuppie-brokers-only" produce section. Next trip, scoop out hefty portions from the edible-flowers bin and plan to make pasta al fiorella that night. You start with a nice pesto sauce. Here's what I do:

1 1-pound package angel-hair pasta

1 1-pound package frozen spinach *or* fresh spinach leaves

2 small onions, chopped

2 cups edible flowers such as violets, pansies, *or* daisies

½ cup chopped black olives

½ cup freshly grated Romano *or* Pecorino cheese

2¼ tablespoons virgin olive oil

4 cloves fresh garlic, sliced

Begin by cooking your angel-hair pasta, but test it frequently for al dente because angel-hair cooks in nanoseconds. Don't let it get too soft, because the pasta's texture is important for this recipe. In a medium saucepan also cook your spinach in just enough water to cover the leaves and cook for 5 minutes on medium heat. For frozen spinach follow package directions. When the spinach is done, drain it and run it once through your food processor with a tablespoon of virgin olive oil so that it is coarsely chopped. Now heat the garlic and onions in another tablespoon of olive oil in a skillet. Just as they begin to sizzle, add the spinach and the remaining ¼ teaspoon of olive oil and half of your cheese, and stir until the cheese melts through and you have a soft pesto sauce. When the pasta is done, drain it and pour the pesto sauce over the pasta and toss. Now add the rest of the cheese and toss again.

Finally, wash your flowers and add them to the pasta, reserving some of the petals as a garnish, and toss through. Serve with a very sharp Italian white wine. Serves a very romantic two.

Fungilli

For me the saddest story of Chief Engineer Geordi La Forge is the story of a romantic dream, imagined love on the holodeck with a creature that inhabits the aspirations of the human spirit, but, alas, does not exist. He created a holoprogram that would ultimately save the *Enterprise*; however, the engineer would lose his heart. The holodeck created Dr. Leah Brahms. Geordi La Forge saw this holoimage as his ideal woman, and then fell in love with her. But when, years later, the real Leah appeared in his life in the flesh—all married, all business, all the time—their relationship was not to be. Poor Geordi! He was just about to establish a friendly relationship with the real Leah when she stumbled upon the holo-Leah and even the friendly relationship had to be repaired. And if this makes sense to you, you should look into a career handling peerage reports for the Borg or, even better, getting a job in politics. In any event, and there were many of them, Leah's favorite recipe was for fungilli, which Geordi replicated for her. Here's my version of Geordi's romantic meal with Leah Brahms—real Leah, holo-Leah.

If you like to make your own pasta and have some form of a bread maker and pasta machine, you can have pasta as fresh as today's harvest. If you don't, you can still enjoy fungilli in your own kitchen with some of the fresh refrigerated pastas on the market or the veggie pastas in some of the many health-food stores in your town.

Leah Brahms's and La Forge's fungilli is actually a heartily spicy pasta made from fresh mushrooms and garlic ground into a pasta dough and served piping hot with garlic-and-olive-oil sauce. You can try to Alfredo it up with a Romano cheese and cream sauce, but I wouldn't recommend it because the cream and cheese will overpower the subtle flavor of the mushrooms. The garlic will take care of itself.

1 dozen fresh mushrooms (wild are better), chopped

10 cloves garlic

4 teaspoons olive oil

½ cup freshly grated Romano cheese

P A S T A

2 cups semolina flour

2 eggs, beaten

1 teaspoon salt

2 tablespoons olive oil

½ cup water

Wash thoroughly about 1 dozen mushrooms of your choice, the more exotic the better. Wild mushrooms have a gamier flavor and usually make a better pasta, but just about any mushroom will do. Next, following the instructions for your brand of bread maker, mix the mushrooms and 6 cloves of crushed garlic into your pasta dough and prepare the pasta dough for your pasta maker. Now prepare the pasta, slice it into the shape you want, and cook it in boiling water until al dente. Drain and set aside while you brown 4 sliced garlic cloves in a teaspoon of olive oil. Just as the cloves begin to sizzle, pour the remaining olive oil over the pasta, add the garlic, and toss with fresh-grated Romano cheese, and serve.

You can also make a version of this dish using store-bought black squid pasta. Follow the same directions for the olive-oil-and-garlic sauce with cheese.

CHIEF MILES O'BRIEN

Miles O'Brien's life actually improved: from being the most put-upon individual onboard the *Enterprise,* he became the most put-upon individual onboard Deep Space 9. At least the *Enterprise* worked. When you threw a switch, something happened. But Deep Space 9 was run-down even before the Cardassians abandoned it to the Bajorans. It's a rough life, but what's a man to do? Roll your sleeves up, and get the station working, then spend some time down at the local pub for a pint of bitters. And indeed, that's what he does. Miles is an uncomplicated man with simple wants. He loves his family and he likes his pint. He also likes a very ancient Earth dish that he thinks was named after one of his ancestors in Dublin.

Potatoes O'Brien

Miles O'Brien didn't invent potatoes O'Brien; they've been around as a way to push yesterday's spuds on the kids long before Miles was ever born. There are plenty of different ways to make this dish; here's the easiest one from the chief's personal log.

> 3–6 leftover baked potatoes
> 1 green bell pepper, chopped *or* frozen chopped pepper right out
>   of the bag
> 1 medium onion chopped *or* also frozen out of the bag
> 1 cup grated cheddar cheese *or* more, to taste

1 tablespoon all-purpose flour

1 teaspoon celery seed

1 cup very hot milk

sea salt and red cayenne pepper or paprika to taste

Preheat oven to 350 degrees. Scoop out and chop up the meat from leftover boiled or baked potatoes. Then, in a large mixing bowl combine the pepper, onions, and celery seed. Mix in the chopped potato. Add the flour, salt, and half the cheese, and stir through. Spoon this mixture into a greased shallow baking dish. Pour the milk over the top, maybe add a pat or two of butter, and sprinkle on the rest of the cheese. Bake at 350 degrees for a ½ hour.

Plankton Loaf

Miles was a meat-and-potatoes man, but his new bride, Keiko, was strictly a vegetarian. Try as she might to get used to Miles's love of meat, she could not. But Keiko had another idea. Maybe she could wean Miles away from his hard-eating ways and lure him over to the world of the vegetarian. Since Miles liked his bread—every hardworking man does, you know—she figured that she might be able to awaken the subtleties of his taste buds by creating a totally vegetarian bread. Since she liked what plankton did for the food chain, she figured she'd start with it for her new husband. Hence, plankton loaf, as created by Keiko O'Brien.

Miles tried his best, but he hated it, and his disappointment was etched all over his face. Keiko should have tried this version of plankton loaf, made with zucchini, infused green tea leaves, and a touch of seaweed, that I intend to serve at tea. Use this recipe in your automatic bread maker.

1¾ cups bread flour

½ cup whole-wheat flour

1 teaspoon dry active yeast

1 cup finely chopped zucchini

½ teaspoon salt

½ cup lung jing *or* shou-mei warm green tea

¼ cup infused tea leaves

1 tablespoon finely chopped seaweed (dried or roasted, and you
     can add more to your taste)

1 teaspoon sugar

½ teaspoon ground ginger

Follow your bread machine's directions for adding ingredients to the hopper, and after the baking sequence has begun, add one nice leaf on top for decoration.

LIFE ON
DEEP SPACE 9

After the Cardassians retreated from Terok Nor and left it to the Bajorans, and after the Bajorans asked the Federation to administer it, and after the new station commander discovered the Bajoran wormhole into the Gamma Quadrant, and after the station was navigated into a protective position near the wormhole, Benjamin Sisko was upgraded from commander of a backwater station in nowherespace to protector of one of the most important facilities in the entire quadrant. Sisko's career quotient went right through the roof of the galaxy, and he began attracting enemies even more dangerous than some of the folks *Voyager's* had the pleasure to meet. Maybe there were no Kazon or Krenim, phage, Hirogen, or Species 8472, but the Jem'Hadar and shape-shifting Founders were trouble enough.

Sisko had his hands full from the moment he set foot on Deep Space 9, but at least he had the Promenade for fun and lots of commercial business to oversee. That's why I want to visit Deep Space 9 if we ever get back to the Alpha Quadrant and maybe even play a game of dabo with Quark. I know the business opportunities will be enormous, especially if I get the chance to talk to Quark, or the nagus, in private.

But enough about me, the food's what's the most important thing about Deep Space 9, and there are real restaurants that serve it. I could make a living there just by opening up Neelix's Delta Quadrant Warp Drive-In or The Wormhole Bar where the folks of the Gamma Quadrant meet the people of the Delta Quadrant. It would be the talk of the galaxy. Commander Sisko, a scion of an important restaurant-owning family on Earth, would be my first customer. Jake Sisko would write me a great review, and maybe even Papa Joe would give me a few tips here and there. There are lots of favorites I'd serve up for the Siskos, père, grand-père, et fils, on my eclectic menu of transgalactic treats.

COMMANDER BENJAMIN SISKO

Benjamin Sisko wasn't overwhelmed with joy when he was assigned to the ramshackle mining facility previously called Terok Nor by its Cardassian builders. Deep Space 9, as it was renamed, could barely stay in position, there were so many things wrong with it, but Sisko had run fleetyard facilities before and knew how to administer a supply and logistics command. He was in for a shock when he first saw the condition of Deep Space 9 and worked hard to bring the station to a Starfleet level of operational capability. That's when Commander Sisko—who had grown up in his father's bistro, Sisko's in *le vieux carré* in New Orleans, and knows his gumbo from his jambalaya—hit the jackpot. Not only did he get a wormhole to run, but he became the Emissary, one of the icons of the Bajoran religion. He learned how to appreciate Bajoran delicacies as well as the hot Tabasco-laced stews from his hometown. Sometimes he even combined the two cultures in a single dish like *ratamba* stew.

Ratamba Stew

This traditional Bajoran dish is much like an Earth vegetable stew. You can make it spicy—with garlic, chili peppers (red or green), a whiff of jalapeños, oregano, and parsley—or you can prepare it like a very garlicky mushroom and red or green bell pepper stew with chunky tomatoes, or you can prepare it with eggplant, squash, and rosemary, à la grecque, so to speak. Because Sisko prepared his *ratamba* stew over spinach linguini, we'll start with the mushroom stew, which is perfect for any spinach pasta. Chili pepper stew belongs over angel-hair pasta or even spinach pastina, and Greek vegetable stew belongs over rice. You can prepare the rice with sautéed spinach stirred through it, too.

Mushroom-and-Pepper Ratamba Stew

1 16-ounce package spinach linguini

2 12-ounce packages fresh mushrooms, chopped *or* **3 8-ounce cans canned mushrooms, drained and chopped**

3 red or green bell peppers, sliced thin

3 whole tomatoes, chopped

2 medium onions, chopped

6 cloves garlic, sliced thin or crushed

3 tablespoons olive oil

2 tablespoons oregano

1 tablespoon dried parsley

salt and pepper to taste

freshly grated Romano or Pecorino cheese to taste

Cook the spinach linguine according to the package instructions or until al dente. While the pasta is cooking, heat the olive oil in a large skillet and add the garlic. Just as soon as it begins to sizzle, add the peppers. Wait 5 minutes and add the onions, then the tomatoes and mushrooms. Stir rapidly over medium heat until the tomatoes begin to dissolve. Add the oregano and parsley and cover. When the pasta is cooked, drain and set aside. Simmer the mushroom and pepper stew for 15 minutes. Stir, correct the salt and pepper seasoning, and pour over the spinach pasta, toss through, grate the cheese over the top, and stir through one more time before serving. Serves four to six.

Chili-Pepper *Ratamba Stew*

1 or 2 16-ounce cans of pinto beans or kidney beans (to taste), rinsed and drained

6 large, juicy, ripe tomatoes *or* 2 8-ounce cans whole tomatoes (juice included), chopped

1 cup tomato juice

6 cloves garlic, crushed or sliced, *or* 5 tablespoons garlic powder

1 medium onion, chopped

1 medium green bell pepper, chopped

2 fresh chili peppers, chopped, *or* 3 tablespoons chili powder (or less, to taste)

½ 6-or 8-ounce can jalapeños or more to taste

1 handful of celery leaves, hand shredded *or* 1 cup chopped celery stalks

½ cup water or more as needed

1 bay leaf

2 tablespoons olive oil

1 teaspoon cumin seeds (You can use ground cumin, but the seeds are more potent, even though you have to score or bruise them with your hands as you drop them in.)

2 tablespoons oregano

2 or 3 fresh whole basil leaves, savagely torn apart in a Klingon manner

In a large skillet, sauté first your garlic in the olive oil, then chopped green pepper next and onion last. Don't let them burn. Next add the tomatoes, juice, ¼ cup water, celery leaves, and beans, and stir through. Bring the mixture just to the point of boiling and reduce heat. Add the bay leaf, jalapeños and chili peppers or powder and cumin seeds. Cook for 15 minutes, then add basil leaves and oregano. Cover and simmer for at least 1 hour. Taste to make sure the flavors have blended, and cook for another 15 minutes. Serve over angel-hair pasta, homemade spinach-and-garlic angel-hair pasta, plain or spinach pastina. Or 1 cup rice prepared with 1 cup chili stew mixed and 1 cup water. Serves four to six.

Eggplant *Ratamba* Stew

Here's a dish you can keep warm all day in your Crock-Pot or cook up in just under 1 hour. Serve it over spinach pasta or rice for a healthy vegetarian dinner.

1 large eggplant, sliced thin

1 large onion, chopped

2 green bell peppers, chopped

3 medium-sized fresh, juicy tomatoes, chopped, *or* 1 8-ounce can of tomatoes in juice, chopped

1 or 2 large carrots, cubed

1 handful celery leaves

½ cup olive oil

5 cloves garlic, sliced

1 pinch fresh basil

½ tablespoon oregano

Preheat oven to 350 degrees and slice your eggplant. You can either peel it or not, depending on the texture you like. Grease a flat baking dish with ¼ cup olive oil and 2 garlic cloves and heat in oven for about 5 minutes. Then arrange the eggplant slices in the dish, turn once or twice to coat them with oil and bake for 15 minutes while you prepare the rest of the stew.

Brown the pepper, onion, and remaining garlic cloves in a large pot in ¼ cup of olive oil. Next add the tomatoes, celery leaves, and carrots, and cover. When eggplant has browned, add it to the pot and continue cooking for another 30 minutes over medium heat. Add the remaining ingredients and spices and cook for another 30 minutes or until the carrots are tender. Serve this over spinach pasta, angel-hair pasta, or rice that you've prepared with some of the olive oil, garlic, and tomato liquid from the stew. Serves four to six.

Pasta Boudin

**½ pound Klingon blood sausage, *or* Creole sausage, *or* even, fresh
Italian hot sausage, cooked, this can be sliced or left whole**

1 1-pound package of linguini

6 cloves garlic, crushed

½ cup grated Romano cheese

¼ cup (½ stick) butter, sliced

⅛ cup olive oil

1 teaspoon dried parsley

fresh-ground black pepper to taste

At Sisko's, Joseph Sisko prepares a traditional French Creole dish, boudin sausage, or blood sausage, over whatever pasta is his favorite for the day. Some days it's angel-hair, others it's linguini, one time Papa Sisko even experimented with fettucini, but that was only because he wanted to try out a new cream sauce and put the boudin sausage on the side. His son, Benjamin, prepares his pasta boudin with linguini ripping with garlic because he likes his Klingon blood sausage nice and spicy.

To make this dish at home for yourself, start with about a ½ pound of Worf's Klingon blood sausage, or Creole or Italian sausage, and set it aside. Then begin cooking the linguini, and while the water's boiling slice the butter, put the olive oil in a cup, and peel the garlic cloves that you will crush between spoons or in a garlic press. Also grate the cheese in advance. The secret to making great pasta boudin is that all the flavors come together in about 60 seconds, so you have to work fast.

As soon as the pasta's al dente, drain it and stir through a smidgen of olive oil so the noodles don't stick. Put it into a large bowl and immediately stir through the remaining olive oil and the garlic, so that it melts and coats. Then stir through the butter and cheese; top with parsley and pepper. When it's just a tick shy of creamy, stir in the sausage and serve. You can also serve the blood sausage on the side. Serves four to six.

Chicken à la Sisko

The commander likes to prepare this one-dish chicken-in-the-pot meal with Cajun spices and rice. The rice can be plain, or made with some of the rosemary, gumbo filé, bay leaf, and tomato juice you are cooking in the chicken pot. This makes a great dinner for four to six or even eight, if they eat like Kes did, but it also works when you're flying solo and want the leftovers for lunch the next day, especially if you can brown-bag it to the office in a microwavable container that you can nuke and take back to your desk with a mug of Chiraltan tea with a cinnamon stick, Bajoran style.

1 frying chicken, quartered, with legs and wings separated

2 large red-skinned potatoes, chopped

4 carrots, cubed or thickly sliced

2 medium-sized onions, thinly sliced

3 large juicy tomatoes, quartered

2 celery stalks and 1 handful celery leaves, chopped

1 green bell pepper, sliced (optional)

½ cup (1 stick) butter

¼ cup olive oil

2 cloves garlic, sliced

1 bay leaf

1 teaspoon gumbo filé

1 teaspoon rosemary

1 teaspoon thyme

1 teaspoon dried parsley *or* chopped fresh parsley to taste

1 teaspoon red cayenne pepper

1 teaspoon Tabasco sauce

salt and additional pepper to taste

1 to 2 cups rice, depending upon number of servings

      (1 cup uncooked rice equals 4 servings)

2 to 4 cups water (that is, double the quantity of the rice)

1 or 2 chicken bouillon cubes (one cube for each cup of rice)

Begin preparing the chicken by quartering, separating legs and wings, and rinsing away blood and organ parts thoroughly. Then, in a large stew pot like a Le Creuset, brown chicken slowly in a ½ stick of butter and a touch of olive oil. You will brown the chicken for at least a ½ hour before adding any other ingredients.

In a separate pot, brown the garlic in the rest of the olive oil and a ½ stick of butter. Then add the carrots and potatoes and cook for 15 minutes. Next add the onions and green pepper, brown them, and add the tomatoes, bay leaf, and celery. Cook for another ½ hour. Add a few tablespoons of water to the chicken and add all of the remaining seasonings. When the vegetables have cooked for a ½ hour, add them to the chicken and cook for at least 2 hours over low heat. Keep checking the chicken and vegetables for tenderness and doneness, particularly the carrots and potatoes. The dish is ready when the chicken is nice and white and cooked completely through and the carrots and potatoes are nice and soft. The tomatoes will dissolve into a very mild chunky sauce, with bits of skin for color.

During the last 30 to 40 minutes, prepare the rice with chicken bouillon cubes added to the water. After the rice has started to boil, add a bit of the vegetable mixture and some of the tomatoes for color and taste. You may also use garlic salt instead of regular salt for a little more flavor. When the rice and chicken are done, serve by spooning chicken and vegetables over rice and topping with a sprig of parsley or even watercress. You'd be surprised how good this tastes accompanied by a hot, steaming mug of Chiraltan tea, especially laced with lots of Bajoran spices, and a chunk of greenbread slathered in Rigelian yak butter. Serves four to six.

Chiraltan Tea

Chiraltan tea has all the heft and kick of *raktajino* without the bitter aftertaste you sometimes get when *raktajino* is left to heat in the pot most of the morning. Good *raktajino* has to be made fresh, and replicators just don't give you the same blast at the beginning of an early morning watch. The closest equivalent to the smoked flavor of Chiraltan tea leaves is Tibetan Lapsang souchong tea, the tea of the hidden cities in the Himalayas. The heavy smokiness of the leaves and the rich, rich flavor around the edge makes it a late-night beverage of choice for workaholics, like Sisko, who gets coffeed out during a brutal 26-7 after the invasion of the Alpha Quadrant by the Dominion. As a perfect complement to green-bread or even a hefty dinner, this tea stands up to the flavor. If you want to drink it Sisko-style, that is, Bajoran-style the way the Emissary likes it, order it with a cinnamon stick; swizzle it around, but take it out before you drink it. Even the Bajorans don't take their cinnamon straight, because the stick gets caught in those little ridges in the bridges of their noses and itches like crazy.

Greenbread

Commander Sisko likes this Yaderan staple for breakfast, as a late lunch, but particularly with his Chiraltan tea. Rather than hunt all around the Bajoran wormhole for the roots the Yaderans use, you simply substitute either a mild or spicy pesto sauce. You can also bake it with green tea for a dessert version. But if you really want to achieve an exotic taste to complement Chiraltan tea or any of the other spicy teas that turn up on Deep Space 9, try to prepare yours with a few flakes of either dried or roasted seaweed.

You can buy seaweed at any Asian market, where you'll find scores of varieties. There's rolled seaweed, flattened seaweed, roasted-for-sushi seaweed, and dried seaweed by the bag. You probably have to rehydrate the dried stuff by following the package instructions. Don't use too much seaweed, maybe ¼ cup at most, because the stuff is truly intense.

To make this in your automatic bread maker, begin by following the instructions for basic white bread that came with your appliance and add either ½ cup pesto sauce—you can use packaged—for a sharp taste that will go with chicken à la Sisko or *ratamba* stew, or infused green tea leaves for a dessert bread. But add just ¼ cup of seaweed as the last dry ingredient, and enjoy the fresh aroma as it bakes.

Don't have an automatic bread maker? No problem! You can buy what's known as "quick bread" mix from the supermarket and bake bread right in your own oven just like the pros do. Again, use the white bread mix, follow the package instructions for your particular oven and baking pan setup, add either the ½ cup pesto sauce or the infused green tea leaves, and don't forget the ¼ cup of seaweed. The Yaderans will wish they had your recipe, especially when the aroma wafts skyward.

Sisko's Shrimp Creole with Mandalay Sauce

Just what is a "Creole" anyway? Is it like jambalaya, gumbo, or even a bayou bouillabaisse? I researched this long and hard after I came across the menus from Sisko's and discovered that a "Shrimp Creole" is, basically, shrimp in a tomato sauce made from Creole tomatoes grown only in southern Louisiana. The essential tomato sauce itself has what twentieth-century Louisiana natives referred to as the "holy trinity" of ingredients, Creole tomatoes, celery, and bell peppers. You have to sauté these in garlic and oil, mix in some hot sauce like Tabasco, add a pinch of sugar to cut the sour taste of the tomatoes, and simmer for 20 minutes. While you're doing this, peel and boil shrimp and add to the mixture to cook for another 20 minutes. You can also add ½ cup of the shrimp stock—the shrimp-boiling water that has in it onions, celery leaves, garlic, bay leaf, and pepper—to the Creole sauce and simmer for another 10 minutes. The sauce is done in under 1 hour and can be served over rice.

Joe Sisko's recipe is a version of this, a good old-fashioned shrimp or crab boil with a hearty tomato, celery, and bell pepper sauce served over rice. It was one of Joe Sisko's favorite dishes and a favorite of his son, Benjamin, and his grandson, Jake. You can start by boiling your shrimp in beer with a mixture of bay leaves, pickling spices, and cloves. You can use any size shrimp; however, I recommend large because it allows you to slice them any way you want. Use the jumbos you can ride for barbecuing. Save the shrimp boil with beer and spices for the Mandalay sauce which is, itself, a base for jambalaya or gumbo.

3 pounds medium-to-large shrimp, peeled

4 quarts water

16 ounces beer

1 teaspoon cloves, 1 teaspoon shredded bay leaves (*or* 2 teaspoons Old Bay seasoning), and 1 teaspoon pickling spice (You can also use 1½ tablespoons of a seasoning product called crab boil.)

6 fresh tomatoes, chopped

1 8-ounce can whole tomatoes in juice

1 6-ounce can tomato paste

2 medium-sized onions, chopped

1 large green *or* red bell pepper, chopped

5 stalks celery with leaves, chopped

8 cloves garlic, sliced

¼ cup olive oil

1 tablespoon butter

2 bay leaves *or* 2 tablespoons Old Bay seasoning

1 handful peppercorns

1 handful cumin seed, bruised

1 teaspoon pickling spice

1 teaspoon rosemary

1 teaspoon cayenne pepper

1 teaspoon Tabasco sauce

2 cups uncooked rice, to be prepared in shrimp-boil-and-beer
mixture with tomato juice from your Mandalay sauce.

Begin by peeling then boiling your shrimp in a mix of 4 quarts water with 8 ounces beer to which you've added the cloves, bay leaves, pickling spice mixture *or* Old Bay *or* crab boil. While the shrimp are boiling—and they only have to turn from gray to a nice pinkish red—prepare your deep skillet by simmering the garlic in the olive oil, adding peppers and onions, and then the butter. What you'll have is a sizzling olive oil and butter sauce with garlic, bell peppers, and onions. You can actually stop here if you want and pour this over the shrimp for shrimp Cajun style. However, if you would like to prepare the Mandalay sauce, you must continue.

After the garlic, peppers, and onions have combined, add the shrimp to the skillet and stir through. Next add all the fresh tomatoes, the canned tomatoes, ½ cup of the strained shrimp boil, and the tomato paste, and simmer on low for at least 20 minutes. When the tomatoes have begun to dissolve, add the rest of the seasonings and simmer for 1 hour to let all the flavors combine. If it still tastes a bit too harsh, simmer for another ½ hour. This is not a quick meal.

After your spices and tomatoes have begun to combine, draw off about ½ cup of liquid for the rice and set aside. You will need an additional 2½ cups water and 8 ounces of beer to cook the rice. During the last ½ hour of cooking your shrimp in Mandalay sauce, prepare the rice using the Mandalay sauce liquid you've set aside. You can serve 4 hearty portions or 8 regular portions. You can also serve 1 disgustingly intense portion stretched over any number of hours. Once you start gorging on this, resistance . . . You get the picture.

Jambalaya

"Jambalaya, crawfish pie, filé gumbo"

—OLD CAJUN FOLK SONG

Technically a Creole stew, jambalaya is a rice dish that can be prepared any way you like it with any leftovers you have on hand. It's description sounds like its name, a jumble of vegetables, fish, meat, or poultry. I can make it vegetarian style, baked, with mushrooms and olives. I can also make it in a skillet with any meat, fish, game, or shellfish that I feel like using. It can be very spicy, loaded with chili and cayenne pepper, or more of a mild, thick tomato–and–rice soup. Jambalaya was a staple at Joseph Sisko's restaurant, where he liked it spicy. He said that his wife and daughter—Commander Sisko's sister, Judith—never put enough cayenne pepper in their jambalaya. Because I'm a Talaxian used to dealing with all different cultures, I can make a jambalaya many ways to satisfy different tastes. I make a vegetarian style jambalaya that I can serve to Tuvok and Commander Chakotay. I also have a meat-and-fish version that I can serve to Tom Paris and B'Elanna Torres for their private dinners, and a true Klingon version with Klingon blood sausage. My Harry Kim version is from California with jalapeños, and my recipe for Quark's, should I ever wind up at Deep Space 9, contains New Mexico green chiles in honor of the crash of an alien vessel near the city of Roswell. It was there that someone, Starfleet records from the mid-twentieth–century on Earth tell us, who looked awfully like a Ferengi, wound up at a military base and inadvertently started this whole UFO business by getting the 509th intelligence officer Jesse Marcel worked up, Colonel Blanchard excited enough to order Lieutenant Walter Haut to write his famous press release, and General Roger Ramey "madder 'n Hell" when he pulled the plug and

called it a weather balloon. Imagine, a Ferengi in a weather balloon. Actually, we all know that it was really a Project Mogul balloon because all Ferengi are the biggest business moguls in the Alpha Quadrant.

1 to 2 cups uncooked rice in 2 to 4 cups water (2 cups water to 1 cup uncooked rice) depending upon number of people you are serving

2 teaspoons crushed bay leaves

1 teaspoon pickling spices

2 stalks celery with leaves, chopped

1 large onion, chopped

1 large bell pepper, chopped

3 large, quartered tomatoes *or* 1 16-ounce can tomatoes

1 dozen mushrooms, sliced (optional)

1 red chili pepper, seeded and chopped (optional)

¼ cup olive oil

½ cup (1 stick) butter

6 cloves garlic, crushed

2 teaspoons cumin seed, bruised

You can prepare this dish two ways: baked or simmered. First, however, boil the rice in water to which you've added the crushed bay leaves and pickling spices. When the rice is boiling, reduce heat to a low simmer and cover. The rice will take about 20 minutes to cook.

For the simmered version, just after you've turned the boiling rice back to simmer, in a skillet, sauté the garlic in the olive oil and butter, then the peppers, the optional chili pepper, and onions. As those begin to cook, add the mushrooms to the pan. After the mushrooms have browned, remove the entire mixture from the skillet and set aside. Now, in the same skillet, combine the tomatoes, celery, and the cumin seed and simmer for at least 40 minutes. Add cooked vegetables back, stir through. Add ¼ cup of jambalaya mixture to the rice just before it's finished cooking and stir through the browned mushrooms, peppers, optional chili pepper, and onions. Set aside. When the jambalaya sauce is finished, pour over the rice and serve. For the baked version, preheat your oven to 300 degrees, and when the sauce is finished cooking add the cooked rice to the mixture, pour into a baking dish, and bake for 40 minutes. Serves six.

You can be very creative with all the different versions. For the meat-and-fish version, I'd begin by frying ½ pound of bacon, along with a slice of ham and some sausage, in a large skillet while the rice is cooking. At the same time, I would also boil about 1½ pounds of medium shrimp in the shrimp boil, along with any other combination of shellfish such as clams and oysters. You can also prepare monkfish or even cod in your broiler and add to the boil. Set the meat aside when done. Prepare the jambalaya sauce as in the vegetarian recipe—I would leave out the mushrooms—and add the meat and shellfish at the very end. Then either pour over rice for individual servings or add the rice to the jambalaya sauce and ladle out into individual bowls. When you're making this meat-and-fish version, I would thin the sauce out with 2 cups water from the shrimp and shellfish boil for a more soup-like instead of sauce-like consistency.

The meat-and-fish version of Sisko's jambalaya can also be enhanced with leftover barbecued or roasted chicken. It can also be served over fried catfish and rice.

For your Roswell 1947, jambalaya, add a finely chopped and seeded green chili pepper instead of a red chili pepper to the mix and another couple of teaspoons of cumin seed, bruised. The result is a mild form of chili jambalaya, combining soft Gulf Coast and fiery southwestern flavors. For a California style jambalaya, in place of the chili pepper, add 5 chopped and seeded jalapeño peppers, but do it in moderation because jalapeños add lots of hot spicy flavor. A great side dish to accompany your jambalaya is Ben Sisko's favorite, sautéed beets. Serves six.

Sautéed Beets

Commander Sisko liked his jambalaya in a sauce made from sautéed salt back or even bacon, flavored with a pat of butter. To this you add thin-sliced canned beets and sauté in a very shallow pan until they're done. You can also shred the beets or cube them, according to your own taste. I don't like the animal fat myself and prefer to use a lot of butter and salt and keep stirring the beets until they start turning brown on the edges.

Endive Salad

The commander has a passion for endive, probably because like his other favorites, it is used a lot in Creole and Cajun cooking. Endive can be used in a lettuce, leek, hearts of palm, and fennel salad. Simply wash all of the ingredients and drain. Chop, toss in a salad bowl, and serve with balsamic vinegar or vinaigrette dressing. A snappy endive salad is a particularly good complement to sautéed beets, with or without jambalaya, or it's even good all by itself for lunch. It's also great for a late snack when you can't sleep but don't want to go to bed after a whole meal. Endive is also quite healthy.

Gumbo

Gumbo was another specialty at Sisko's and a favorite of Benjamin's and Jake's. This is soup made from tomatoes and powdered sassafras leaves—called filé—and contains a generous amount of okra for both taste and texture. As do other Louisiana bayou specialties, gumbo contains the basic celery, garlic, bell pepper, and onion, and may have some bay leaf as well as other spices. It is either piquant or mild, according to taste, can be served with or without meat or chicken, and contains rice. Gumbo is a soup rather than a sauce, so in addition to its being a one-pot dish, it can be a one-meal dish, or something you can have with a nice vegetable and a salad, or a first course to a really sumptuous pasta and shellfish dinner. Gumbo is also a terrific leftover. For either chicken or beef, the base of tomatoes, okra, garlic, bell peppers, celery, onions, and cayenne pepper is the same. You can certainly make it with rice, the way I like it.

1 frying chicken, cut into pieces and floured

¼ pound bacon or fatback

6 quarts water, boiling

1 16-ounce can tomatoes with juice

1 cup tomato juice

2 cups okra, sliced

1 green or red bell pepper, chopped

6 cloves garlic, chopped

4 stalks celery and leaves, chopped

1 medium onion, chopped

2 teaspoon filé (sassafras powder)

1 teaspoon cayenne pepper

1 teaspoon cumin seed, bruised, *or* 1 teaspoon ground cumin

1 tablespoon olive oil

1 teaspoon Tabasco sauce

1 bay leaf

½ cup uncooked rice

Begin by rendering your fatback or frying bacon in a large skillet, remove the meat when rendered, and preserve the cooking grease. In flour seasoned with garlic salt and black peppercorns, coat the chicken pieces and, in the same skillet, brown in the bacon grease. After the chicken has begun to turn brown, about 10 minutes on moderate heat, add the tomatoes, garlic, okra, peppers, onions, celery, and olive oil to the skillet and stir through. This mixture will cook together for another 15 minutes. While the chicken and vegetables are cooking, remove 1 cup of water from the boiling water, add rice, bring back to a boil, then reduce to simmer. When the chicken has browned, remove the chicken and vegetables from skillet, drain, set the vegetables aside in a separate bowl, and return the chicken to the skillet. Next remove enough water from the boiling water to cover the chicken completely in the skillet and let simmer for approximately 30 minutes or until the chicken meat separates from the bone. Remove chicken from skillet and debone. Add the vegetables, chicken meat, and the stock back, then add the rest of the seasonings and simmer. At this point your rice should also be done, so remove it from the heat and set it aside. Simmer, but do not boil the chicken and vegetables, for about 30 to 45 minutes or until all the vegetables are nice and soft. Serve with rice on the side.

For beef gumbo, you do not need to flour the beef, although you can if you want to. Whether you flour or not, you should cook your beef in the grease of either fatback or bacon. Begin with about 2 pounds of any cut of cubed stewing meat or a cut of roast that you cube yourself and brown in bacon grease or fatback in a large stew pot. Add 3 quarts water, your bay leaf, garlic, celery, onion, some sprigs of fresh parsley, and pepper. Simmer for at least 2 hours, then skim the fat. Now add the tomatoes and okra to liquid and bring to a rapid boil for about five minutes. Reduce heat to simmer and add the gumbo filé, cumin, more salt to taste, cayenne pepper, and Tabasco, and simmer for an hour during which time you should cook the rice separately in 1 cup of the stock drawn off from the gumbo. Simmer rice in the gumbo stock until soft, about 25 to 30 minutes. When the rice and gumbo are done, combine in individual serving bowls or let your guests add their own rice at the table.

This is an absolutely perfect soup to serve with another Sisko favorite, bread pudding. Serves four.

Bread-Pudding Soufflé

This specialty of Sisko's is made with three-day-old or stale bread. It works especially well with greenbread made with infused green tea leaves—no pesto or seaweed here, please. Greenbread from green tea is pungent and is nicely enhanced by the judicious use of brown sugar or honey, cinnamon, vanilla, and cream in this recipe. When chilled, it tastes surprisingly like the green-tea ice cream you can find in Asian markets. Hot, it tastes more like the pudding it's supposed to be.

> **4 cups or more three-day-old stale bread, chopped into coarse cubes**
>
> **2 cups raisins, dates, *or* figs, chopped**
>
> **4 cups whole milk *or* 3 cups milk and 1 cup light cream**
>
> **3 eggs**
>
> **¼ cup light brown sugar or honey**
>
> **1 teaspoon vanilla extract**

Preheat your oven to 325 degrees. Blend the milk, eggs, brown sugar or honey, and vanilla together with a hand mixer or a blender on low until nice and creamy. Add mixture to the bread cubes and fruit, and either stir through or use your hand mixer on low to combine the ingredients until soggy. Grease a 9-inch baking pan and pour in the mixture, stirring through once or twice to make sure it's thoroughly blended and uniform. Bake for 30 minutes. The top should just turn brown, but don't let it burn.

You can serve this piping hot with cream or a fruit topping, or you can serve it cold. If you serve it at room temperature, you should heat some heavy cream with a splash of honey to use as a topping. Serves four.

Uttaberry Crepes

Uttaberries come from the planet Betazed and are a favorite of the natives there. How they turned up in Quark's, I'll never know, but Quark had a great recipe for crepes prepared with uttaberries that Sisko simply devoured. Harry Kim told me that uttaberries bore a remarkable resemblance to and tasted just like the blueberries you can get on Earth. Harry remembered eating blueberries fresh, packed in those cute little wooden boxes, from the neighborhood markets in San Francisco. I imagine you can get them anywhere. Crepes are also very easy to make, whether you use the recipe you can find on the boxes of instant pancake batter or make them the way the French used to.

1 cup all-purpose flour

1 cup whole milk

3 eggs, beaten

¼ cup granulated sugar

2 tablespoons butter, melted

1 teaspoon grated orange, *or* **lemon rind,** *or* **1/4 teaspoon orange**
        or lemon extract

½ teaspoon vanilla extract

1 pinch of salt

confectioners' sugar to dust finished crepes

2 cups fresh blueberries, washed and stirred through with ¼ cup
        sugar and 2 tablespoons water to lightly sweeten blueberries

While you're gently melting the butter, combine the flour, salt, and granulated sugar in a medium-sized bowl and set aside. Make sure the butter doesn't burn; remove from heat. Let it cool. Beat the eggs and milk together, and then beat in the cooled melted butter. Now add the orange or lemon extracts or grated rinds and the vanilla extract. Beat until smooth and then combine with the flour mixture, continuing to beat, even with your hand mixer until smooth.

Lightly butter and heat a small skillet or a crepe pan, and pour in just enough batter to cover the bottom. It should be a light, thin layer, and you should rock the skillet back and forth to make sure the layer is an even depth. Just as it begins to set, spoon in the blueberries to form a thin line down the middle of the crepe. As the edges of the crepe brown, quickly flip each side over the middle to wrap the blueberries, then flip the entire crepe over and set aside on a warm platter. Dust each crepe with confectioners' sugar and serve plain, with ice cream, with cream, or even a touch of honey. Yield one dozen crepes.

JADZIA DAX

I do appreciate Klingon culture, as does Jadzia Dax. So here is my encomium to Dax in all of her/his incarnations, especially the present one: Lieutenant Commander Jadzia Dax, the Klingon culture aficionado extraordinaire. She can wield a *bat'leth* with the best of them, whether it be in a holodeck simulation or in the kinds of free-for-all matches Klingons truly relish. She likes wild, loud midnight parties full of Andorian ale and lots of bloodwine. And she has half of Deep Space 9 running around panting after her. I wouldn't mind a Trill like Jadzia beaming around *Voyager*. I'm a spot man myself, although you wouldn't think so just to look at me, and certainly appreciate a fine symmetrical pattern of organized skin pigmentation as well as the next guy. I think Jadzia and I would get along quite well. After all, I can rustle up a Klingon dish fit for Kahless himself and now, since I have led Klingons into battle, you could say that I know what it takes. If she likes the highwayman business spirit of the Ferengi, which she says she does, she'd love the life of a Talaxian trader. We could show the Ferengi a thing or two about business, I can tell you that. And unlike the Ferengi, the Talaxians are born diplomats. I think Jadzia could go for me in a big way.

Azna

Azna is Jadzia's favorite dish. She likes this so much, she recommends it to Commander Sisko, claiming it will add years to his life. What is this stuff, magic? Not at all; it's a kind of vegetable stew that Trills regard very highly because it does provide them a kind of longevity. On Earth, the closest stew is a simple mixed-vegetable curry with carrots, broccoli, and potatoes in a mild sauce.

2 cups fresh *or* frozen chopped broccoli, in large pieces

1 white potato, cubed

2 carrots, sliced

1 cup whole milk

½ cup sour cream *or* light cream

2 tablespoons sifted all-purpose flour

1 tablespoon coriander

1 teaspoon cumin seed, bruised *or* cumin powder

1 teaspoon salt

½ teaspoon turmeric

2 tablespoons (¼ stick) butter

Begin by steaming fresh broccoli on a rack in a saucepan filled with boiling water until the broccoli is tender. You can also use frozen broccoli boiled or microwaved until tender about 2 minutes. Steaming retains more of the vitamins and nutrients. You can boil or microwave potatoes. Boil potatoes with carrots for about 30 minutes or until they are tender. Or microwave the potatoes on high for 10 minutes, check for doneness, and microwave for increments of 5 minutes until they are thoroughly cooked. If you microwave the potatoes, boil or steam the carrots until they are tender. Drain and set aside while you melt the butter in a saucepan and add the flour and milk, and stir until completely mixed. Bring this sauce to a boil and quickly reduce to simmer. Simmer until it thickens, and then add all the seasonings and continue to simmer for 1 more minute. Stir in sour cream or light cream and simmer for 2 minutes. Slowly add vegetables. Stir while you simmer for about 1 more minute, and then serve. Serves four.

Andorian Tuber Root

Andorian potatoes are another one of Jadzia's favorites. You can bake 'em, you can boil 'em, but I like 'em in a pie. My version for your kitchens is a baked sweet potato pie with an optional topping of marshmallows.

2 large sweet potatoes

⅛ cup (¼ stick) butter, melted

½ cup whole milk (you can use half-and-half)

¼ cup light brown sugar

1 tablespoon plain *or* vanilla yogurt

½ teaspoon vanilla extract

1 pinch nutmeg

1 16-ounce package marshmallows (optional)

1 packaged pie crust

Wash and pierce sweet potatoes, then microwave on high for 20 minutes while you preheat your oven to 350 degrees. When potatoes are cooked, mash them in a mixing bowl while they are steaming hot, add the melted butter, and stir thoroughly. Next add the sugar, vanilla, milk, and yogurt. Finally add the nutmeg. Line a pie tin with the crust and spoon in the sweet potato pie filling. Bake for 30 minutes. If you want to top with a nice marshmallow crust, cut marshmallows in half and arrange them over the top of the pie. Bake for an additional 15 minutes, and serve. I'm told that Jadzia liked this dish much more than did Sisko, even though a baked sweet potato pie is exactly what Joe Sisko served at his restaurant. Serves six to eight.

Raktajino

You can enjoy your Andorian tuber root as a side dish or as a dessert. Either way, don't forget the *raktajino,* the hefty, robust Klingon coffee that everybody loves on Deep Space 9 and that Tom Paris would kill for on *Voyager. Raktajino* is not some wimpy coffee you buy in a can; it's real java, aged java you can make even more robust and vigorous by mixing with dark French roast or Italian espresso beans that you grind yourself.

Vary the proportions of dark roast to java for taste and strength. You can prepare it in your drip coffeemaker or, for a jolt of *raktajino* power right through your bionic neural network, in your French plunger coffee carafe. You can also do something really crazy and look for a vacuum coffeemaker. Some of them are still around, especially at secondhand stores, flea markets, and swap meets. Follow the package directions for grinding your coffee really fine and for preparing the brew. Vacuum coffee is interesting because it captures the real essence of the coffee. But it's easy to ruin, and once the seals between the top and bottom vacuum bulbs wear out, the coffeemaker no longer has the pressure to force the flavor out of the grind. So don't be afraid to experiment with different blends—java, mocha java, a dark French or Italian roast—and with different coffeemakers.

Icoberry Juice Cocktail

Jadzia loves the sharp, sweet snap of icoberries, as you know, but she can't drink the juice without scratching herself silly because of her Trill allergies to the stuff. If you don't have allergies and can get your hands on an automatic juicer—like a Juiceman or something like it—or even a straight-out blender, you can create this berry concoction yourself. There are a couple of variations you might try. The first is a basic mix of fresh strawberries in fresh apple juice. You first quarter and remove the seeds from a couple of apples and run them through the juicer; then add strawberries for taste and color, every now and then stirring and sipping the concoction to test for tartness and sweetness. Once you're happy with the result, you're done.

You can also use any version of bottled or canned apple juice—the bottled fresh stuff from fruit stands has a decidedly different taste—along with fresh or frozen strawberries puréed in your blender. If you find strawberries too sweet and want to go for a more exotic taste, try red or black raspberries, both of which come frozen as well. Mixing raspberries and apple juice yields a very interesting taste. Want something even wilder? Add just a touch of cranberries to the mix and watch your kids' eyes pop wide open. The stuff's loaded with vitamin C and it looks like a standard Klingon blood beverage. Mix the proportions according to your own taste and, just the way I do on *Voyager,* experiment, experiment, experiment.

Moba Fruit

Here's another exotic Bajoran fruit delicacy that Dax says tickles her taste buds. I've looked around for something to replace it, but the best I could come up with is a kiwi, a sweet and tangy little fruit with a very fuzzy skin. Slice it really thin and serve it with *jumja* tea or even Earl Grey, hot. You can also add some kiwi as *moba* fruit to a dessert that Jadzia likes called Citrus Blend.

Citrus Blend

Here's a fruit cocktail that Jadzia likes any time, day or night, just as long as it doesn't have too many fresh icoberries. The trick to preparing this is to let the fruit flavors blend in your refrigerator for a few hours—even overnight is better—before you serve. You can sweeten this with some sugar, or you can add a dash of vanilla extract and some lemon juice and let the fruits speak for themselves.

> ½ pint strawberries, sliced
>
> ½ pint raspberries
>
> 2 tablespoons fresh water
>
> ½ cup sliced peaches
>
> ½ cup sliced kiwi
>
> any other favorite fruits, including blueberries, blackberries,
>
> > cantaloupe, honeydew, or other melons
>
> ½ teaspoon vanilla extract
>
> ½ cup sugar (optional)
>
> ½ teaspoon lemon juice

First, wash berries thoroughly in water as cold as you can stand, thinly slicing them under the running water and dropping the slices into a very large punch bowl. After slicing, dribble 2 tablespoons fresh water over them into the bowl. Do not drain. Add peaches, kiwi, and melon or other fruits along with vanilla, sugar, and lemon juice, stir, and let them sit in the liquid for at least 4 hours in your refrigerator before serving. Serves four to five.

MAJOR KIRA NERYS

A freedom fighter from the time she was twelve years old, Kira Nerys was born during the Cardassian occupation of Bajor and joined the Shakaar resistance cell of the Bajoran underground. She had a hard life before the Cardassians were finally driven out: an internee at a Singha refugee camp, a secret agent sent to Terok Nor to retrieve a list of Bajoran collaborators, and the member of a military expedition to liberate the infamous Gallitep labor camp from the Cardassians. So she knows how to fight. She also knows how to kill, having blown away the chemist Vaatrik after he figured out Kira's real identity on Terok Nor. Ironically, she could have been in deep trouble when Odo first suspected her of pulling off the murder, but she tricked him into thinking her innocent. It wasn't until years later that Odo learned the truth.

Kira—like most Bajorans who lived under the tyrannical Cardassian colonial regime that systematically starved them by taking food off the planet—loves to eat.

Matopin Rock Fungi

Kira is really into fungus in a big way, a 'shroom lover from the time she first routed around for the wildest species of these delicacies while hiding from the Cardassians on Bajor. Her favorites are the Matopin rock fungi, tasty little morsels you can find only on the underside of rocks—kind of like the Cardassians, she says, especially Dukat. While I lichen Matopin rock fungi more to the conventional spotted spores of Talax than to the commercially harvested mushrooms on Earth, we can't be too choosy. I like to prepare an Earth version of Matopin rock fungi with oversized mushrooms that I sauté in butter and then combine with a canned mushroom soup and spices. You can serve this as a sauce, but I like to make a mushroom pastry out of it by folding it into refrigerated crescent rolls. Here it is:

> 1 pound packaged raw mushrooms
>
> 1 8-ounce package refrigerated crescent roll dough (Pillsbury crescent rolls, for example)
>
> 1 8-ounce can of cream of mushroom soup (Campbell's, for example)
>
> ½ cup (1 stick) butter
>
> 3 cloves garlic
>
> 1 tablespoon heavy cream
>
> 2 teaspoons rosemary
>
> 1 teaspoon thyme leaves
>
> salt and pepper to taste

While you preheat your oven to 350 degrees, heat can of Campbell's, or another brand, condensed cream of mushroom soup in a small saucepan over very low heat following the directions on the can. Wash and then scrub the fresh mushrooms. Slice the mushrooms, making sure to discard the very bottoms of the stems; then slice the garlic cloves into the butter in a large skillet on medium heat and add the sliced mushrooms. Keep turning and stirring constantly so they don't burn. When the mushrooms are tender, add the soup and stir through. Simmer and add the seasonings. Keep the mixture warm while buttering a baking sheet and then heating it in the oven for about 2 minutes. Remove from oven and arrange the flat dough for each crescent roll on it. Now spoon onto each triangle of dough just enough mushroom filling from the skillet to allow you to fold one corner of the dough over it. Heat them for about 15 minutes, or whatever the package directions call for. The rolls should brown, but not burn. When they are done, remove from oven, top with the rest of the mushroom sauce, and serve. Serves two to four.

Tuwaly Pie

This is a Bajoran dessert that's more of a staple than a delicacy. I mean, for a cook, everything is a delicacy, because the trickier it is to get the ingredients to make it, the greater the praise heaped upon you when the dish is set before the mess. However, not even I can claim that tuwaly pie is anything more than it really is, the best darned coconut cream pie in the entire galaxy.

COCONUT CREAM FILLING

2 cups milk

1 cup shredded coconut

¾ cup sugar

⅓ cup sifted all-purpose flour

½ teaspoon salt

2 eggs, slightly beaten

1 teaspoon vanilla extract

CREAM PIE BATTER

1 cup sugar

½ cup (1 stick) butter

2 eggs

1¾ cups sifted all-purpose flour

½ cup milk

2½ teaspoons baking powder

½ teaspoon salt

Packaged pastry piecrust or packaged graham cracker pie shell

Preheat oven to 350 degrees while you prepare the cream filling. In a medium-sized bowl, combine sugar, flour, and salt. Next beat the eggs and combine with the dry ingredients. Next, scald the milk—in other words, heat to just short of boiling so that a thin film appears on the sides of the pan, but don't boil. When it is scalded, stir the milk into the ingredients in the bowl. Now put the mixture in a saucepan and cook over very low heat for about 15 minutes, adding the vanilla and the shredded coconut. When the mixture has thickened, set aside and allow to cool while you prepare the batter for the cream pie.

For the cream pie batter, again, combine the sugar, flour, salt, and baking powder in a small mixing bowl first; then add eggs, butter, and milk. I like graham cracker crust pie shells best, so pour half the batter into one graham cracker crust pie shell and the rest into one greased pie tin, and bake them for 30 minutes. Remove them from the oven, let cool for 5 minutes, and then pour the coconut cream filling on top of the batter in the graham cracker crust. Return to oven, and bake for another 10 minutes. Remove from the oven, let cool and refrigerate for 2 hours.

Delvin Fluff Pastries

You've probably figured out by now that Kira has a major sweet tooth. I think it goes with that cute Bajoran nose that she likes to crinkle even when she's talking trash about Gul Dukat and the rest of the Cardassians. But when she's not kicking the stuffings out of a Jem'Hadar, she's nosing around for something sweet to eat. One of her favorite desserts—it has to be because it's too sweet for regular breakfast—is Delvin fluff pastries, little happy cakes that are so light, even though they have a filling, that they just disintegrate into a containment field of taste in your mouth. And they're tiny. My Terran equivalent is a French pastry called a petit four.

SHEET CAKE

5 eggs

1¼ cups cake flour

¾ cup granulated sugar

3 tablespoons butter

¼ teaspoon vanilla extract

⅛ teaspoon almond extract

FILLING

1 cup heavy cream, whipped,
_or_ 2 cups ready-made
whipped cream

3 tablespoons confectioners'
sugar

1 teaspoon vanilla extract

½ teaspoon mocha java _or_
French roast coffee
(or Earl Grey tea, for a
Jean-Luc Picard touch)

¼ teaspoon orange extract

GLAZE

3 cups granulated sugar

1½ cups water

¼ teaspoon cream of tartar

¼ teaspoon vanilla extract

1 or 2 drops food color of your choosing

Preheat oven to 325 degrees, and butter the bottoms of 2 jelly roll pans, approximately 10 by 15 inches. After you've buttered them, cover them with waxed paper so that the thin sheet cakes will be easy to cut into shapes and remove while still somewhat warm from the oven without breaking them. Next melt the 3 tablespoons of butter and set aside. You should have a double boiler for this recipe. If not, heat your eggs and sugar very carefully in a heavy saucepan while you beat them slowly with a hand mixer. If you have a double boiler, beat this mixture in the top of the double boiler until the mixture is thick and piles softly (about 10 minutes). Remove from heat and keep beating as it cools. After it has cooled, add the vanilla and almond extracts. Then, in four stages add the flour. At each stage, fold the flour in completely. When all the flour has been folded in, stir in the melted butter. Pour the batter into the baking pans, and bake at 325 degrees for 45 minutes.

While your cakes are baking, prepare the filling. In a medium-sized bowl, whip the heavy cream until the cream is stiff or measure in the store-bought whipped cream; then add the vanilla, coffee or tea, and sugar, blending them all completely, and set the filling aside in your refrigerator.

When the filling's completed, prepare the glaze by combining the sugar, water, and cream of tartar in a heavy saucepan and stirring over low heat. When the sugar is dissolved, increase heat to bring the mixture to a boil; then cover the saucepan and reduce to a slow boil for 5 minutes. After the first 2 minutes on a low boil, uncover and wipe any sugar crystals off the sides of the pan. When the cooking's completed, remove from heat and pour the sugar mixture into a mixing bowl and add the vanilla and any food coloring. Refrigerate this until the sheet cakes have completed baking and are completely cool. Remove from refrigerator and shape into a ball and let set up for 15 minutes.

While the glaze is setting, spoon the filling onto the lower layer of your petit four sheet cake and place the upper layer over top. Let the filling cool. After the frosting has set, 15 minutes in your refrigerator, knead frosting into ball, working it into a soft, spreadable dough-like mixture which you will spread as a frosting that you can apply to the surface of your sheet cake with a spoon or narrow spatula. When you've finished frosting, cut the cake into small shapes—any designs that strike your fancy—and remove from the baking tray with the edges of the waxed paper. Serve.

Jumja Tea

This is actually blackberry currant tea, which goes well with Delvan fluff pastries, or petit fours, or tuwaly pie. For a relaxing dessert tea or even as a late-night tea, add just a touch of honey per cup and a spritz of lemon juice.

Alvinian Melons

You can find these green-flesh melons on Earth as well as on Bajor, where they are among the favorites of Major Kira. On Earth, they're called honeydews, and you can serve them plain, with a dash of lemon juice, with a nice scoop of ice cream, or as an accompaniment to *jumja* tea.

DR. JULIAN BASHIR

O n *Voyager* we have an Emergency Medical Hologram; on Deep Space 9, they get the real McCoy, a living, breathing doctor with a bedside manner and everything. Dr. Bashir may be an expert at medicine, but he's a sucker for Quark's tricks. His favorite at Quark's is Tarkalian tea, a dark penetrating brew that you can drink at night and not be afraid it will keep you up.

Alexander Siddig's "Bashir's Spam-and-Beans Bolognese"

When I was younger—so much younger than today—I was at university, where I used to cook a bastardization (bastardisation, actually) of spaghetti Bolognese with beans. It's a British thing. Four ravenous students could easily be fed in 30 short minutes from a single electric burner, and all for less than half a pound sterling a head, which, in those days, really meant something. The Spam was easy because it ain't just junk e-mail. The tricky part was getting the spaghetti just right. You can try this in your own dorm as long as you don't tell anyone that Julian Bashir gave you the recipe.

> 1 16-ounce can Italian plum tomatoes
>
> 1 can Spam, cut into cubes
>
> 1 8-ounce can baked (not barbecued) beans
>
> 1 16-ounce package #8 spaghetti
>
> 1 teaspoon olive oil
>
> 1 pinch each oregano, parsley, and basil
>
> garlic salt and ground pepper to taste

Bring water to a boil, add spaghetti, and reduce to slow boil. Cook al dente. Drain in a strainer, mix with a little oil, and set aside. Heat some more olive oil in the spaghetti pot, where you will first cube then brown the Spam but not burn it. Set aside. Next, in the same pot, simmer the tomatoes in their juice, with oregano, parsley, basil, and garlic salt to taste. When mixture is fully heated through and seasoned, add the browned Spam and stir through. Next add the beans and stir through, and reseason to taste. Pour over the spaghetti, top with your favorite cheese, bung on a life, and gather around the telly for the latest episode of *Deep Space Nine*.

Tarkalian Tea

Julian orders up a pot of tea from Quark's; the equivalent is really a bracing and tart cranberry tea. You can serve it with lemon, the traditional way, or with a sliver of orange rind. I especially like to float a piece of orange rind in my tea and add a squeeze of lime juice. For a cold night, it's very soothing. But try this iced for a summer afternoon or a dessert drink at a picnic.

ODO

I'd like to say that Odo has a favorite dish, but without a real digestive system—because he's a changeling—it's problematical. Odo does drink, however, kind of, by turning part of himself into a glass. It looks weird, but then so's Odo, whose name even means "unknown" in Bajoran.

Rene Auberjonois's
"Odo's Baked Tomato Bruschetta"

This may sound too simple to be true, but I guarantee it's a knockout appetizer, hors d'oeuvre, or just plain snack. I'm telling you, people go crazy for this stuff. They think you're a genius, especially when you tell them it's a vegetarian version of Klingon heart of baby *targ*.

1 loaf crusty Italian white bread

1 dozen Roma tomatoes, cut in half, stems removed

2 or 3 cloves garlic, sliced

2 cups virgin olive oil (cold-pressed is best)

1 tablespoon ground red pepper

1 teaspoon fresh minced or dried crushed basil

salt and pepper to taste

Preheat oven to 350 degrees. After tomatoes have been sliced in half and laid out cut-side up on a flat, lightly oiled baking tray, mix the garlic cloves with the olive oil and stir. Let it sit for at least 15 minutes. Split the bread in half lengthwise. Spoon the olive oil-garlic mixture over the tomatoes (at least 1 tablespoon or more per tomato) and sprinkle with salt and pepper. Bake the tomatoes on the upper oven shelf for 15–20 minutes, until they are completely roasted—almost unrecognizable as tomatoes—and have the consistency of jam. Then sprinkle them with chopped basil. At the same time bake the bread until it's hot and toasted, but not burnt. Remove bread from oven, cut into bite-sized chunks, and serve alongside the tomatoes. Let your guests spread the jam-like roasted garlic tomato on individual pieces of bread and sprinkle with ground pepper. Serve with red Italian wine or Klingon bloodwine. Serves six.

CHIEF MILES O'BRIEN

Miles O'Brien transferred over to Deep Space 9 from a starship. As a reward for the courage to change, he received a promotion and a real increase in status. Granted, DS9 wasn't the *Enterprise,* the flagship of the fleet, but there was an even greater challenge in trying to keep the run-down Cardassian operating systems from completely falling apart on the baling-wire space station. The *Enterprise* was first-class White Star Line luxury compared to what they had to live with on Deep Space 9, and Miles had a wife and daughter to worry about. So Miles threw himself into his work and into developing new culinary tastes. He enjoyed himself at Quark's, played darts, sampled Bajoran food, nibbled on Klingon food, and tried a Cardassian dish here and there. But mostly, Miles came back to good old-fashioned home cooking, especially when the dish included his very favorite meat no matter what quadrant he was sent to—veal.

Fricandeau Stew

This version of fricandeau of veal is Miles's favorite dish on Deep Space 9 because Chief O'Brien loves veal any way he can get it, especially when it's larded over with pork and braised until all its juices are sealed nice and tight inside and then dredged in flour and stewed with hearty red-skinned potatoes with the skins on, some celery, an onion, and a couple of tomatoes to flavor the gravy. I like to spice it up with some garlic, a handful of whole cloves, and a bay leaf, but these are optional and totally nontraditional. This is an Earth dish that you can make yourself, but if you want it to be a true fricandeau, you have to ask your butcher to give you the "cushion" of the veal, the meaty portion cut from the thickest part of the leg.

2 pounds cushion of veal, boned at the market

¼ pound salt port, fatback, *or* thick-cut bacon, cubed

½ cup (1 stick) butter

2 tablespoons butter melted

5 medium red-skin potatoes, thickly cubed

1 large onion, chopped

5 stalks celery, with leaves, chopped

4 medium tomatoes, chopped

½ cup all-purpose flour

2 cloves garlic, whole

4 cloves garlic, sliced

3 or 4 whole cloves (optional)

1 bay leaf

salt and pepper to taste

Preheat oven to 350 degrees. Wash the cushion of veal and cut ¼-inch slits into the flesh. Into these slits, press in pieces of your fatback, salt pork, or the fatty portions of the bacon, and wipe down the entire piece of meat with 2 cloves of garlic. Now stick the whole cloves into the meat, if you want, but it's entirely optional. I like to because cloves provide a very exotic taste, just the kind of experience you'd encounter were you to sit down to a bowl of fricandeau stew with Chief O'Brien after a brutal day working the plasma injector coils on the *Defiant*. Now salt and pepper the meat and sew the slit where the bone was removed together, along with the slits into which you inserted the pork lard. You can also use toothpicks.

Place a roasting-pan rack in a pan, making sure the pan beneath is deep enough to catch the drippings, for the gravy you'll need for the stew. Dredge the meat in flour, allowing flour to fall to the bottom of the pan, so it will form a gravy and place meat on rack, arrange more bacon or fatback around the meat. Now roast for about 3½ hours, basting every 15 minutes or so with some butter that you've melted in about 1 cup of boiling water and drippings.

While the fricandeau of veal is cooking, wash and cube your potatoes, then cover with water in a medium-sized saucepan and boil for about 45 minutes or until fork tender. When the potatoes are almost done, begin frying the sliced garlic in ½ cup of butter in a large skillet and then add the chopped onion and the celery. Next, add the tomatoes, bay leaf, ½ cup of water, and some of the drippings from the bottom of the fricandeau roast. Simmer slowly for about 1½ hours and then set aside. When the fricandeau is done, combine the roast, the gravy drippings, and the vegetables in a large saucepan. You can leave the fricandeau whole or you can slice it into large pieces. If you decide to slice the veal, it will cook faster. Cook for 1 more hour. Test the meat after 40 minutes to make sure that it is getting nice and tender and the flavors are blending. After 1 hour, serve with nice thick, crusty bread and maybe a salad. Serves four to six.

Eggs and Bacon and Corned Beef Hash

Here's the hearty breakfast that the chief likes the most: 2 eggs over easy with 3 pieces of Irish bacon and corned beef hash. I'm not really a big over-easy man myself, preferring my eggs the way the celebrated Earth naval hero Captain Horatio Hornblower prepared them, over well. But Miles likes them over easy, with the yolks just ready to burst so they flavor the hash.

There's an easy way to prepare this and a trickier way, but the trickier way tastes better. Here's the easy way: you buy a can of corned beef hash—and there are plenty of brands—and cut off a nice slice, roughly ⅓ of the can. Start frying yourself a few strips of thick-cut Irish bacon, a cross between Canadian bacon and American bacon, and when you have enough bacon fat, drop a pat of butter in it and fry the corned beef hash too. When the bacon's done, remove the bacon and hash, and fry 2 eggs in the same skillet. Just let them set, then flip them over and let the other side set for about 90 seconds, and then flip them back. Serve the corned beef hash on an English muffin with the eggs right on top and the bacon alongside.

Even better tasting than canned corned beef hash is the stuff you make yourself on the day after St. Patrick's Day.

1 pound cooked *or* leftover corned beef, chopped

2 cups finely chopped leftover boiled potatoes

2 tablespoons cream, half-and-half, or whole milk

1 teaspoon dried parsley

salt and pepper to taste

Remove all the fat from the corned beef and chop the meat. Peel and then chop the potatoes. Combine the meat and potatoes in a mixing bowl and sprinkle with parsley. Spread the hash on a hot, buttered skillet and stir. Add the cream or milk to moisten, and keep stirring. Just after it begins to brown, push it to one side. Now add the bacon and let the hash brown slowly. When the bacon's done, cook the eggs and proceed as above. For the chief this is a single serving, but it usually serves two.

Chee'lash

This dish is actually prisoner's rations. It's a kind of staple that's made from sliced green apples in their own juices. You can make as a dessert, not unlike apple compote, but without the brandy that compotes sometimes have.

2 to 3 pounds green apples (Granny Smith apples are the best)

3 cups ice-cold water

1 cup white grape juice

1½ cups sugar

1 teaspoon lemon or lime juice

1 teaspoon vanilla extract

1 teaspoon cinnamon

Wash and core the apples and slice them into a large saucepan, leaving them in their own juice. Add grape juice, water, sugar, lime or lemon juice, vanilla, and cinnamon, and bring to boil. Simmer for about 1 hour until the apples become tender. Refrigerate for about 2 hours. Serve cold. You can add whipped cream or heavy cream, or serve over a pound cake, or if you're an ice cream fan, drop a scoop of vanilla ice cream into the apple compote or serve the compote as a topping over ice cream and pound cake. Serves two to four.

Senarian Egg Broth

Keiko and Miles are soup fans and love the swirling magic of Senarian egg broth. You can make two versions of this soup yourself: one is a standard chicken egg-drop soup, and the other is a spinach-and-chicken-broth egg-drop soup. Both are very quick soups to make if you use already prepared ingredients, such as frozen spinach and canned chicken broth.

2 8-ounce cans clear chicken broth

1 egg, well beaten

Heat chicken broth to boiling and reduce to simmer. Simmer for about 5 minutes, and beat the egg in a separate bowl, thoroughly combining the yolk and the white. Now, while stirring the soup, very slowly pour in the egg so that it barely dribbles into the soup and forms a long spiraling string as you stir. The trick is not to combine the egg and the soup but to get the egg to hang in a suspension. For a Greek version, you can add ¼ cup of lemon juice now. When the egg is suspended in long filaments, carefully spoon or ladle the soup into bowls for serving.

For a spinach version of egg-drop soup, sauté a ½ cup of finely chopped fresh or frozen spinach in a saucepan with about ¼ stick of butter and chopped onion. When spinach is tender, remove from pan and process it in a food processor or blender so that it's almost puréed. Return to saucepan over low heat and add an 8-ounce can of chicken stock. Bring it up to boiling, simmer for 10 minutes, and then slowly add the beaten egg until it swirls. Again, you can add lemon juice now for a Greek version of spinach egg-drop soup. Serves four.

Q'parol

Keiko's favorite dish is a version of stuffed shells with spinach, featuring ricotta cheese mixed with feta cheese, baked in a casserole and topped with parsley and oregano. I like this with lots of garlic and zipped up with fresh-ground black pepper.

1 cup ricotta cheese

1 16-ounce package large pasta shells

2 cups washed and finely chopped spinach

1 egg, well beaten

4 ounces feta cheese

2 tablespoons oregano

2 tablespoons olive oil

4 cloves garlic, crushed

2 teaspoons dried parsley

salt and pepper to taste

grated Romano or Parmesan cheese to taste

Preheat oven to 325 degrees. While you cook the large shells according to the package's instructions, mix the ricotta cheese, feta cheese, olive oil, spinach, and egg until you have a stiff cheese stuffing. Now crush the cloves of garlic and fold them into the stuffing along with 1 tablespoon of oregano and salt and black pepper to taste. Set this aside in your refrigerator. When shells are done, drain, and stuff them with the ricotta-cheese-and-spinach filling. Lightly grease an 8-inch glass baking dish with olive oil, and arrange the stuffed shells in the dish. Sprinkle the parsley and the remaining oregano over the top and bake at 325 degrees for 45 minutes, checking after 30 minutes to make sure the shells don't burn. Just as the shells become crisp, after about 45 minutes, remove from oven, sprinkle with your favorite grated Romano or Parmesan cheese, remove from baking dish, and serve. Serves four.

QUARK

"You can get anything you want

At Quark's Bar 'n' Restaurant

From raktajino to hasperat"

—CHORUS FROM A CONTEMPORARY FERENGI FOLK SONG

Quark—now there's a Ferengi I'd like to do some business with if I ever warp myself over to Deep Space 9. At the rate *Voyager*'s going, it would probably be easier for me to find a way through the Gamma Quadrant to the Bajoran wormhole and right to the station. I'd have me a drink at Quark's, maybe share a few recipes with him, and see if there's any trading we could do. Indeed, there's a lot I could learn from Quark if I only had the chance. Maybe I'd open a bar just like his somewhere in a distant quadrant and let my clientele bring the business right to my very door. Maybe, but the next quadrant is many light-years away and I'm not getting any younger.

The food and drink Quark serves at his famous Bar, Grill, Gaming House, and Holosuite Arcade represent the best in both the Alpha and Beta Quadrants. And the replicator, programmed with special recipes and fine-quality food, is one of the reasons you'd want to visit Deep Space 9. With Quark's own favorite foods, his special drinks, the menu at his restaurant, and the list of foods available from the replicator, you could fill an entire tour of duty with different foods every week. Here's just a sample of what you can get at Quark's.

Armin Shimerman's "Poulet Ferengé from Quark's"

1½ pounds chicken breast (skinless, boneless, white meat only, and cut into bite-sized pieces)

1 16-ounce can peeled tomatoes (a dabo girl will not do)

1 Bermuda onion, thinly sliced

½ cup thinly sliced black olives

12 garlic cloves, crushed (or pulverized, preferably by your Moogie)

1 tablespoon imported virgin olive oil

2 teaspoons thyme

1 teaspoon imported hot chili paste (*sambal delek*—we have a fine collection at Quark's)

2 bay leaves

1 teaspoon coarsely ground kosher salt

½ teaspoon coarsely ground black pepper (You can grind this yourself.)

¼ teaspoon saffron threads (now, this stuff is really expensive)

1 sprig fresh parsley, chopped

Make sure that you've removed all the skin and pieces of bone from your chicken, and then cut it into easy bite-sized pieces. Now brown it in the olive oil in a heavy skillet, making very sure that you don't burn it. Remove from heat just as it browns and place on paper towel to drain the oil from the chicken. Now sauté the onion slices in the remaining oil for 5 minutes. When they just begin to turn translucent, add the garlic and let it brown. Now add the tomatoes, thyme, salt, and pepper, and bring to a simmer for 10 minutes. Add the chicken, chili paste (*sambal delek*), and bay leaves, and turn the heat back to a slow simmer (we on *Deep Space Nine* call it a "shimmer") for 20 minutes. Now add the saffron and olives, and continue to simmer for 10 minutes. Test chicken for tenderness and doneness. When you're satisfied that it is thoroughly cooked (no pink spots) and tender, add the parsley, stir through, and serve. Take a Quark bow, which means you smile without showing too much teeth and incline forward ceremoniously, but not too submissively, at the waist, without ever taking your eyes off the customer or his latinum. Serves four.

Millipede Juice

The Ferengi like to start off each day with the juice of a hard-shelled insect. It's pure protein and gives them the oomph they need to strike the kinds of deals that would cross the eyes of most galactic traders. I'm not especially fond of millipedes myself, but I can whip up a clam-juice cocktail that does the same thing for me that a millipede does for Quark. You can have your clam juice two ways: one, warm and straight-up with a twist of lemon; and two, mixed with tomato or vegetable juice. Either way, start with about a dozen chowder clams, which you wash and steam. Then draw off the juice and strain to remove the sand. Serve the juice nice and hot with lemon. Raw clam juice too strong? After you've drawn the juice and strained it, chill it for about ½ hour and combine it half-and-half with vegetable or tomato juice, lemon, and a smattering of salt and Tabasco. Serve it over ice to start the day, and watch out world.

Purée of Beetle

The Ferengi seem to have a thing for insects. Maybe it's me, but the idea of mashing some winged hard-shelled thing with your fingers, squeezing a bag of green puss for blood, and watching lots of legs that squirm in all directions when you go to eat it doesn't seem like gourmet dining no matter how you serve it. So, although the Ferengi like purée of beetle as a common breakfast food, I can see where humans might have a problem. Short of flattening insects for a morning repast with a hot cup of *raktaji-*

no, you might try the closest thing to an insect that Earthlings consider a delicacy, with a lobster pâté on your toast points. Lobsters are insects, too, you know. Can't get any lobster? Try crabmeat or even shrimp. Here's a basic pâté recipe for all three of them.

1 to 1½ pounds cooked lobster meat, *or* **lump crabmeat,** *or*
      boiled, peeled, deveined shrimp
1 cup dry white wine
1 slice stale white bread, ground into bread crumbs *or* **⅓ cup**
      store-bought bread crumbs
2 porcini mushrooms *or* **canned truffles, finely chopped**
2 egg yolks
1 tablespoon melted butter
½ teaspoon salt
black or red pepper to taste

Cut the lobster, crab, or shrimp meat into 1-inch pieces and marinate them in the wine 2 to 3 hours. After the marinating period, preheat oven to 350 degrees and combine the marinated lobster, crab, or shrimp—including the wine—with the bread crumbs and mushrooms or truffles. Beat the egg yolks thoroughly; then stir the egg yolks into the pâté mixture. Blend in the melted butter, salt, and pepper. Arrange in a baking dish, cover, and bake for 45 minutes. Remove cover and bake for another 15 minutes, checking the top to make sure it turns crisp and browns lightly but does not burn. Serve over toast. Serves four.

Slug Liver

Ferengi do share with humans a perverse taste for a variety of little shelled creatures who creep upon the surface of the earth or beneath the sea, processing through their bodies any toxins and poisons that civilized society can manufacture or throw off as a by-product of a manufacturing process. It is simply astounding what chemicals human society can generate and even more astounding what creatures they eat that process these toxins. However, far be it from me to judge, given what I've served up to our resident half-Klingon during my tour of duty in *Voyager*'s galley.

The closest animals to slugs, whose livers the Ferengi simply adore, are snails, which can be prepared raw right out of the shell, as it were, or, for those people who cannot find the time to pick through the day's catch at the local fish market, come canned or prepackaged. I suggest the latter because snails are a tricky deal and are better left to the pros. My recipe calls for canned snails cooked in a nice bouillon or consommé of beef or chicken with bay leaf and lots of pickling spice, served with a hearty Rhombolian butter which, on Earth, is called "snail butter."

1 8-ounce can beef consommé

1 cup sherry *or* white wine

1 4- to 6-ounce store-bought canned, cooked, and cleaned snails

1 bay leaf

1 tablespoon pickling spice

1 to 3 cloves garlic, crushed, to taste

SNAIL BUTTER

1 cup (2 sticks) butter, melted

½ cup green onions (scallions), finely chopped

4 cloves garlic, chopped

1 teaspoon celery powder *or* minced fresh celery leaves

Combine the consommé and sherry or wine and bring to boil. Add bay leaf, pickling spice, and crushed garlic to taste. Stir and reduce to simmer. Wash snails thoroughly, and then add them to the broth and let simmer for about 5 minutes. Remove, drain, and serve with a sauce for dipping you've made by melting the two sticks of butter and adding the green onions, celery powder or leaves, and garlic until all ingredients are thoroughly combined and blended. Serves four.

Wentlian Condor Snake

Here's a Quark specialty, battered and fried fresh condor snake, served steaming hot. The tastiest (and easiest) replacement for the condor snake on Earth is a standard eel from your fish market or Asian market.

1 to 2 pounds fresh eel

2 cups cornmeal

½ pound fatback

salt and pepper to taste

Slice the eel into 2-inch pieces and boil for about 10 minutes in vigorously boiling water. As the eel pieces cook, season the cornmeal with salt and pepper on a flat plate, because that's where you'll be rolling the eel pieces before you fry them. Now heat the fatback in a heavy skillet so that it is reduced to liquid fat. When the eel is tender, remove from water, dry, and roll it in the seasoned cornmeal. Now sauté in the pork fat and serve over heavily seasoned rice. Serves four.

Tube Grubs

The Ferengi, like the Klingons, enjoy their share of living organisms as a snack or light meal. Tube grubs are one of their favorites. You can make this at home in your own replicators by getting nice fresh squid or octopus from your Asian market and slicing it real thin over packaged udon noodles that you've chilled and tossed with soy sauce and sesame salad dressing or tahini.

Alterian Chowder

Quark's may not be recognized as the gourmet hot spot of the Alpha Quadrant, but the Ferengi restaurateur knows how to program a replicator. Take a stroll along the Promenade any afternoon and you'll find patrons from cultures across the quadrant and through the wormhole queuing up to sample the cultural delights Quark has assembled to satisfy his diverse clientele. Even Commander Sisko has his favorites at Quark's, one of which is a creamy soup called Alterian chowder. This is a smooth vegetarian dish that would tend to be oversweet were it not for the peppery spices Quark programs as a seasoning. You can order your Alterian chowder spicy hot or mild. It's easy to make in your own kitchen with frozen or canned corn nibblets, cream, some bell peppers and even jalapeños, and butter. Season it with salt and celery seed or celery salt and, for a walk on the wild side with Tom Paris, a splash of Tabasco.

1 16-ounce package frozen corn kernels, thawed, *or* 2 8-ounce cans corn (You can also scrape the kernels from leftover cooked whole corn as long as you get 2 full cups.)

1 cup cream, half-and-half, or whole milk (or more, depending how you vary the amount of corn kernels)

½ cup (less or more to taste) green *or* red bell peppers (fresh or frozen), chopped

1 handful jalapeños, seeded and chopped, to taste

¼ stick (⅛ cup) butter

2 teaspoons celery salt or salt

2 teaspoons celery seed

Tabasco sauce to taste

coarse-ground pepper to taste

Blend the corn kernels with cream or milk in your blender or with your hand mixer until you have a chowder. Pour into a medium-sized saucepan and add the rest of the ingredients. You can thin the mixture out with more milk or cream, or blend more corn kernels. Heat, on medium for 10 minutes correcting the seasoning as necessary, and serve. Yields two servings.

Vulcan Mollusks

Vulcan mollusks, another treat from Quark's, are green mussels served nice and hot with a Rhombolian butter sauce. Begin with 1 dozen or more fresh mussels and plunge them into boiling water seasoned with lots of Old Bay seasoning and pickling spices. When the mussels open, they're done. Arrange them around a dish of snail butter for dipping in, with a garnish of watercress for spice, and serve. Serves two.

Jumbo Romulan Mollusks

Low on Vulcan mollusks? Try the Romulan variety. They're much bigger and only a tad tougher than the Vulcan. Romulans and Vulcans are cousins, you understand, probably having descended from common ancestry. But sometimes shipments from Romulus are slow and you have to improvise. In that instance, I suggest good old-fashioned cold-water oysters. Serve them fresh and raw for your Klingon friends, dipped in a cornmeal-and-beer batter and fried on a skillet for Cardassians, and boiled in beer, put back in the shell, and baked with spinach, bacon, and bread crumbs for any Romulans with whom you have the pleasure of dining. For fried oysters you'll need the following:

1 dozen oysters, shucked

2 cups cornmeal

¼ cup all-purpose flour

¼ cup of milk

1 12-ounce bottles beer

½ cup (1 stick) melted butter

red pepper to taste

sea salt to taste

Tabasco to taste

Combine cornmeal with flour and sea salt and pepper; add beer and milk to form a thick batter. Wash oysters and dip in cornmeal batter, then fry in melted butter in a skillet. Sprinkle red pepper and sea salt and add Tabasco to taste. Serve steaming hot. Serves two.

FOR OYSTERS BAKED ON THE SHELL:

1 dozen oysters, shucked

1 8-ounce can creamed spinach

½ pound bacon

1 teaspoon dried parsley

1 teaspoon Worcestershire sauce

1 teaspoon Tabasco sauce

1 teaspoon lemon juice

Preheat oven to 450 degrees. Shuck and clean oysters, then clean the shells because you'll use them again. Spoon a dollop of creamed spinach into each shell and top with an oyster. Top the oyster with a square of bacon and sprinkle with Worcestershire sauce, lemon juice, and Tabasco. Bake for 10 minutes at 450 degrees, and then broil for about 5 minutes in a broiler on high. Sprinkle a pinch of parsley over each oyster just prior to serving. You can also heat very coarsely ground salt in a baking tray and serve the shells on the salt. Serves two to three.

Palamarian Sea Urchin

Quark's Ferengi version of sea urchin sashimi lives on in the computerized annals of Starfleet cuisine. You can use regular sea urchin sashimi on Earth, served raw, of course, on beds of lettuce. At your Asian market you can find sea urchin that's tasty and a delightful appetizer when sliced very thin. In many Asian supermarkets, you can find the sea urchin already sliced and ready to arrange on a bed of white rice for individual servings. I would arrange 8 or so pieces for each serving on about a cup of fluffed white rice liberally mixed with sesame seeds and some rice vinegar. Garnish with sliced pickled ginger, also available at any Asian market, and you have an appetizer as well as a delicious lunch.

Icoberry Torte

Another one of the favorite desserts from Quark's is this berry delight. Icoberries are sweet as well as pungent, and if you overindulge, you can get an allergic reaction. The straight icoberry juice is so strong that when Jadzia Dax tried some, her spots began to itch. It seemed the juice went through her Trill system so rapidly it overloaded its delicate balance. I'm told many races have negative reactions to icoberries. Not so with humans.

Quark's version of this torte has a strange rectangular shape, which you can make in your own kitchen, after you let the torte itself cool. Of course you can't find icoberries at any street-corner market, but you can use red raspberries. Some people don't like the overpowering taste of raspberries, so I've included an alternate version with the sometimes more popular strawberry. Remember, also, that real tortes are made with almonds instead of flour. You have to grind the almonds, or buy them finely ground at the store, and mix them with ground bread crumbs for the cake. This recipe's tricky, but it's worth the effort:

1 cup ground almonds (store-bought are best)

½ cup honey-whole-wheat bread crumbs (Let a few slices of honey wheat bread go stale and grind them up into bread crumbs.)

6 egg yolks

6 egg whites

1 cup light brown sugar (You can mix this with 2 teaspoons cinnamon if you like.)

½ teaspoon orange extract *or* 1 teaspoon orange juice

½ teaspoon lemon extract *or* 1 teaspoon fresh-squeezed lemon juice

1 cup or more (as needed) raspberry *or* strawberry preserves

⅓ cup confectioners' sugar

1 cup heavy cream, whipped, *or* 2 cups store-bought whipped cream (Homemade whipped cream is far fresher and tastier, but in the middle of the hard night with crushing work deadlines bearing down upon you, no sound is happier than the *whoosh* of a whipped-cream container.)

Preheat oven to 350 degrees. Traditionalists will tell you to use a greased circular baking pan with a spring-loaded removable rim. There's a reason for this: the torte is so delicate that you can't remove it from a normal pie tin or cake pan without breaking it. The spring-form pan lets you remove the rim and let the torte cool on the pan bottom. When it's cool, you can trim it into the rectangular shape served at Quark's.

With a hand mixer, beat the brown sugar into the egg yolks until the result is creamy. Add the orange and lemon extract or juice; keep beating so that it blends thoroughly. Now add the ground almonds and bread crumbs, and keep beating. Set aside and whip the egg whites in a separate bowl, until they begin to stiffen. Then stir them into the almond torte mixture until they are blended. Spoon the torte mixture into the pan and bake for 45 minutes. Allow it to cool, remove from pan, trim into a rectangular shape, and spoon over the raspberry or strawberry preserves. You can even have a raspberry/strawberry mixture. Place in refrigerator to chill. When ready to serve, sprinkle with confectioners' sugar and spoon on whipped cream. If you make it yourself, you'll find it's actually better than you can get at Quark's. Serves four to six.

Ferengi Spore Pie

Here's a pastry dish that's right from Quark's replicator. This spore pie is easy to make and can be reheated as a leftover. The spores I'd recommend—the nonreplicator version—are fresh mushrooms that you bake into a custard pie filing. Basically, this is a mushroom quiche, which, when done right, is a magnificent dish for a light lunch, a weekend breakfast, or a wonderful snack. You can make this with or without bacon. Traditionally, a mushroom quiche Lorraine is a bacon quiche. For Ferengi spore pie, I suggest you leave the bacon out. No matter how you prepare it, the trick is to add nice purple cabbage to the quiche as a garnish for both texture and flavor.

1 store-bought frozen pastry shell or refrigerated packaged
    pastry piecrust

1 pound fresh mushrooms, cleaned, trimmed, and sliced

6 ounces Gruyère cheese (Swiss Knight is perfect), shredded

6 ounces imported or domestic Swiss cheese, sliced

1 clove garlic, sliced thin

2 cups whole milk *or* half-and-half

3 eggs

½ cup (1 stick) butter

½ teaspoon salt

¼ teaspoon nutmeg

1 pinch of dried parsley

pepper to taste

½ cup small red cabbage, shredded, as a garnish

Preheat oven to 450 degrees, and arrange your pastry shell in a 9-inch pie tin. Wash, trim the ends off, and slice the fresh mushrooms, and sauté them in the butter and garlic in a medium skillet. After the mushrooms are nice and soft, shred the Gruyère cheese and cut the Swiss cheese slices into long strips and set aside. Heat the milk or half-and-half to scalding. Beat the eggs and add the salt, nutmeg, and pepper. Stir in the milk. Layer the mushrooms in the pie shell, cover with both cheeses, and pour in the egg mixture. Bake at

450 degrees for 10 minutes; reduce heat to 350 degrees and bake for another 15 minutes; remove from oven and sprinkle on the parsley, then bake for an additional 10 minutes. During the final 10 minutes, wash the cabbage and shred it into small strips, which you will use as a garnish for the completed servings of quiche to your guests. Serves four to six.

Augergine Stew

Quark had been trying to curry favor with the grand nagus for the longest time before the old Ferengi himself decided to pay a visit to Deep Space 9 to see how Quark was making out. After all, Quark's was the only Ferengi business in close proximity to this most valuable wormhole. Quark, trying to impress the one person who could have made him his fortune for the rest of his life, served up his famous Augergine stew, which turned out to be a hit. Unfortunately, it was a hit with Jadzia Dax, who scarfed up additional helpings of this stuff because it's so tasty. I've worked up a version of this dish for you, an eggplant-tinted Irish stew with lamb, of course, and an optional mild curry. Why is the stew the color of an eggplant? Because aubergine, in French, means eggplant, but it also means the purple color of eggplant. So you can have an eggplant-colored lamb stew with—grape jelly—or a veggie version of this curry stew with sliced and grilled eggplant.

2 to 3 pounds lamb roast, cut into bite-sized cubes (Preserve the bones for flavor.)

2 large carrots, peeled and thick-sliced

2 large turnips, peeled and thick-sliced

4 medium potatoes, peeled and cubed into large pieces

1 medium onion, sliced

2 quarts water

¼ cup all-purpose flour

1 to 2 tablespoons grape jelly for color

1 teaspoon thyme

1 teaspoon dried parsley

1 teaspoon curry powder (optional)

Wash your lamb roast and cut into bite-sized chunks while you boil enough water to cover the lamb bones. Boil the lamb bones for about 1½ hours, skimming off the surface scum. Remove bones, strain the water, and return to the soup pot. Add the lamb pieces and cover with an additional 2 quarts of water and heat to a vigorous boil. Cover and reduce to a simmer for 1½ hours. Strain every 20 minutes or so. After 1½ hours add grape jelly for color and simmer for 10 minutes. Next, add the vegetables and seasonings and simmer for 1 more hour. Mix the ¼ cup of flour with just enough cold water to form a thick paste, and add it to the stew. Cook for another 30 minutes and serve.

For a vegetarian version, with or without grape jelly, slice very thinly, then sauté in olive oil, a whole eggplant. Or you can broil the sliced eggplant in your broiler. Prepare the other vegetables and seasonings by boiling in 2 quarts of water for 30 minutes. Mix ¼ cup of flour with just enough cold water to form a thick paste, and add it to the stew. Then, at the very end, add the eggplant and serve in shallow bowls. Serves four to six.

Kohlanese Stew

The replicator makes Kohlanese stew easy because the beef marinade is automatic. Punch in the replicator codes and, bingo, your meat is ready. However, it's not that easy on Earth, even though you can punch in the settings for how you want your microwave oven to defrost the cut of meat you're preparing for your version of this stew. The Neelix secret here is to marinate the beef—and it can be anything from a chuck roast to a top round—with ginger and cloves as well as garlic. The result is a stew in which the meat jumps into your mouth and dissolves in a wash of flavor. It also helps to add just the right red wine at the end, and I don't mean Klingon bloodwine either.

2 to 3 pounds chuck or round roast cut into 1 inch cubes

1 medium-sized onion, chopped

4 carrots, sliced

2 medium-sized tomatoes, chopped

½ pound bacon

6 whole black peppercorns

1 tablespoon olive oil

½ teaspoon thyme

½ teaspoon chopped fresh ginger root

3 whole cloves

2 cloves garlic, sliced

1 sprig whole fresh parsley

2 cups dry red wine

Believe it or not, this can be a one-dish meal that you can begin the night before and set on slow-cook during the day in your automatic Crock-Pot. When you come home from work, the aroma of fresh Kohlanese stew will invigorate even the most beaten-upon middle manager.

Begin by marinating the beef in a deep heavy skillet for at least 3 hours (or the night before) in 1 cup of red wine, onions, carrots, and seasonings, but not the tomatoes. Those are for later. You should turn the marinating meat every 30 minutes or so, just to make sure that all parts of the meat marinate evenly. If you're using a Crock-Pot instead of a skillet, you will be able to cover the meat in the wine and can turn it every hour or so. Marinating adds flavor to meat and tenderizes the tougher cuts.

After 3 hours, remove the meat from the marinade and let it drain. Now, in a separate skillet, dice the bacon and cook it slowly. When it is evenly brown, remove from skillet and allow to drain. Reserve the bacon grease in the skillet and add the olive oil. Now add the meat and brown it thoroughly. Add the vegetables from the marinade as well as the bacon pieces, and heat for about 5 minutes. Next add the tomatoes, which you've chopped, and allow to simmer. Finally, you can strain the marinade juices and pour over the simmering meat. Next add an additional cup of red wine, cover, and simmer for 2 hours, at which point the meat should be so tender you begin to taste it as soon as you remove the cover from the skillet.

You can serve Kohlanese stew over rice or over any type of pasta that strikes your fancy on any particular night. Traditionally, it's served over macaroni, but you can serve it over radiatore, fusilli, rotini, or even good old-fashioned spaghetti. Serves four to six.

Vak Clover Soup

This is another specialty at Quark's. In place of Vak clover you can use basic watercress, for a spicy bite, laced with cream. It's also a great way to start a meal that includes either Augergine or Kohlanese stew.

2 8-ounce cans clear chicken stock

2 bunches fresh watercress, chopped

½ cup milk

1 egg yolk, slightly beaten

3 tablespoons butter

2 tablespoons all-purpose flour

salt and pepper to taste

parsley, dried or minced fresh, for garnish

After you've washed and chopped your watercress, sauté it for 2 minutes in 1 tablespoon butter to soften it; then add the stock, bring it to a boil, reduce it to a low boil, and cook for 5 minutes. In a separate saucepan combine the remaining butter and the flour, and cook gently until the mixture is thick and smooth. Combine with watercress and stock, add salt and pepper, and simmer for about 5 minutes. Next add the milk, stir through, and finally remove 2 tablespoons of the hot mixture beat in egg yolk and then stir back in. Serve immediately, sprinkled with a bit of parsley. Serves four.

Yigrish Cream Pie

Here's a no-nonsense dessert straight from Quark's food replicators that everyone likes. Even Deanna Troi, were she to spend a weekend on Deep Space 9, would find her way to Quark's Yigrish cream pie once someone described the tantalizing chocolate icing that sets off the vanilla cream custard filling.

Needless to say, you can make packaged-cake-mix cream pie from the store. Many manufacturers make this product or you can make it yourself in various stages of "from scratch." Chocolate frosting comes packaged as well as canned, as does the cream filling. But knowing that everything is packaged, here's how you make it from scratch. Feel free to replace anything with a packaged version.

CAKE

1¼ cups cake flour

1 cup sugar

⅓ cup water

3 egg yolks

3 egg whites

2 tablespoons lemon juice

1 teaspoon double-acting baking powder

1 teaspoon grated lemon rind

½ teaspoon salt

½ teaspoon vanilla extract

CREAM FILLING

1½ cups milk

2 egg yolks, only slightly beaten

⅓ cup all-purpose flour

⅓ cup sugar

2 tablespoons butter

1 teaspoon vanilla extract

¼ teaspoon salt

CHOCOLATE FROSTING

1 1-ounce square semisweet baking chocolate

¼ cup milk

¼ cup sugar

1 tablespoon all-purpose flour

1 teaspoon butter

½ teaspoon vanilla extract

⅛ teaspoon salt

Preheat oven to 325 degrees. To prepare the cake batter, combine by sifting together the cake flour, baking powder, and salt; set aside. Now separate the egg yolks from the whites and combine the yolks with the water, lemon rind, and vanilla. Beat with a hand mixer on low or with a rotary mixer, while you add the sugar and lemon juice. Now add the dry ingredients to the egg mixture, stirring slowly to remove all lumps. Set aside. In a separate bowl, beat the egg whites until they stiffen, and fold into the cake batter. Grease 2 8-inch cake pans, line them with waxed paper, and pour in the batter. Bake at 325 degrees for 35 to 40 minutes. Test for doneness by inserting a knife or toothpick. Insert and remove, the cake is done when removed the knife comes out clean. Set aside to let cool.

For the cream filling, which you should make while the cake layers are baking, heat 1 cup of milk in a saucepan and add the butter. Combine the flour with the salt and the sugar. Add the additional ½ cup of milk to the dry ingredients and stir until smooth. Then add this to the hot milk and butter in the saucepan, stirring thoroughly until the mixture thickens. Add the slightly beaten egg yolks and cook for 2 to 3 minutes. Remove from heat, add the vanilla, and let the filling cool in a separate bowl while your cake continues to bake and you prepare the frosting.

While the cake is baking and the filling is cooling, melt the square of chocolate in the milk over low heat in a saucepan. Separately, combine the flour, sugar, and salt. Now add these dry ingredients to the milk and chocolate and stir until smooth. Remove from heat and add the butter and vanilla. Beat until thick and set aside.

When the cake layers have cooled enough for you to handle without them crumbling, spread the cream filling on one layer and top with the second layer. Now spread the chocolate icing over the cake swirling it for effect and making sure you cover all of the sides. Refrigerate before serving.

Pyrellian Ginger Tea

After a deep bowl of Vak clover soup, hearty plate of stew, and a Troi-sized slice of Yigrish cream pie, rather than keeling over with a heart attack that requires the doctor to work you over in sickbay, have a cup of Pyrellian ginger tea to reduce your skyrocketing blood pressure. A combination of ginger and ginseng teas, Pyrellian ginger tea was so valuable, Quark actually risked his little life by hoarding the stuff on Terek Nor during the occupation, for resale on the black market.

Here's how to brew an Earth version using standard black or oolong tea. For every bag of tea or teaspoon of loose tea you infuse, snip one good-sized piece of ginger from a fresh ginger root and a similarly sized piece of ginseng from a ginseng root. Steep both the ginger and the ginseng with the bag of oolong or black for a serious pick-me-up. Warning! Don't drink this brew just before going to bed, especially if this is your first major hit of ginseng, unless you're prepared to bounce off the walls all night. Ginseng is powerful stuff. So drink this as an afternoon beverage, because it's quite stimulating. I can see why Quark found a ready market for it.

Lokar Beans and Gramillan Sand Peas

Any good bartender knows that whatever encourages his patrons to drink is good for business. That's why Quark serves *lokar* beans and Gramillan sand peas to all his customers; they're hot and sweet and get people drinking. If you want to make these snacks instead of buying red-hot spiced peanuts or honey-toasted beer nuts at your package store or supermarket, you can. Both are roasted on a flat baking sheet in your oven at 350 degrees for 15 minutes. You can use your electric toaster oven, too. For *lokar* beans, start with dry-roasted peanuts, or shell your own roasted peanuts, and first roll them in honey and then dust them with coarse-milled kosher salt. Grease a flat baking pan and spread out the peanuts. Roast for 15 minutes and then let them cool.

Hot spiced peanuts are just that. Take dry-roasted peanuts and stir them through a mixture of melted butter and hot Tabasco sauce, remove to a seperate plate and sprinkle the whole thing with salt. For a milder peanut, use green Tabasco sauce. The more Tabasco or hot pepper sauce you use, the hotter the peanuts, so you'll have to experiment. I'd start gradually, because too much hot pepper sauce can actually burn the inside of your mouth. Not even the coldest German brew will wash down burning pepper sauce, hence the need for care. Be very careful with this recipe, and keep it away from children. Also, make sure you wash your hands after mixing up these nuts, and don't rub your eyes before you do. When you've coated all the peanuts, roast them in an oven at 350 degrees for 15 minutes. You can also heat them in your microwave for 2 to 3 minutes. Eat these peanuts only a few at a time because they're, quite literally, dynamite.

Alan Sims on How to Re-create Quark's Bar

We tried to make Quark's into more than just a bar; it was a tavern just like you'd find in your old neighborhood, where people came to party and be together. But Quark's is more than just a neighborhood hangout; we wanted it also to be like a happening every night, with gambling, drinking, dabo girls, and holo-suites. It's Miss Kitty's "Long Branch" in Dodge, a saloon in an old-time Western where cowboys, traders, and drifters, as well as the local male population, could find a cold glass of Andorian ale, a wheel of chance, and more than one hostess, in this case of some unknown species, willing to take their money in exchange for a bit of companionship and a friendly touch.

To make drinks like the ones in Quark's, you'd use watered-down cola syrup, either Coke syrup or some other kind of cola syrup, to make the dark

brandies. For the cognac, you'd lighten up the syrup with more water; for the brandies you'd keep it dark or nut-colored. For things like Saurian brandy or Andorian ale, if you don't use fruit juice, you can use either cola syrup or lime soda syrup thinned out with as much water as you need to make it pour as if it's real brandy or liquor. So you have to experiment both with color and with how it pours, the actual texture of the drink.

I have also become really intrigued with the look of some of the new Gatorade flavors such as Riptide Rush, Glacier Freeze, Blue Raspberry, and the translucent white fruit drink Alpine Snow. Because translucent white, for example, isn't clear, but a light milky color, it allows you to shine various colors through it so as to get a refraction through the lens. When you dress the beverage even more by putting it in a glass, mug, or fluted cup with lots of different angles, you can play with the refraction by changing the angle of focus of the light source and even the colored gels over the lens. So by angle and color of lighting, most of which you can do at home with all kinds of party lights and Christmas lights, you can get a drink with a rainbow of colors.

Glacier Freeze also gives me the opportunity to play with color and reflection because the drink is a very light blue, just enough to look otherworldly, but not enough to create its own presence on the set. Because it's muted, I can use it in a variety of settings. It's also noncarbonated, so I can add sparkling water, ginger ale, or any carbonated drink—including Dr. Brown's Cel-Ray—to change the color and activity inside the glass.

Some of Quark's drinks are legendary. Here are ways we captured their look and essence for the show. By combining presentation and design and even some imaginative lighting, you can do these same things in your own home even if you don't want to use alcohol.

Aldebaran Whiskey

The whiskeys at Quark's, and at Guinan's, too, for that matter, are usually quite dark, though not as dark as a brandy. Aldebaran whiskey is green, and I would use the dark green lemon-lime flavor of Gatorade called, oddly enough, Whitewater Splash. If you want to make it sparkle, cut it with a little sparkling water or Welch's white grape juice.

Andorian Ale

This is a yellowish nut-like drink that I would concoct by mixing Vernor's or Schweppes ginger ale and giving it a head with just a half teaspoon of milk so it looks like an egg cream. You can also use a lemonade concentrate mixed in lighter-than-usual proportions with club soda or ginger ale instead of plain water, and mixed with a half teaspoon of milk and stirred to give it a head.

Alvanian Brandy

This is a pinkish drink that you can make with Gatorade Strawberry Kiwi, pink-lemonade concentrate, or even pink grapefruit juice in bottles or in frozen concentrate. If you want to darken it, use just a touch of Welch's regular grape juice or even one of the darker cranberry juice cocktails or Knudsen unadulterated cranberry juice.

Black Hole

Here's a Ferengi drink that is exactly what it says it is. Make this at home with dark espresso coffee sweetened with as much sugar or aspartame as it takes. If you want to carbonate it, chill it and serve over ice mixed with sparkling water, vanilla extract, and sweetener. You can serve it hot or cold.

Brestanti Ale

This rich brown color should remind you of Watney's or any one of the British or Irish ales you can find in a package store. You can get this color by mixing All Sport Cherry Slam drink with Knudsen natural cranberry juice for a dark, almost brownish color; add just a hint of club soda or seltzer or sparkling water for carbonation.

Calaman Sherry

Here's a blush-colored drink that should look like pink champagne. Strawberry Kiwi is again your base drink of choice, lightened with Martinelli's sparkling apple cider, which also provides effervescence, or straight club soda if you don't want it too sweet. Serve in a tall, long-stemmed champagne glass so you can watch the bubbles rise.

Fanalian Toddy

Actually a cough remedy, according to Dr. Bashir, which he once ordered from Quark's. This drink is hot, of course, and has a clear color, almost beige, kind of like a schnapps. It's not thin and watery, but has almost the consistency of syrup. There are at least three ways to make this by the mug. One is to use just a touch of light molasses or light Karo corn syrup with a clear Gatorade lemon-lime. There are two versions of this drink in the supermarket. You can get a dark green lemon-lime and a clear, much lighter lemon-lime. I would use the second, clear lemon-lime, thicken it with just a little light Karo syrup, and heat it. Then I'd float cinnamon on the surface of the mug.

Another way is to heat lemon Jell-O but to cut it with lots of water so that it never thickens and serve it hot. Now it's a beige drink that will stay liquefied as long as you keep it warm.

Finally, you can mix lemon Kool-Aid with Knox unflavored gelatin, keeping the gelatin consistency very thin and, again, serve it nice and warm with cinnamon or a touch of brown sugar on top of it in the mug. When you use gelatin mixes to thicken your drinks, make sure you use extra water and cut it by at least two-thirds to make sure you don't wind up with a glass of gelatin at the end of the day when the mixture reaches room temperature. If you need to reheat the mugs, microwave them for about thirty seconds, making sure the surface of the mug has cooled before serving it to anybody, so it is safe to handle.

Gallia Nectar

Although *Gallia* is actually a drink made from a blossom that grows only in the Delta Quadrant on the planet Paxau, its beautiful pale yellow color can be duplicated by mixing lemon yellow Kool-Aid with Welch's white grape juice and serving it over ice.

Gamzian Wine

This heavily intoxicating beverage is really plum juice or plum nectar. To darken it, mix mostly plum juice with just a smidgen of prune juice to darken it, and serve it in small glasses, not large ones. Plum juice or nectar and prune juice make a drink that's nice and thick, just the kind of beverage you'd want to serve if someone as mysterious, as exotically beautiful, and as intriguing as Vash sat down across from you at Quark's and tried to get you to reveal your secrets of archeological finds in the galaxy.

Kanar

Kanar is a legendary dark-brown Cardassian drink that has, from time to time, also turned up as purple on some of the episodes. Although it's not necessarily carbonated, the closest look you can achieve is with a deep-colored chocolate syrup in sparking soda. It's official name is a "plain chocolate soda," dif-

ferent from an East Coast "chocolate egg cream" in that it has no white foamy head and is darker because it has no milk. The darker the chocolate syrup the better. Bosco and Fox's are the deepest in color, but you can also use Hershey's with some coffee extract to darken the drink. For purple *kanar*, just use Welch's grape juice mixed with a base of Gatorade's Riptide Rush.

Karvino Juice

This is a bright green drink; actually it's a green Gatorade called Whitewater Splash. It's funny that green Gatorade is Whitewater, while the opaque Gatorade is called Alpine Snow. Alpine Snow, by the way, looks just like ketracel-white, which is what the Jem'Hadar live on.

Klingon Bloodwine

Really simple to make on the set and at home. You use a very dark grape juice or cranberry juice, but you use a food processor, maybe a blender, or, even better, a juicer like a Juiceman and fresh cranberries. Then you use the juice and the cranberry residue—it looks like bloody organic tissue, very clotty, and you can even put some red Jell-O in there to make it seem like it's clotting up even more. Again, for people who can't drink sugar beverages, use straight-up cranberry juice, the blender mash of cranberries, and sugar-free strawberry, raspberry, grape, or cherry Jell-O that's just beginning to congeal.

Maporian Ale

Grilka's favorite drink should be served in a thick heavy glass mug. Use Martinelli's as a base with a splash of Welch's dark grape juice or a soft drink that's still available in some supermarkets called Coffee Time, a coffee soda. You can also use Dr. Brown's Cream Soda, or Stewart's Cream Ale. Grilka orders her Maporian ale with *pazafer* on top. You can find this at any Indian restaurant or any Indian grocer on Earth. It is called hot chutney spice. Float just a bit of it on your cream ale and see how it tastes.

Maraltian *Seev*-ale

From Quark's private stock, this ale has either a strange deep burgundy or purple color or a deep brown nut color. These most interesting colored drinks are created from both Reed's: raspberry-flavored ginger ale or dark ginger beer. Or any of the imported ginger beers or birch beers, especially, have the right color. Serve this drink in the kinds of Asian import mugs you find at a Pier 1 or another imported goods store that has a catalogue of exotic-looking glassware or dishware.

Rekarri Starbursts

This has a combination of colors, the Gatorade Alpine Snow with thick cherry or grape soda syrup floating on top. If you let the syrup float, especially if you drizzle it around the side of the Alpine Snow, it will gradually settle along the inside of the glass and will look like a star burst. But you can't let these sit. You have to make these drinks one at a time.

Romulan Ale

This cobalt blue drink that you have to serve in a tall schooner glass is either a straightforward Gatorade Cool Blue Raspberry, which has a luminous quality to it, or a Powerade Mountain Blast, which is a deeper blue. Either way, the drink is served, Romulan style, in a tall spiral glass or schooner glass, and is meant to be sipped, not downed in a single slug like the Klingon ales. You can also serve it in a very tall champagne glass, and mix a few teaspoons of Martinelli sparkling cider or club soda which allows the sparkling effervescent bubbles to rise to the surface.

Saurian Brandy

The distinctive curved-neck bottles of this liqueur provided quite a decorative touch at Quark's, even though anybody that drank this stuff knew in a minute that it was a valuable, highly-prized brew. The bottle is a commemorative design from the Dickel Company of Tennessee. Like Earth brandies from the eighteenth and nineteenth centuries, Saurian brandy was a commodity as well as an exquisite pleasure. The gold, nut-like color of Saurian brandy is best captured by O'Doul's nonalcoholic beer. You can use other nonalcoholic beers as well. These have a strong taste and a moderate head, but the color's just right.

Stardrifter

Here's a Ferengi drink Quark served at the bar that, believe it or not, allows you a variety of colors to mix. As a base, you can use either the Alpine Snow or the clear lemon-lime Gatorade topped with straight-off-the-shelf blueberry pancake syrup. Instead of the Alpine Snow, you can use any orangeade or orangeade concentrate topped with blueberry pancake syrup, grape drink syrup, or cherry syrup. You can even mix lime or lemon-lime syrup with sparkling water and drop cherry syrup on top.

For any stardrifter drinks you can also use this trick: you can have a smaller glass within your larger glass—and use plastic, not real glass—with two different liquids. For example, you can have Welch's grape juice in the inner glass and Gatorade orange in the outer glass. You serve these with a double straw, the Y-shaped clear plastic straws you get from party stores that are supposed to be used when people share the same drink. But for a stardrifter, reverse the straw so that one end of the Y is in the grape juice and the other end is in the orange drink. When you or your guests drink from the single straw, they'll actually be drawing two differently colored liquids through the bottom of the straw's branches that mix when the branches meet. If you can find these straws, it's a great special effect you can create in your own home.

Synthehol

Here's a drink you can make by using cola syrup, which you can buy from any soft-drink or beer warehouse, and experiment with proportions of sparking water until you get the shade you want. It's supposed to be bourbon-colored, which is a light, almost transparent, brown or amber color. Straight cola is almost the right color, but you have to lighten it by adding more sparkling water. If you can't get cola syrup, try one of the supermarket-brand colas for color and lighten it with club soda or ginger ale. You can also use a very dark apple juice or unfiltered or nonpasteurized apple cider, lightened with water.

Takarian Mead

Mead is a honey-colored foamy drink that is easy to make with lemonade, especially from lemonade mixes, sparkling water, and the nonalcoholic "Mr. Frothee" fizz mix you can get from any liquor store. By adding cans of frozen lemonade concentrate to the lemonade, you'll get a thicker drink that looks more like mead than like lemonade.

Tamarian Frost

You can use Gatorade's Alpine Snow mixed with a splash of milk and sparkling water for a foamy head. Even better, if you can find vanilla syrup at any soft-drink warehouse, you can create a New York-style vanilla egg cream, which is two to three tablespoons of vanilla syrup in a glass of sparkling water with a spritz of milk. This makes a white frosty drink with a thick head.

Trixian Bubble Juice

Here's a pink, highly carbonated drink that you can make with pink lemonade mixed with Martinelli's or sparkling water. You can also use pink grapefruit juice concentrate instead of pink lemonade and mix with sparkling water, carbonated mineral water, or even ginger ale instead of plain tap water.

Yridian Brandy

Use a cola syrup or a supermarket cola, lightened with either ginger ale or plain water.

THE KLINGON DELI

Ever have a craving for Klingon takeout? On Deep Space 9 it's only a com-badge call away. I've developed a real taste for Klingon food, and not just as a chef. You wouldn't think it to look at me, but I have the singular distinction of being the only Talaxian in history to have led a band of Klingon warriors into battle. Sure this was a holo-simulation, but did I know it at the time? And, guess what, those bloodthirsty Hirogen disabled the safety protocols on the holodeck, so, simulation or not, K'Neelix faced the certainty of injury or death when he led his forces against the Mauser-marauding holo-Nazis. There I was, good old Neelix, singing battle songs around the campfire, getting drunk on heady Klingon ale, swinging a *bat'leth* as if I really knew how to use it, and holding a *d'ktahg* to the throat of anyone who dared disobey me. Better still, I did this even after my neurostimulator had been turned off and I was Neelix once again.

Now that I am, or was, a Klingon, let me tell you what I share with those armor-clad warriors more than anyone will ever appreciate. I now know the song of battle; my pulse quickens at the thrill of blood, and I love the smell of photon-torpedo bursts in the morning. Bring on the skull stew, the *gagh,* and the bloodwine.

Klingons like meat, all kinds. They like body organs, hearts and guts. And they rejoice in the taste of blood. Here are some of the more intense dishes you can feast on from the traditional menu at the Deep Space 9 Klingon deli.

When the three moons align on the planet Eromt-Sew, the Marzonion plant springs forth with large beautiful buds. These buds are most delectable when boiled with the juice from the *krasie* tree. But at last, you can only enjoy the sublime taste of artichokes in white wine.

1 artichoke per person

¼ teaspoon olive oil per artichoke

¼ teaspoon salt per artichoke

1 clove garlic per artichoke, minced

1 cup Chablis per artichoke (or half wine, half water)

First, cut off the artichoke stems so the base is flat and the artichokes can sit on the bottom of the pot without falling over. Next, rinse the artichokes thoroughly in cold tap water. Slice off ½ inch from the top to remove sharp ends and open the bud. Next discard the small leaves around the base.

In a mixing bowl, combine the olive oil, salt, garlic, and wine or wine-and-water mixture. Then place artichokes on the bottom of a large, deep saucepan, making sure that each one sits on the bottom of the saucepan and that they all fit comfortably. Pour the wine or wine-water mixture over the artichokes. Cover and bring to a boil. Reduce heat to a gentle boil and cook for about 30 to 40 minutes or until a leaf from the center of the artichoke pulls out easily. This is your test for doneness.

Serve the artichokes in their own bowl. Pour the cooking liquid into a separate bowl. This is for dipping the leaves. Add another bowl for discarding the uneaten portion of the leaves.

Klingon Skull Stew with Tripe

Not for the fainthearted, this dish is exactly what it says it is: a skull with the meat stewed off and served on a nice bed of entrails. Sound appetizing? It did to me when I was Klingon for those few days on Holodeck 2. Of course, les petits fours also tantalized my taste buds when I was delivering food for Kathrine, leader of the French Underground on Holodeck 1 during the Hirogen invasion. Before the Khitomer Accords and the alliance between the Federation and the Klingon Empire, skull stew was once thought of as only a myth. If you're up for this, you can make it at home if you prepare it very carefully and slowly. Don't worry, there's always enough skull stew to go around, so tell your guests to enjoy it in moderation and then come back for seconds.

1 medium-to-large-sized calf's skull

1 to 2 pounds honeycomb tripe

1 medium-sized onion, chopped

1 small green bell pepper, chopped

4 small tomatoes, chopped *or* 1 8-ounce can peeled tomatoes, chopped

½ pound mushrooms, chopped (optional)

1 tablespoon vegetable oil

½ cup cream

2 eggs

2 tablespoons butter, melted

3 tablespoons flour

1 tablespoon cooking oil

2 beef bouillon cubes

2 tablespoons dry sherry

½ teaspoon salt

pepper to taste

cayenne pepper to taste

Tabasco to taste

You will prepare the tripe and the calf's head separately in 2 stew pots and then combine them about ½ hour before the stew's done. Begin by washing and cleaning the calf's head, removing the brains and blood. Then cover with water and bring to a boil; remove the surface scum, cover with lid, reduce heat, and continue boiling for at least 2 hours until the cheek meat is tender. After you've set the calf's head on boil, wash and clean the honeycomb tripe. If you've purchased it from a supermarket, chances are the blood vessels will already have been removed, but give it a good cleaning nevertheless. Chop the tripe into 2 or 3 long pieces. Cover with water in a 6-8 quart pot, cover, and set it to boil. Reduce to simmer for about 2 hours or until it is tender. When the tripe is tender, drain it and then bake it in a deep pan at 350 degrees for about 30 minutes, then set it aside.

When the calf's head cheek meat is tender, remove head from pot and let cool. When it is sufficiently cooled, cut the cheek meat away from the bone, cube, and set aside. Wash and save the skull. In a separate baking dish, combine 2 tablespoons melted butter and two tablespoons of flour with just enough water to make a thick paste. Season this with the salt, pepper, cayenne, and Tabasco, add the cubed cheek meat, and stir in the beef bouillon. Heat in oven with the tripe.

Now in a medium skillet brown the onion and bell pepper in oil (if you are using mushrooms, add them at this time), and then add the tomatoes and heat until they begin to dissolve. Remove the tripe from the oven when done and the calf's head stew. Add the onion, pepper, and tomato mixture to the tripe and return to oven for about 10 minutes. Mix the eggs and cream together, and add to the calf's head stew. Return stew to oven. When the ten minutes are up, remove the tripe from its own cooking pan. Set aside. Remove the calf's head stew. Combine the tripe sauce with the calf's head stew and return to oven for 5 more minutes. Remove and stir in the cooking sherry.

Place the calf's skull in the center of a large, large serving bowl and over it pour the combined stew mixture. Now drape and arrange the pieces of the tripe around the skull and dish. Serve in a ceremonial manner while chanting Klingon songs of battle victory. No one will ever forget this meal. Serves six to eight.

Klingon Organ Stew

How best to serve your enemies, especially to your friends? The Klingons have a unique tradition called organ stew. This wild-game hunter's stew is another complicated dish that will be sure to please at your Klingon parties. It is not for your vegetarian friends, who should have been invited to your Vulcan party, you know, the one where you serve *plomeek* soup and lots of green leafy things and everyone sits around claiming the other person is illogical.

Unless you personally know the creature who's being consumed, you have to appreciate that Klingon organ stew is the ultimate in galactic recycling. You eat everything: heart, liver, ears, tongue, stomach, tail, and, if you want, the intestines also. The only thing you don't eat is the skin, but you can make something out of it if you know how to tan and stitch a hide. I've been told that Klingon blue suede moccasins are among the finest in the galaxy, prized possessions handed down through the generations. So if you're going to make organ stew anywhere else but planet Earth, make it out of the innards of an animal whose hide you can use for clothing, shoes, braces, your laptop attaché case, anything. This is something the Hirogen might look into someday if they ever get tired of simply hanging their trophies from the walls and ceilings.

My version is a pork stew, and the trick to preparing this dish so that it's edible for humans, or for anyone else this side of the Caretaker's space station, is to cook the toughest organs first until they're nice and soft. Then cook the tender organs, like the liver and heart, separately. After cooking, you purée the tender organs to make a thick stock for the stew of the ears, tongue, and stomach. The tail meat is very strong, and we use it as flavoring. Any bones you want to use, scrape and wash thoroughly, boil separately, then add at the end as presentation and decoration. The intense meat flavor of this dish is mitigated by the hefty pasilla chili pepper and the 2 or 3 large juicy tomatoes. If you want to prepare this with an American southwestern flavor, add green chilies to the stew. If you want a strong Central American flavor, add more garlic and ground pumpkin seeds.

½ pound pork liver

½ pound pork heart

½ pound pig's ears

½ pound pork meat such as a roast

½ pound pork tongue

½ pound pork stomach

½ pound pigtails

2 tablespoons olive oil

2 large tomatoes, chopped

1 whole pasilla (chili pepper), seeded and chopped

1 medium onion, chopped

6 tortillas, lightly toasted

4 ounces ground pumpkin seeds

1 teaspoon powdered garlic

1 teaspoon thyme

salt and pepper to taste

Begin by cleaning the ears, stomach, and tail thoroughly, scraping off all the veins, waste, and blood. Cover them with water. Then boil them for at least 2 to 3 hours or until they have become tender, skimming continually to remove scum and crud from the surface of the water. After they've cooked, discard the water and dry the organs. Next purée ½ the liver with the olive oil and cook in a saucepan with the dry organs until lightly browned. Remove from heat and save. Now place the remaining liver, heart, and tongue, cover with water, and cook for about 1 hour. Drain the water. While your soft organs are cooking, in a saucepan add the seasonings, vegetables, and tomatoes and just enough water to cover, and simmer for about 1 hour. When your liver and soft organs and vegetable sauce are done, combine them with the hard organs. Add a few teaspoons of water, if necessary, to thin the sauce, and simmer for about 1 hour. Make sure that the flavors have blended and that all of the organs are tender. Correct the seasoning with additional salt and pepper and even some Tabasco, according to your own taste. This can serve 6 hearty Klingons who like to dip their tortillas or even wrap the tortillas around the stew. Serves six.

El Bouche: Klingon Throat Stew

The Klingons believe that the best way to celebrate a successful hunt is to eat your prey for dinner that very night. A stew is their preferred method. Happily enough, there is a recipe from Earth, Central America to be exact—El Bouche—that you can prepare to enjoy the fruits of your hunt. In this recipe your prey is a wild boar, but it could have been anything from a caribou to a fully grown bull *targ*.

> 1 pound pork cheek meat
> 1 pound pork throat (bouche), scrubbed, boiled in water until
> tender, then chopped
> 1 medium-sized onion
> 5 tomatoes, chopped
> 3 cups water
> ¼ cup seeded and chopped jalapeño pepper
> 1 tablespoon chopped cilantro
> 1 teaspoon fresh lemon juice
> salt and black pepper to taste

While you're boiling the throat, boil the pork cheek in a separate saucepan for about 1 hour and set aside. After about an hour, when the throat is tender enough to chop, remove and do so. Set it aside, and combine the tomatoes, onion, jalapeño, and seasonings with 3 cups water and bring to a boil. Simmer for a ½ hour and add the throat and pork meat. Simmer for 1 more hour, correct the seasonings. Serves four to six.

Racht

"Nothing's worse than half-dead racht.*"*

1 16-ounce package soba noodles

¼ cup teriyaki sauce

¼ cup soy sauce

sesame salad dressing or tahini as needed

Although most Klingons say that these serpent worms are best when served live, if nice cold recently dead *racht* is the only thing available, they won't throw them out into the disposal unit. I suggest 1 or 2 packages of the thickest white soba noodles you can find at your Asian market, boiled, and then chilled and served with a combination of soy and teriyaki sauces with just enough sesame salad dressing to give it color and taste. You can serve soba warm in a mixture of soy and teriyaki sauce as well, but serving it cold makes it easier to scarf up with your hands, the way the Klingons do.

The trick to *racht* is the presentation, and I suggest lining the plate with raw Asian sea squid or whole octopus tentacles, maybe a very large purple eggplant or an Asian melon cut wide-open with the seeds left in. It will look like a Horta egg and only add to the exotic quality of the visual presentation. Serves two.

If you use raw or live shellfish as garnishes, please remember that they are highly perishable foods and spoil very rapidly. They can contaminate the foods they come in contact with, particularly if they're all on the same platter or dish. So please don't leave raw or live shellfish sitting on a table for any extended period of time. Keep them under refrigeration until ready to serve. If you are using them as a garnish, I suggest that you place the food you are serving in a clear bowl, and wrap the garnish around the bowl on another dish or platter, so that they do not touch! You can become sick from spoiled fish so extra care must be taken.

Zilm'kach

Zilm'kach is a special Klingon fruit that cuts the intensity of skull stew, organ stew, and skull stew. If you can't find them on Earth, you can replace them with a hybrid citrus called a tangelo. It's acidic, less sweet than you'd imagine, and complements the intensity of any meat dish.

Yridian Brandy

Worf, as most Klingons do, appreciates the heady taste of the traditional Yridian brandy consumed only on special occasions. If you're celebrating a big Kahless event, lamenting over the massacre at Khitomer, or even getting married, Yridian brandy is the nectar of the homeworld. In your kitchen, the trick to Yridian brandy is the texture as well as the color and the taste. To serve, just about any vessel will do, especially a thin flask that forces you to sip, but you can also use the thoroughly washed fish-shaped bottle from a Verdicchio, the wicker basket bottle from a Chianti, or even the odd-looking Frascati bottle.

For the brandy itself, you can use a cup of dark apple juice, darkened further with ½ teaspoon of vanilla extract. If you want a heavy consistency, try mixing the cup of apple juice and vanilla with just 1 teaspoon of unflavored gelatin and let it sit in your refrigerator for a couple of hours. If you've used too much gelatin and it thickens too much, cut it with water and stir. With the proper bottle and right lighting, you've got Yridian brandy for any Klingon occasion.

Alan Sims on Klingon Food

Some raw Asian seafoods, especially the sea slug, look almost like a big snake or giant eel. When they're served as part of an Asian dish, they are supposed to be cut up or sliced in large enough pieces to create an effect. I lay them out whole right around the dish for decoration and they look fabulous to dress the dish. I never tasted one, but I hear they're salty as hell.

Just as raw seafood and crawling-type Asian delicacies are used for presentation, so is the actual dish you serve the food in a part of your presentation. I used pewter or a plated pewter look for all my Klingon setups on *The Next Generation*, and we use it on *Deep Space Nine* as well. Pewter, the heavy metal goblets, pitchers, and plates, all have that ancient barbaric-warrior look that defines the Klingon presentation. Use odd shapes like ovals, triangles, and rectangles. Don't go for the conventional round dishes, go for ones in the out-

of-the-way shapes that you can sometimes find in flea markets, secondhand stores, or swap meets. You can even lay these foods directly onto cloth—make sure they are clean, and that if the cloth is colored that the dyes will not leach into the food—that cover a plate.

If you use raw or live shellfish as garnishes or props, please remember that they are highly perishable foods and spoil very rapidly. They can contaminate the foods they come in contact with, particularly if they're all on the same platter or dish. So please don't leave raw or live shellfish sitting on a table for any extended period of time. Keep them under refrigeration until ready to serve. If you are using them as a garnish, I suggest that you place the food you are serving in a clear bowl, and wrap the garnish around the bowl on another dish or platter, so that they do not touch! You can become sick from spoiled shellfish so extra care must be taken.

If you do a Klingon wedding feast, drape cloth over plates. Go for metal plates that are completely clean and have no rust, chipping paint, lead paint, or enamel, dishes that you know are perfectly clean. Use mugs for the ale, metallic-looking goblets or flagons for the bloodwine and Klingon ale. You can find strange or bizarre glassware in the Pier 1 stores. You can mix lemonade with sparkling water or sweeten iced coffee and mix with club soda for mead or brandy, or you can create a look with cranberry juice and water, but if you put it into a well-designed goblet from one of the restaurant supply or import/export stores, you have the makings of an alien table set. Develop the heavy, barbarian look. It's all part of the package.

Flatware is also important. It may be expensive, and there's no easy way out of spending the money unless you can find odd-looking forks or rectangular spoons at a yard or garage sale or at a flea market. And don't think you always have to have regular forks; you can always poke things with long sticks or fondue forks. I recommend chopsticks as a really inexpensive way to get a kabob look for all barbarian feasts; you can pick them up free from the sushi counters or Asian food counters at the big supermarkets. Grab a handful every time you go and keep them for your parties.

Let your imagination create the meal, the look, the entire attitude. In an episode like Worf's wedding we had to make the food look different with garnishes, vegetarian or sashimi. Vegetables are an inexpensive way to express your alien imagination. I like to use things like endive or fennel or chard. I use different types of herbs like chives or rosemary leaves. I use tarragon as an accent. Rosemary is great because it looks alien. But stay away from the conventional pasta shapes like rotini or rigatoni because they're at every restaurant and everyone serves them. You can create your own alien dishes by thinking of what you don't see every day on a table. Rice noodles look odd and they can replace pasta. Udon noodles are good, of course, because they look like *gagh*. Soba noodles also look unconventional. Another great prop food for Klingons and maybe other alien cultures as well is tongue. Tongue, a nice, big pickled tongue, which you get from a butcher, is perfect because when you arrange it on a dish that's too small, it looks like it's moving, crawling off the plate. If you arrange an oversized tongue on an undersized plate full of dark lentils, you have the perfect Klingon, Ferengi, Romulan, or even Cardassian dish, and you can eat it and enjoy it.

I'll tell you something else that always works well as an alien food—borscht, basic bottled borscht from the store. It's bright red and beety, so it has chunks of stuff in it. You can throw in anything and it's immediately dyed red in natural beet dye. You have to be careful, though, because red beet dye tends to stain. Borscht is the perfect alien soup. If you add thick-curd cottage cheese, you get Klingon corpuscles.

Ferengi food is different; it's more ornamental and we don't have to make real food. For the Ferengi we like to use straight-out props.

Rom

How would you feel if your only moniker in the place where you work and live was "my idiot brother"? Since I never met Rom personally, I can't answer that question, but it's clear that the assistant manager of Quark's has more skills than simply whupping up a stardrifter or a glass of Icoberry Fizz every now and then. He is an engineer of some repute, but he's humble and takes the browbeating—and Ferengi have a lot of brow—in the spirit of genuine brotherly love. But be careful, even Ferengi brothers are supposed to be treacherous—it's the Ferengi way. Remember the 139th Rule of Acquisition, "Wives serve, brothers inherit."

Pancakes

Rom likes basic foods. His favorite, a short stack of pancakes for breakfast. Here's Rom's replicator recipe for combadge-sized banana pancakes.

1 cup pancake mix, Bisquick or any other brand

⅓ cup milk

1 egg

2 bananas, 1 mashed, 1 sliced thin

¼ cup (½ stick) butter

1 teaspoon vanilla extract

½ teaspoon cinnamon

Combine pancake mix, milk, egg, vanilla, and cinnamon in a medium-sized mixing bowl. Next fold in the mashed banana until it's completely blended. A few lumps here and there are okay as long as the banana is mixed through. Then add the slices of the second banana on top. Melt the butter in a large skillet until it sizzles and just begins to turn brown, then spoon the pancake batter into the skillet forming 2-inch pancakes. As bubbles appear in the batter, flip the pancakes quickly, flatten with a spatula to make sure all the batter cooks, flip a couple of more times, and serve with butter, syrup, sugar, fruit, or any combination of your favorite toppings. Yields two dozen pancakes.

GUL DUKAT

One of the most complex adversaries the Federation ever faced, Dukat has had a career that has twined around the lives of Sisko and Kira just like a strand of DNA. He was a bitter enemy when he was commander of Terok Nor, and Sisko and Dukat battled each other after the Federation took control of Deep Space 9.

Dukat has always displayed fishy behavior toward Sisko. That's no mystery, because the Cardassians have a fondness for fishy things: hot fish juice accompanied by red leaf tea, or mollusks in *yamok* sauce and stews made from exotic game meats with *yamok* sauce. How they love their *yamok* sauce. They put it on everything. You could shine shoes with the stuff and they'd eat it off the shoe leather, if they didn't eat the leather itself.

Tojal in *Yamok Sauce*

The secret of this Cardassian appetizer is that you can eat a lot of it and still have room for your main dish, probably *zabo* meat. The Cardassians skewer pieces of *tojal* on tiny forks and swirl it around in the *yamok* sauce. I'm told that at formal Cardassian dinners, they only stop bringing out the *tojal* when there's not enough *yamok* sauce for the *zabo* meat. You can use either small or medium shrimp, boiled and deveined, and serve it with a mixture of teriyaki and soy sauce as a cocktail dip. You can also use cooked lump crabmeat and even prepackaged oysters. If you're using shrimp, I suggest you cook them in a concoction of crab boil and beer.

2 dozen medium shrimp, deveined

2 12-ounce bottles beer

2 tablespoons crab boil or Old Bay seasoning

6 whole cloves

4 cloves garlic, sliced

1 tablespoon pickling spice

YAMOK SAUCE

1 cup teriyaki sauce

½ cup soy sauce

1 teaspoon fresh-squeezed lemon juice

Boil shrimp in beer, Old Bay or crab boil seasoning, cloves, pickling spice, and garlic for 15 minutes when the shrimp turn pink and become tender. Drain and set aside. Mix teriyaki and soy sauces and spritz in the lemon juice. Serve in individual cocktail glasses over ice. You can replace shrimp with raw oysters or cooked crab meat. Serves four.

Zabo

This exotic game meat served by Keiko O'Brien is actually a favorite of the Cardassians even though it's not native to Cardassia. It's actually venison, served as a cutlet with either currant or mint jelly.

1 to 1½ pounds fresh venison loin, sliced

½ cup olive oil

¼ cup (½ stick) butter

5 cloves garlic

½ cup olive oil

1 cup bread crumbs

6 ounces currant jelly *or* mint jelly

Crush garlic cloves into ½ cup of olive oil. Insert pieces of butter into the loin-of-venison slices, and brush the olive oil onto the meat. Roll oiled slices in bread crumbs, and broil for 5 minutes. Venison should always be served rare. Serve with currant or mint jelly on the side. Serves four to six.

Sem'hal Stew

Here's another meat stew favorite of Cardassians served with a *yamok* sauce. It's a lamb kidney stew, which as a leftover can double as a filling you can bake in a pastry.

6 fresh lamb kidneys

1 cup beef consommé or bouillon *or* 1 bouillon cube in 1 cup
       boiling water

1 cup dry white wine

½ cup all-purpose flour

⅔ cup boiling water

2 tablespoons butter

1 teaspoon onion juice

1 teaspoon lemon juice

salt and pepper to taste

Soak and then slice the kidneys and sprinkle with salt and pepper. In a deep skillet sauté them in butter for 5 minutes and remove them. Dredge them with flour and return to skillet. Add the consommé or bouillon and ⅔ cup boiling water. Simmer for 5 more minutes and add the onion and lemon juices and wine, and simmer for 10 minutes. Serve with own juice and with *yamok* sauce for Cardassian style—½ cup teriyaki, ¼ cup soy sauce—as a dip. Because kidneys tend to toughen after cooking for 15 minutes or so, if you don't serve them right away, you'll need to cook them slowly for another 2 hours to serve them again. So this is not a dish that keeps well. Serves six.

Hot Fish Juice

Here's a Cardassian breakfast beverage that's made from the juice you've drawn off steamed clams. You can serve it straight and hot or, for an eye-opening Terran breakfast drink, mix it with bottled tomato juice, Tabasco sauce, some celery salt, and pepper—especially Tabasco sauce—for a morning pick-me-up. You can squeeze a wedge of lemon into your glass or replace the standard Tabasco with a teaspoon of salsa verde or green pepper sauce.

Red Leaf Tea

Cardassians swear by the restorative powers of red leaf tea that's available only in certain sectors of the Alpha and Beta Quadrants. I've discovered, through another one of my exhaustive searches through the Starfleet database of Earth's Amazon herbs and teas, an herb tea called uña de gato or cat's claw tea. This is actually more of a bark than a real tea, but it's brewed just like tea and available from most health food stores as well as from supermarkets specializing in natural or organic foods. I don't want to sound like an EMH, but I've heard that if you boil the bark in water for about 20 minutes and then drink the water, just about any infection you have will be purged from your system. This concoction is such a diuretic I can't imagine that anything could last in your system for twenty-four hours. Tea herbalists swear by it and say that it rids the body of all types of germs, bugs, and even intestinal influenza bacteria. You can reboil the same bark over again and reheat the tea you don't drink on the first night. You have to develop a taste for it, however, because the stuff's incredibly bitter.

Jake Sisko

Benjamin Sisko's son, Jake, grew up on Deep Space 9 far from his family home in Louisiana and his grandfather's restaurant. But the commander prided himself on home cooking—he learned it from his father—and Jake learned to appreciate a good meal. He's a kid after my own heart, and I'd love to prepare a freshly cooked hot bowl of oatmeal one day for him. Here are some of his favorites:

Jumja

As a young kid running around Deep Space 9, Jake loved a candy called *jumja,* made from sap of the *jumja* tree on Bajor. The *jumja* tree also produces a fine leaf for tea. Just ask Lysia Arlin, who runs the *jumja* kiosk. You can't find the *jumja* tree on Earth, but I'm told that you can actually buy a pretty satisfactory replacement for *jumja* made out of maple syrup candy. You can find prepackaged maple sugar candy on popsicle sticks, or you can make your own by buying maple sugar cubes and inserting your own sticks, then chilling them in a refrigerator so that they last a little longer on summer days and kids don't get sticky fingers that leave sugar spots around the house. If you want the candy-making experience in your own kitchen, you can buy the fixings for caramel apples, follow the package directions, but add maple syrup after the caramels have liquefied and are ready for apple dipping. Maple caramel apples are sweet, to be sure, but they're a different flavor for kids and are a great variation on *jumja.*

Oatmeal

This is one of Jake's favorite breakfasts, even though there are no cold, snowy mornings waiting at the shuttle stop on Deep Space 9. For those of us on *Voyager*, I use Tabrikian oats (the Tabric are a band of merceneries operating in Kazon space), but any plain rolled oats will substitute, and *frezzles,* a small dried berry from the third moon of Gorybore, can be replaced with raisins. For added zip, spoon in some cinnamon, nutmeg, a splash of maple syrup, and some brown sugar. Everyone loves this dish. For Jake, however, I'd start with quick-cooking John McCann's Irish Oatmeal or Quaker rolled oats and cook them with a splash of vanilla and lots of cinnamon.

1 cup quick-cooking rolled oats or Irish oatmeal

1 cup milk

⅛ cup (¼ stick) butter

1 teaspoon cinnamon

¼ teaspoon vanilla extract

honey to taste

Combine all the ingredients except the honey in a small saucepan while the milk is still cold. Slowly bring to a boil, stirring constantly, and let cook at a low simmer for about 5 minutes. Add the honey just before serving. You can also prepare this in a microwave-safe bowl by combining in it all the ingredients, including the honey, microwaving them on high for 2 minutes, stirring, microwaving for 1 additional minute, and then letting it stand for 1 minute; and then serve.

Don't let your kids remove dishes straight from the microwave until you're sure the dishes have cooled sufficiently. It's always safer not to let young children handle anything from the microwave under any circumstances, and you should always use hot pads when removing anything. It's too easy to get burned. Serves two.

I'danian Spice Pudding

Jake's favorite dessert is just as easy to make on Earth as it is on Deep Space 9. I like to start with a basic store-bought package of vanilla pudding, either instant or quick-cooked, spiced with lots of cinnamon and a touch of nutmeg. I also suggest this variation: add cooked rice for texture and body. If you do, a few raisins also add to the flavor.

1 8-ounce package instant or quick-cook vanilla pudding

¼ cup raisins

¼ cup uncooked rice

1 tablespoon cinnamon

1 teaspoon cinnamon

¼ teaspoon nutmeg

In a saucepan prepare the vanilla pudding according to package directions. In another saucepan prepare the rice: ½ cup of water for ¼ cup of rice, bring to a boil with a little butter, cover, and let simmer for about 20 minutes. Now add the rice to the warm pudding, add the spices and raisins, and let cool. Serve with a splash of milk or cream and top it off with whipped cream for approximately 4 servings.

GARAK

Cardassians are spooky, to say the least, and Garak is perhaps the spookiest. A man who calls himself a tailor, Garak was forced to stay behind on Deep Space 9 after the Cardassians evacuated the station. Garak is a sucker for sweets, and his favorites are the Cardassian delicacy, the ultra-sweet and ultra-silky Delavian chocolates that might well have been genetically designed to appeal to the Cardassian chocolate pleasure centers; they're that satisfying.

Delavian Chocolates

There are a variety of chocolates that fill the bill as replacements for Delavians on Earth, including not only the world-famous Godiva chocolates, but the very special Hershey's Select, which, I'm told, are so exclusive you can't even find them except in some high-priced catalogues. Chocolate making is an art, and even though it was a homemade recipe during the nineteenth and early twentieth centuries on Earth, the raw materials for it have become too hard to get. You need a really top-quality double boiler to start, as well as the raw ingredients. You can make your own chocolate sauce from unsweetened baking chocolate melted down in the top of a double boiler with some sugar, vanilla extract, and maybe even extracts of orange or mint; but nothing beats roasting and cooking with your own cocoa beans—it's just that it takes forever. Here's a special chocolate fudge recipe from one of the vedeks, Diana Rosen, whose history of Earth tea and coffee is still recorded as standard reading for all aspiring chefs.

½ cup (1 stick) unsalted butter

¼ cup brewed dark-roasted coffee

2 tablespoons unsweetened dark (bittersweet) cocoa powder

2 tablespoons real maple syrup (Others are just maple-flavored
      corn syrup; why bother?)

3 cups sugar

¾ cups plus 2 tablespoons sweetened condensed milk

1 cup chopped walnuts

1 cup cold water (for testing the fudge)

4 to 6 ounces shredded or flaked coconut (optional)

Grease a 9-inch-square baking pan. Next, in a large saucepan, gently heat together the following ingredients: butter, coffee, cocoa, maple syrup, and sugar. Using a wooden spoon, stir occasionally until the sugar is completely dissolved. *Do not allow to boil.* Slowly add the condensed milk, and now bring it to a boil and stir constantly. Boil about 8 minutes, or until bubbles in the mixture look like erupting craters on Delavia. Continue to cook about 3 more minutes or more, until a small amount forms a soft ball when dropped into a cup of cold water. This is your test for doneness. Remove from heat and allow the entire mixture to cool, until the bubbling stops. Beat well about five minutes until the mixture thickens.

Add chopped walnuts (and optional coconut) and blend them in well. Pour fudge mixture into the pan and allow to stand 30 minutes until about half set. Using a very sharp, clean knife, mark off 1-inch squares. Let stand until cold. Cut out the 1-inch squares and remove them from the pan. Makes about 1½ pounds. The fudge squares can be stored in jars with tight-fitting lids for the shuttle trip back to the surface of Bajor—that is, if Garak doesn't sneak into your quarters and get to them first.

Joe Longo on *Deep Space Nine* Food Props

Yamok sauce

The basic sauce for all Klingon and Cardassian dishes is *yamok* sauce. We use it with *gagh* and refer to it as a basic food. It is dark Karo syrup and Worcestershire sauce, mixed together to get a deep brown color. You can put it right over white udon noodles and it's just the color of the worms. I would use the white udon noodles all the time because white noodles take color better than the whole-wheat noodles. We have both hot and cold noodles.

For an interesting variation of *gagh,* we put baby crabs in the noodles. These look just like big cockroaches. You can also use oyster crabs. I have heard that as long as you have a dish of butter alongside, you can eat the oyster crabs live, just like clams. This would really be eating Klingon style.

Blood pie for me is a mixture of cranberry juice and cranberries crushed in a blender, and I mix it with my *yamok* sauce for my Cardassian friends.

I also like to make leg of lamb and cover it with my *yamok* sauce. It's an odd taste—the combination of Karo syrup, Worcestershire sauce, and sometimes puréed cranberries on lamb—but it works and makes a great effect.

Bloodwine is a composition of cranberries in a fruit-drink base like cherry punch.

For the Ferengi food, which is different, we use the baby crabs or oyster crabs, we use lots of sea slugs cut to different lengths, and we use fresh, living mealworms or night crawlers as props.

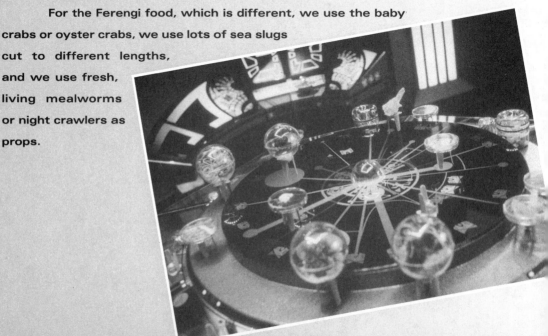

LIFE ON VOYAGER

The Strange New Worlds of the Delta Quadrant

I should think the crew stumbled into some good fortune when the captain welcomed me aboard. They needed a cook, and I believe I was the answer to their prayers. With my background as a trader, I'd already sampled a great deal of the Delta Quadrant's cuisine. It seemed I was always eating at a strange table, finalizing a deal over some new dish. That's always been a real thrill for me, sitting down to eat something I couldn't name, couldn't recognize, biting into a new, alive, exotic taste! And it happened often; traveling about as I was, I never knew where my next meal was coming from.

I was neither a beggar nor a chooser. I didn't have the luxury of turning up my nose at an opportunity to fuel up. I ate what came my way, and I've learned that a trader can use anything he finds. I once cooked *festle* lichen in a steam that rose off the wet trees of the Dorian moon at dawn. I've eaten raw *fud,* a kind of ground clam from Iziox that's 92% genitalia. They make rabbits look like puritans. The Yax once fed me a feast of rattlefish nipples, wire smelts, and paradise snails that made me ill for a month. They called it sashimi; I called it bait. While bartering with the Tak Tak, I sampled some of their deep-fried Tak Tak toes. Or were they tic tac toes? So many meals, I can't remember: was it ocean cocoa, sand candy, or lightning lice?

Eating the food of a species is a terrific way to learn about them, too. In the following section I show you an assortment of the many different

recipes I've prepared in the mess hall over the last few years. I've cooked many dishes, some of which the crew was not too fond of, some they've disliked, others they wouldn't eat, and a few they claimed were not even food. It would be dishonest of me to say my feelings are not hurt. Indeed, I consider myself a renowned chef. But it seems to me that they sometimes treat me like a badly programmed replicator. Still, we'll be together for a while yet, and I'm hoping that thrill in encountering new foods I spoke of will be contagious. Talaxians are famous for their hope and optimism.

All that notwithstanding, I get a lot of complaints in the galley. In fact, Harry Kim and Tom Paris thought it would be very funny, after staying up all night when they were off-shift and watching ancient videos of twentieth-century Earth late-night television, to put this notice up all over the ship's computer. Captain Janeway laughed so hard she spilled her one and only *raktajino* ration for the day and then got mad at me. Even Mr. Vulcan cracked a smile, although I'm sure it was out of politeness, because he didn't know what everyone was laughing at. He took it seriously.

Top Ten Reasons the Crew Hates Neelix's Cooking

10: Two words: Kazon saliva.

 9: Kidney is not a breakfast food.

 8: A little confused by the soup fork.

 7: Can't take any more "cream of yesterday."

 6: Swill du Jour.

 5: Square meals means diced carrots.

 4: Tuesday is fungus night!

 3: The fruitcake leaks.

 2: Pleeka rind.

 1: Jelly à la Neelix.

This wasn't funny. But I do have other dishes that some people on *Voyager* find intriguing. After all, we've been to so many worlds I had to pick up some tricks along the way. One of the first, after figuring out the favorite foods of the crew, was using the raw ingredients and culinary cultures we encountered as we wended our way through the Delta Quadrant.

Artilotian Loosedine

This is a weird one, the only chow I know that comes from the Lambda System, where the Artilotians live. My friend Sirix, a renowned traveler from my home planet, first gave me this recipe. It includes the thigh meat from a *miphrop*, a fourteen-legged dog that is precognizant, but only about others of its kind; it knows when another *miphrop* is about to itch, or groom, or pee. Other ingredients are the wings from Gonazian smoke flies, fleece needles that grow in fields of stardust, and blood leaf. Artilotians also add mermaid egg, but I don't have a clue where they get that from.

You'll need a heavy saucepan or stew pot for this recipe, which on Earth is called rosemary chicken. It's based on a simple principle: you wash and then brown a quartered chicken in lots of butter and its own juices, add vegetables such as carrots and potatoes along with a few stalks of celery and a tomato or two, and simmer for hours until it's tender. This is the kind of dish you can also make in your Crock-Pot if you throw a little chicken bouillon into the recipe. It can cook slowly for 8 hours and be ready for supper.

2-pound frying chicken, quartered, legs and wings separated

2 large carrots, sliced

4 medium potatoes, peeled and sliced or cubed

2 tomatoes

3 stalks celery

½ cup (1 stick) butter

2 tablespoons rosemary

2 garlic cloves, sliced

1 teaspoon parsley

1 chicken bouillon cube (optional)

salt and pepper to taste

Wash chicken thoroughly. Melt a half stick of butter in a very heavy saucepan and brown garlic. Then add chicken pieces and brown. Add 2½ cups water, and for extra chicken flavor add the cube, and all the vegetables. Reduce heat and add herbs and the remaining butter. Cover tightly and cook for at least 3 hours. Check vegetables and chicken for doneness. Serves four.

Deep-Fried Blue Tashmanian Spiders

I prepared this once for B'Elanna and she really liked it. Unlike the chocolate-covered ants of Earth, deep-fried Tashmanian spiders are served live. Don't scoff, they're delicious. These spiders (found only on the Klingon Homeworld) are so tough they survive the boiling oil they're dipped in. The average Klingon can easily put away a hundred or more at a sitting. It's quite a sight to see thousands of these tiny blue delicacies crawling inside the encased serving trays at the beginning of a Klingon banquet alongside the vats of scalding oil. The guests can help themselves to the spiders and spoon out bowls of hot oil.

An Earth replacement for the spiders you can try are tiny deep-fried oyster crabs. Like the Klingons, you can also eat them living and squirming right out of the shell, but since they live inside the oysters' shell and oysters live in some very toxic places, it's best to buy your oyster crabs from some entity you can sue if you notice a third eye popping out after a night of heavy indulgence. Once you've thoroughly vetted your source of oyster crabs, here's what you'll need. You can prepare these in one of the many automatic deep-fat fryers on the market or just a deep skillet with incredibly hot oil. If you use the latter, be very, very careful, because boiling oil can splatter and burn, not to mention catch fire. It's best to prepare in your kitchen. If you use a skillet, make sure it has a tight-fitting lid. If the oil does catch fire use the lid to smother the fire. *Never* use water. I also recommend having a bowl of ice water handy, in case the oil splatters on you. I recommend a deep-fat fryer because they're safer than a skillet of hot oil.

3 or 4 dozen oyster crabs, washed and kept alive—or at least in stasis—on ice

2 quarts seasoned cooking oil (I suggest seasoning with garlic salt and even a little hot pepper sauce. You can also buy a hot pepper oil just for this occasion.)

3 or 4 cups flour, seasoned with 1 teaspoon garlic salt and ¼ teaspoon black pepper

1 teaspoon sea salt

1 teaspoon fresh ground pepper

1 teaspoon garlic powder

1 teaspoon celery seed

paper bags for dusting the crabs with flour

colander *or* sieve

drain board and plenty of absorbent paper

First prepare your seasoned oil and your flour. You can prepare your own seasoned oil with a vegetable oil such as corn or canola in mason or other types of bottles or jars. You can make your own garlic, chili pepper, rosemary, thyme, or any other seasoned oil by pouring oil over the spice or seasoning and allowing it to age for about a week before you use it. Seasoned or spiced oils in attractive bottles are also great seasonal or housewarming gifts because they are as great-looking as they are practical. For your seasoned flour, rather than using garlic salt and black pepper, you can also season your flour by shaking in freshly ground pepper, garlic powder, celery seed, and sea salt.

If you're using a deep-fat fryer, follow the manufacturer's instructions for the appliance. If you're using a skillet, make sure it's deep and heavy to prevent splattering and only fill it with oil half way. Heat the oil gradually in the heavy skillet until it just begins to bubble. Reduce heat so that the oil simmers without splattering.

Begin preparing the individual crabs by washing and drying each one very carefully. Drying is especially important because water tends to splatter oil, and unless you're working in a professional restaurant kitchen with a deep, deep fat fryer, splattering oil can be dangerous. Once the crabs are dried, dust them in the flour and bounce them around in a sieve to get as much flour off them as possible. Then, with a wire basket or a similar utensil—*but not a table* fork or a knife—immerse the crabs in the hot oil for about 30 to 45 seconds, remove, and stack on absorbent paper.

The best way to prepare these safely is to form a Borg drone work detail—Seven can show you how—in which one person flours, next person immerses, next person stacks and brings the platters out to starving dinner guests. The trick is to have an enforcement procedure to make sure the cooks and stackers actually get the crabs out to the guests. These little babies are so crispy and tasty, you can pop them in your mouth, swill them down with a mug of Dixie, Rolling Rock, or Lone Star beer, and forget which planet you're on. Serves six to eight.

Throck

I'd say we've been pretty successful on *Voyager;* given all the danger we've faced, we've been eating pretty well and have avoided being eaten. From Planet Hell to the Nekrit Supply Depot, we're always running into nasty critters. In my opinion, the nastiest are the Kazon because they lack class of any kind. They're a sick, twisted, malevolent race, consumed with cosmic rage and intense disgust for all other species. But few people are aware that the Kazon founded the CID, the Culinary Institute of the Delta Quadrant. This was eons ago when they were among the most culturally advanced peoples in the quadrant. After the Trabe conquered them, all their goodness was leached out. But I'll always have a soft spot for them in the corner of my belly for creating that astounding cooking school. Deviled *throck* (a *throck* is the tender tongue of a paradise angel-peach, a fruit bird from Porakas), which I've made often for Captain Janeway, was developed at the CID, and its delicacy and savor are characteristic of the kind of cuisine the institute is known for.

You can prepare this dish using either fresh or an 8-ounce can of peaches. If you decide to use store-bought canned peaches, cut into slices—the same size as *throck*—prepare in a large bowl with just a hint of confectioners' sugar and about 1 tablespoon of cinnamon. Mix and allow to sit for about 15 minutes in your refrigerator before serving topped with light cream or whipped cream.

If you want to use freshly canned peaches that you can probably find at farmers' markets or roadside stands, especially in late summer or early fall after the first peach harvest has come in, remove peaches, drain, and slice. Then marinate for about 15 minutes in your refrigerator in a solution of 1 tablespoon sugar, 1 tablespoon cinnamon, and 1 cup water. Again, serve with cream or whipped cream.

You can also make this dessert from fresh peaches, the fresher the better, especially if you bring them home from the roadside garden stand. Wash, peel, and slice. Marinate in 1 cup water with 1 tablespoon sugar and 1 tablespoon cinnamon, and, for an extra-special touch, you can also add washed whole red or black raspberries. Now let this mixture marinate for at least 1 hour, and serve exactly as is—no cream, no fuss, just straight peaches, raspberries, and cinnamon.

Sweetened-and-Pickled Wild Fantasia Beans

A delicacy. The wild fantasia bean grows on the dark side of the Nijian moon, making them arduous to pick because, obviously, they're so hard to see. While the color of the fantasia bean is normally bright pink, during the picking season (a brief three days) they turn pitch black, no doubt Nature's way of safeguarding the fantasia from extinction. However, with the invention of the "Black Fantasia Bean Picking Glasses," especially designed for picking the fantasia, the Nijians have managed to gather enough beans to satisfy most of the planet.

On *Voyager,* this is a tricky dish to make, not only because you need the space of a cargo bay to prepare it but also because you need at least 1 bushel of wild fantasia beans, 15 cups salt, 35 cups sugar, the roots of 6 dried and stretched *boodo* leaves, a large wooden barrel, 3 buckets sap of the sacred wala wala tree, 1 teaspoon of Bavadian *smaka sedge,* 1 large and preferably fresh-killed roasted gazala, and at least ½

barrel of *roda* water. Place all the ingredients, except the beans, into the barrel and allow to stand overnight at exactly life-support temperature (72.5 degrees) in computer preset ¾ dim light. When the color of the water is a sort of putrid green (it only looks putrid), throw in the beans from a distance of 3 feet. You have to do this because when they hit the bacteria-filled *roda* water they smoke something fierce and give off what to a Talaxian seem to be noxious fumes. They're not. They only *seem* noxious. Wait 2½ minutes for the clouds of smoke to dissipate by falling back into the bubbling *roda* water. Now, rinse beans in water. Serve them over *gladst*.

For a delightful Earth variation, in not even a fraction of the preparation time, try this recipe for frijoles negros.

3 15-ounce cans prepared black beans, rinsed and drained

1 cup boiling beef bouillon (1 bouillon cube added to 8 ounces
      boiling water *or* 1 8-ounce can store-bought bouillon)

2 tablespoons chili powder

2 tablespoons garlic in oil *or* 4 cloves garlic, crushed, in 2
      tablespoons of olive oil

2 teaspoons whole cumin seed

2 teaspoons dried oregano

1 teaspoon red pepper

salt to taste

Heat the beans and the bouillon in a medium-sized saucepan. Bring to a simmer and add the garlic and oil first, stir through, then add the chili powder. Add the whole cumin seeds by rubbing them in your hands to bruise the surface as you drop them in. Next add the oregano and red pepper. Simmer for 20 minutes, and add salt to taste. Serve these over hot tortilla chips or alongside corn or flour tortillas and some lettuce and tomatoes. For a picnic, you can wrap the black beans in soft tortillas and immediately wrap in aluminum foil. This should keep them warm. You can also serve black-bean tortillas for lunch or dinner. Serves six.

Goorizian Fish Stew

Want a great soup to go with your black beans? Try this. It's made from a very rare fish called the *gooriza*. The tiny *gooriza* fish lives in a sugar sea—on Earth, you have fresh water and salt water, but on Gooriz, the smallest moon of my home planet, there are seas of sugar water! The *gooriza* fish is the size of a human's thumb and tastes like a Krenim candy bar. I crush the whole thing, bones and all, into a pot and add vegetables, but the stew is way too sweet for most humans. I tried serving it for dessert, until the crew caught on that they were eating what was basically fish pudding. That turned them off very quickly. Now I just make it for myself. But if you use other, less sweet fish, such as cod, monk, lumpfish, bass, or perch, it's still a heck of a good recipe for a fish stew, and can be as inexpensive as you want to make it, according to the ingredients you elect to use. I include the whole shebang here, but you can mix and match the fish and shellfish. On Earth, this is called bouillabaisse, but don't tell the French because that is one of their regional dishes. They tend to get nasty, as well they should, when you mess with their traditional ingredients.

1½ pounds cod *or* monkfish meat

1 pound perch

1 pound bass

½ pound lumpfish (optional)

1 pound fresh small shrimp, deveined

2 dozen littleneck clams, washed, but still nice and alive

2 dozen oysters, shucked (optional)

1 dozen green mussels, washed and boiled but in their shells
    (optional)

1½ pounds boiled lobster meat, cut into bite-sized pieces (Can be
    packaged or prepared at the supermarket, or you can boil
    the lobsters yourself, remove the meat, and prepare.)

¼ cup olive oil

1 small onion, chopped

2 small tomatoes *or* plum tomatoes, chopped

2 leeks, white part only, chopped

1 clove garlic, crushed

½ bay leaf

1 tablespoon dried parsley

½ teaspoon savory

½ teaspoon fennel

⅛ teaspoon saffron

1½ teaspoons salt (or to taste)

½ teaspoon black pepper or to taste (or red pepper)

You will need a large—really large—soup or stew kettle.

Clean your fish by washing them in salty cold water. Cut fish into two-inch–thick bite-sized pieces and set aside. Clean and peel the shrimp, rinse, and set aside. Prepare the lobster by cutting the boiled meat into bite-sized pieces, and set aside. Wash the clams and mussels, and boil the mussels if they're still uncooked. Drain the shucked oysters, but preserve the liquid, and set them aside.

Heat the olive oil in the stew kettle and add your onions, the chopped white section of the leeks, and your garlic clove. Brown these ever so slightly before adding the tomatoes and seasonings except the salt and pepper. Cook just enough for the flavors to blend, tasting frequently, but not so frequently as to eat up all the good stuff before anybody else gets to eat any, and add the lobster and bass. Stir and add enough water to cover the fish and lobster. Now add the salt and pepper. Bring to a rapid boil and then immediately reduce the heat to a simmer and add the rest of the fish. Simmer for another 15 minutes, making sure the fish and lobster are tender, and add the shrimp, clams, and mussels. While the shellfish are simmering, simmer the oysters in their own juices for just 5 minutes and then add to the fish stew. Simmer for another 3 minutes or so, just to make sure the flavors have blended, while you toast some thick French bread with lots of garlic and butter on it.

Arrange the bread in a deep serving bowl and ladle the stew right over the bread. Serve it as hot as you can, with a white wine so dry it actually cracks the glass when you try to drink it. You can get away with any French dry white, but if you want your house to ring with the sound of applause, serve this with a frascati and stand back to accept the accolades. Serves six.

Fried Mochana Shoots

Mochana shoots is the local staple of the Yudoos. They grow in abundance on Yudoo in the very far reaches of the Delta Quadrant, but the fierce ailurus lizard makes them extremely hazardous to harvest. The Yudoos go to great lengths to gather the *mochana,* because of their importance to their economy. They export the shoots throughout the quadrant and the *mochana* is responsible for their entire fiscal health. But because of the ferocity of the dreaded ailurus, hundreds of thousands of Yudoos are killed at each harvest. The Yudoo population, once in the hundreds of millions, is now down to forty-two. I prepare these shoots by dropping the cut, dried and washed *mochana* shoots in boiling gax oil. I fry until they're completely black. Strain, drain, and serve with a sour cream dip.

You can do the same thing with bean sprouts in your wok for your salads, especially Chinese chicken salad, or pita bread sandwiches. You need about ½ pound of bean sprouts and 1 tablespoon of peanut oil. Heat the oil in your wok, spreading it all around the edges until it just starts to smoke. You can also use a heavy skillet. Stir in the dry bean sprouts and keep stirring as they fry and turn crispy. This only takes about 5 minutes, and they're done.

Jimbalian Seven-World Omelette

This is a Talaxian trade secret. I discovered that you need ingredients from seven worlds. I only been using ingredients from six worlds, when it was a seven-world omelette. The eggs are Eskarian (I once predicted this type of egg would be on Tuvok's face when he learned what a fine investigative reporter I was). The other ingredients are Spith basil, *prishic* (a yellow moonweed unique to Rinax), *thriv* (cheese from the milk of the ronrat, a small rodent with hallucinogenic dandruff), *ekky* berry, thunder lily, pepper, and the ingredient I'd failed to add for so long, Nimian sea salt. By the way, this is a particular favorite with the captain.

I suggest an Earthly version called on the West Coast of the United States a Denver omelette, while on the East Coast it's known as a western omelette. It includes the following:

> **3 eggs**
> **¼ pound sliced ham *or* 1 small ham steak, chopped**
> **½ cup chopped red and green bell peppers**
> **½ small onion, chopped**
> **1 tablespoon butter, melted**
> **½ teaspoon celery seed**
> **½ teaspoon cumin seed**
> **⅛ teaspoon Tabasco**
> **⅛ teaspoon cayenne pepper**

Melt about 1 tablespoon of butter in a skillet while you chop the ham, peppers, and onion. Brown them in the skillet over low heat while you beat 3 eggs and add the celery seed, bruised whole cumin seed, Tabasco, and cayenne pepper. You can salt to taste or even use garlic salt. Remove the ham, onions, and pepper from the skillet and set aside. Pour egg mixture in and increase heat. Lift the edges of the egg as it begins to set, to make sure that all the egg is cooking, then add the ham, pepper, and onions back to the skillet and quickly fold the edges over the filling. Let it bubble and brown and then quickly flip it. Press down on the omelette with your spatula to make sure all the liquid egg runs out and cooks, flip 2 or 3 more times, slide onto a plate, and serve with a sprig of parsley, a portion of Hakonian hash, hot *raktajino*, and maybe a glass of vegetable juice. Serves one.

Komar Cookies

When I was courting Kes, I was a lot leaner—in fact I spent a few years
as a swimsuit model on Talax—but now I've filled out, and why not? I
always say, "Beware the skinny cook." One of the reasons I've gained a
little weight is this dish created by the Komar. They live in a nebula and
feed off the neural energy of other species. They're not real nice, but
they make a great cookie. They don't bake theirs—they zap the dough
with a magnetodynamic TL 5 solar-photox blast, but you don't have to do
that, unless you know how. The dough is made from rattle fern caviar,
Turian stardust, and Betelgeuse butter. The Komar also add wineworm
blood, but I think this detracts from the already intense taste. I hope you
like these!

1 cup all-purpose flour

½ cup (1 stick) of butter

½ cup light brown sugar

1 egg

1 egg white

1 teaspoon cinnamon

½ teaspoon vanilla extract

¼ teaspoon salt

granulated sugar, as needed for coating

raspberry *or* strawberry jelly or preserves

Cream the butter and brown sugar and beat in the whole egg, flour, vanilla, cinnamon, and salt. Roll the dough into a ball and chill in your refrigerator for about 15 minutes while you preheat your oven to 375 degrees. When the dough has been chilled, break off individual 1-inch pieces and roll into small balls. Separate egg white and beat lightly in a small bowl until it's slightly frothy, not membranous. Next, fill a small bowl with granulated sugar. Coat the balls in the egg white and then roll them in the sugar to coat them. Now arrange them on a flat greased baking sheet and make a slight impression in each with your finger—or you can use the broad end of a chopstick or even a thimble. Drop a small amount of raspberry or strawberry jelly or preserves into each depression and close over the depression with the cookie dough. Bake at 375 for about 10 minutes. Allow to cool before serving.

These make incredible Christmas and holiday gifts, by the way, and can become a holiday tradition. Wrap them in fancy paper and fancy bows for friends and neighbors. Yields two dozen cookies.

Laurellian Rice Pudding

I often serve a dessert called Laurellian rice pudding. The main ingredient is a Finorian flutter fly, found only on the frosty fields of far north-central Finor, which you stir through warm swamp rice. It is named after Taxzdf Laurel, a great Finorian chef famous for having his esophagus and stomach on the *outside* of his body. I never met him myself, but my good friend, Wixiban, encountered him once at a barbecue on Finor's moon. Wix said he was so ugly that he wasn't listed in "Who's Who" but in "What's That?" Anyway, the dish is wonderful, but strange. When Tuvok first tried it, he developed an odd side effect. He broke out in this rash, really a very interesting pattern, Tom told me that it is called "polka-dot." But I worked out the kinks, and now this dish is one of the most popular on the ship, especially among Vulcans! Ensign Vorik frequently requests seconds and even thirds.

1½ cups uncooked Thai rice

1½ cups canned unsweetened coconut milk

4 tablespoons sugar

2 ripe mangos

If you have a steamer, steam the rice on high for 25 minutes. You can also boil the rice for 20 to 25 minutes instead, in 3 cups of water and a small pat of butter. When the rice is done, heat the coconut milk in a medium saucepan and add the rice. Cook on low heat for 5 minutes. Add sugar. While rice is cooking, peel the mangos and slice into ½-inch slices. When pudding is done, serve in individual bowls topped with mango slices. Serves four to six.

Mehaxian Sod

This is a dangerous dish, one that B'Elanna loves, but no one else will touch. It contains a stinger from the mehax wasp, and if not cooked just right, causes insanity. It also makes you grow a tail. Before the meal is consumed, it's important the stomach be coated with enzymes secreted during nausea. I usually just ruminate on Seska to accomplish this. Besides the mehax stinger, the Zolian air snake is a main ingredient. The sweat from the Mokra mist monkey adds a tangy touch, and I serve it with prairie gourd-ade. It takes six days to digest, so it's great for an away mission when you can't bring a lot with you!

1 16-ounce package lasagna noodles

1 pound fresh mushrooms, sliced very thin

2 cups chopped fresh spinach

1 small onion, finely chopped

4 eggs

6 cloves garlic, finely chopped

½ cup (1 stick) butter

1 cup grated Parmesan *or* Romano cheese

2 teaspoons oregano

2 teaspoons minced fresh *or* crushed dried basil

1 teaspoon minced parsley

salt and pepper to taste

Preheat oven to 350 degrees. Cook lasagna according to package directions, drain, and set aside. In a skillet, brown garlic and onion in melted butter. Add spinach and mushrooms and sauté until soft; then stir through oregano, basil, salt, and pepper. Arrange mushrooms and spinach and lasagna in alternate layers in an 8- by 10-inch baking dish, or a dish of a similar size, and top with parsley and Parmesan or Romano cheese. Cover dish with foil and bake at 350 degrees for 45 minutes. Serves two to four.

Mokra Couscous

The Mokra, a paranoid, hostile race, make an amazing fried dish with *weequa,* a grain that during lightning storms falls from the Mokra *bannoo* stalk. It's similar to rice. They are fond of using fish cabbage (the cabbage lives under water and has gills!) and *holiax,* something like broccoli that glows in the dark. They crush in a variety of seasonings, like camphor dung and Alsuarian sneezeweed, and serve it with a medallion of *slerf* eyelids. Suder was very fond of this dish. Because the *slerf* eyelids can carry sun anthrax (a nasty parasite), I recommend overcooking it, maybe using a smoke detector as a timer.

You can start very easily with a couscous mix right off the supermarket shelves and follow the package directions. Once you have cooked the couscous, you can use it with a variety of recipes. Here's a very basic Middle Eastern vegetable couscous that combines zucchini, chickpeas, eggplant, and red curry powder, for a casserole that you can prepare in under 30 minutes.

1 16-ounce package couscous, prepared according to directions

1 tablespoon olive oil

½ medium-sized eggplant, sliced thin

½ medium-sized zucchini squash, sliced thin

1 15-ounce can chickpeas, drained and rinsed

1 small onion, finely chopped

2 cloves garlic, finely chopped

½ cup chopped fresh parsley

1 teaspoon whole cumin, bruised

½ teaspoon curry powder

½ teaspoon cayenne pepper

½ teaspoon lemon juice

lemon slices as a garnish

Prepare the couscous according to package directions. You can use chicken, vegetable, or even tomato bouillon instead of plain water. Heat the olive oil in a skillet and sauté the garlic and onion, then add the eggplant and squash. Stir through and sauté for 5 minutes, and then add the chickpeas, parsley, and all of the spices. Cook for another 5 minutes, and then stir in the couscous and the lemon juice. Cover and cook for another 5 minutes, and serve topped with lemon slices. Serves four.

Pan-Braised Nako Cutlets

They say a glutton is someone who digs his grave with his teeth, so get ready to die. This meal is one of my favorites! Pan-braised nako cutlets in *favinit* butter oil. Nako is a *magna* fowl from the land of the Drakina Forest dwellers (Drakina Forest dwellers have paranormal abilities; they can walk in a room and "see" images of people who have recently been there; I've told Kes all about these guys time and again). *Favinit* is a Vulcan orchid Tuvok has a special alliance with, and I crush it into Takar cream butter for extra flavor. There's also *likmon,* tartberries, and brill cheese (the kind that doesn't have to go to sickbay). I serve this with Talaxian champagne, moon-ripened, the kind I served Kes in our very last meal together.

> **2 pounds veal cutlets**
>
> **½ pound (2 sticks) butter**
>
> **2 tablespoons tarragon**
>
> **½ cup olive oil**
>
> **½ cup all-purpose flour, seasoned with ⅛ teaspoon tarragon and ⅛ teaspoon thyme**
>
> **½ cup bread crumbs, seasoned with ⅛ teaspoon celery salt**
>
> **1 egg**

Preheat oven to 350 degrees. Slice the veal cutlets very thin and wipe them dry. Melt butter in a large skillet and add olive oil and 2 tablespoons tarragon. Heat very slowly while you season the flour with ⅛ teaspoon each tarragon and thyme in one shallow bowl and the bread crumbs with celery salt in another bowl. Beat the egg in a third bowl. Coat each veal cutlet with egg, then with flour, then with bread crumbs, and sauté slowly in the mixture of tarragon, butter, and oil until the cutlets are nice and brown. Now arrange them in a greased baking pan and roast for 30 minutes at 350 degrees. Serves four to six.

Raktajino Cake

Tom Paris, reveling in the rations he won in a gambling scheme, mentioned to Harry how he'd use the rations: prime rib with mashed potatoes, creamed spinach, Yorkshire pudding, and *raktajino* with whipped cream. I made *raktajino* into a coffee cake. When I first tried to bake this, it was so bad, the raisins walked out. Over time I've perfected it and am very proud of it now. It's a dense cake that achieves it's unique piquancy from Rillan teaberry melon rinds. The Rillans are the race that made that sexy lubricant used to cover scantily clad Vulcans during the *Rumarie,* an ancient pagan festival.

CAKE

2½ cups cake flour

1¼ cups sugar

½ cup shortening

½ cup milk

⅓ cup orange juice (for more flavor, mix frozen concentrate with
 less water than the package instructions call for)

2 eggs, unbeaten

1 tablespoon grated orange rind

3 teaspoons baking powder

1 teaspoon salt

½ teaspoon vanilla extract

LEMON BUTTER ICING

3 cups confectioners' sugar

3 tablespoons butter

3 tablespoons cream, scalded

⅛ teaspoon salt

1 teaspoon lemon juice

1 teaspoon grated lemon rind

½ teaspoon vanilla extract

Preheat oven to 350 degrees. Sift together the flour, baking powder, salt, and sugar in a medium bowl. Add orange rind, shortening, milk, and orange juice. With your hand electric mixer, beat on low for 2 minutes until the batter is blended. Now add two eggs and vanilla, and beat for another 2 minutes. Pour into a greased and floured 8- by 12-inch baking pan and bake at 350 degrees for 30 minutes.

While cake is baking, make the icing. Cream the butter and salt until thoroughly blended. Next gradually add confectioners' sugar, stirring and blending as you do, and gradually blend in the scalded cream, checking for smoothness and consistency. Add lemon rind and lemon juice. Blend thoroughly, and add vanilla.

Test cake for doneness and remove from oven when top springs back when lightly touched. Remove from pan, allow to cool, and frost.

Traggle Nectar

You may remember that I once offered B'Elanna a glass of traggle nectar. She actually requested a cup of coffee, but I told her she'd already consumed two pots of my Landras blend—a coffee so powerful that Tuvok, after a few cups, has been known to go to the bridge and fire off class-4 probes at nothing in particular. Traggle nectar is a blend of traggle, a rocket poppy from the tropics of Talax, and Rinaxian sea bugs. When traggle is fresh, the juice will stain your skin forever, never coming out. We use it for tattoos on Talax, and for anti-Haakonian graffiti. I also add powdered Nimian bud pollen for a little extra jolt.

1½ cups apricot nectar (unsweetened is better)

1 large carrot

1 teaspoon fresh-squeezed lemon juice

1 sprig fresh mint

In your automatic juicer, extract the juice from the large carrot. If you're using a blender, dice the carrot into small pieces and blend on the highest setting. The blended carrot will have more solids than the extracted carrot juice. Either way, combine the carrot juice with the apricot nectar in a tall glass, add the lemon juice, and garnish with mint.

Yallitian Crystal Salad

This dish is a popular summer salad, made with hearts of ice ferns, which grow on the plains of the purple glaciers of Yallitos, the coldest planet in the entire Delta Quadrant. It is, in fact, so cold there that the politicians have their hands in their *own* pockets. The Yallitians are a strange species, with up to three feet of fat under their skin. They harvest the ice ferns during their summer, when they can venture outside their hosts. (Yes, they live for the rest of the time inside the bellies of giant Koko whales!) It was in the summer that I visited Yallitos and tasted this scrumptious salad. In addition to the ice fern, the dish includes Kolian cold peppers, hail berries, Myrigian snow salami, *neptunematoes,* and a dressing made from Perjuta vinegar and Bolpian otter oil.

The crystal salad equivalent I recommend is a very healthy dish based on a very ancient herb, dandelion leaves, those little monsters that take over gardens and drive home owners nuts. They wouldn't want to dump toxins all over their garden if they knew that what they were killing was the basis for tea, tonic, desserts, and a salad. Of course we Talaxians know all about that because we're people of the forest, in a manner of speaking. This dandelion salad is made from the leaves of the plant, bell peppers, green onions, salt, vinegar, and oil. You can add other vegetables if you like, so experiment. But here's the basic recipe:

> **1 pound fresh-picked dandelion leaves, washed and chopped (but *never* use any dandelions from a lawn that has been treated in any manner or has been fertilized or sprayed with any chemicals)**
>
> **1 cup chopped green onions (scallions)**
>
> **1 cup chopped red bell peppers**
>
> **¼ cup red wine vinegar**
>
> **⅛ cup olive oil**
>
> **coarse-ground salt to taste**
>
> **black pepper to taste**

Wash the vegetables thoroughly and make sure they're dry before serving. Arrange vegetables on individual plates or a serving dish. Combine vinegar and oil and any spices you desire, such as garlic, in a separate cruet, shake, and drizzle over salad. Serves four to six.

Top Ten Borg Recipes

10: Blackened Braise à la Borg

9: Borg-a-bob

8: McBorg

7: Borg on a Bun

6: Borg Kibble

5: Borg Bisque with Shredded Borganzola Cheese

4: All-you-can-eat Borg's Big Boy Borscht

3: Borg Berry Cobbler

2: String Cheese

1: Smorgasborg

The Elixir of Life

I vaguely remember that I once prepared a drink for the crew that I called "The Elixir of Life." Actually it was just ration cubes, which the Doctor surmised, but I puréed them, mixed in water, and enhanced it all with Talaxian spices. Here are three elixirs for your automatic juicer or blender that when prepared and taken on a regular basis will keep you just that.

I

6 carrots

wedge of green cabbage

½ apple, cored

II

1 cup of raw, fresh, spinach leaves

6 carrots

III

4 carrots

½ cucumber

1 beet

¼ piece fresh ginger root

Follow the directions for your automatic juicer, or process in a blender on the highest speed and separate the pulp from the juice through a strainer.

Sprid Wings

I couldn't sleep at all last night because of a nightmare—Seven of Nine was lost in a five-and-ten—so I got up and decided to have a little snack. I stumbled on an amazing discovery: certain foods taste better in the middle of the night. This sounds bizarre, but it's true. I'll be darned if the deep-fried *sprid* wings I served the night before didn't taste juicer and more succulent at three in the morning.

At first I attributed this to the wings marinating longer in the *gohog-lohyil* sauce, but when I served it for dinner the following night, it didn't taste nearly as good. So the next night, having woken again (Seven of Nine was driving a four-by-four in a tutu), I tasted the *sprid* wings again, and sure enough they tasted fantastic. Then I wondered if preparing the bird at three in the morning might actually improve the taste.

The next evening (Seven of Nine was starring in *Seven Brides for Seven Brothers,* and she was competent, but lacked focus in the second

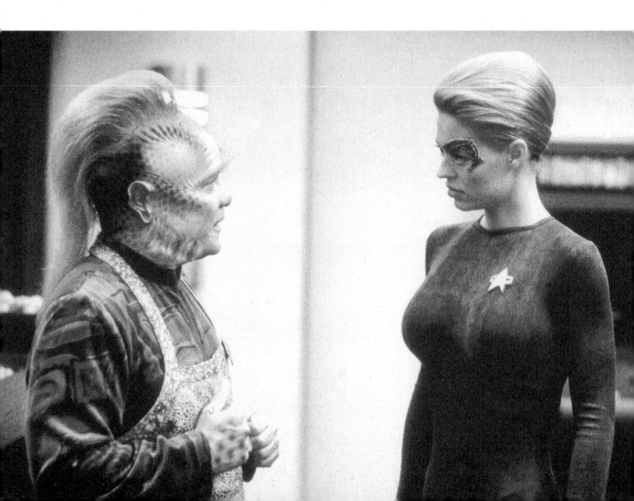

act) I decided to test my theory. Unbelievable, but the *sprid* wings tasted far better cooked at three A.M.! I'm currently experimenting with other dishes. (Last night I dreamt Seven of Nine stole a 3-D copy of a 007 film—Borg, James Borg—and got four to six in the slammer. Boy, was she behind the eight ball.)

Replace *sprid* wings with chicken wings simmered in a peppery red stock with Tabasco and served with blue cheese dressing, and you have Buffalo wings.

2 pounds chicken wings

1½ tablespoons butter

1½ tablespoons vegetable oil

2 tablespoons paprika

¼ cup chicken stock, *or* **¼ cup chicken bouillon straight from an 8-ounce can,** *or* **¼ cup liquid from 1 bouillon cube dissolved in 8 ounces boiling water**

2 teaspoons Tabasco sauce

2 teaspoons garlic salt

1 2-ounce package blue cheese dressing *or* **¼ cup of bottled blue cheese dressing**

1 or 2 celery stalks per serving of chicken

Melt butter and oil in a heavy saucepan such as a Le Creuset and stir in the garlic salt, paprika, and Tabasco. Add the chicken wings and reduce heat to simmer for 15 minutes. When wings are a reddish brown, add chicken stock, and simmer for another 20 to 30 minutes. Serve wings with blue cheese dressing and a 1 or 2 celery stalks per person. Serves four to six.

Alfarian Hair Pasta

This dish, made from the follicles of a mature Alfarian, is high in protein and fiber. In early fall the Tarkannans, a genial race near my home planet, harvest the hair during shedding season from these gentle tri-genital beasts that graze on the lavender mud plains of Central Tarkanna. I served this dish to Tom and Harry in one of my first attempts in the galley. Actually, I served it to Harry, and threw it on Tom, because I was convinced he was trying to steal Kes away from me. My suspicions were not justified, but I was consumed by jealousy, a trait common to male Talaxians who date pretty blond Ocampans. Tom and I patched it up on Planet Hell, but that Nondoran tomato paste left a bad stain Tom never got out.

1 16-ounce package angel-hair pasta

1 6-ounce can anchovy paste

6 large tomatoes, chopped

1 6-ounce can tomato paste

2 medium onions, chopped

1 small green bell pepper, chopped

½ clove garlic, sliced thin

½ clove garlic, crushed

¼ cup fresh chopped parsley

2 tablespoons olive oil

1 bay leaf

1 tablespoon oregano

2 teaspoons sugar

1 teaspoon fresh basil

grated Parmesan cheese to taste

Sauté the sliced garlic in olive oil in a large kettle and add onions and then bell pepper. Next add tomato paste and simmer for 10 minutes, add the tomatoes, and bring to a boil. Reduce heat to simmer and add the anchovy paste and all of the rest of the seasonings. Simmer on low heat for at least 1 hour, taste, correct the seasoning, and simmer for another ½ hour. During final

10 minutes of cooking, cook the angel-hair pasta according to the directions on the package, drain, and put in a serving bowl. Stir through some of the sauce and some Parmesan cheese. Serve with sauce on the side. Serves four.

Mool

Here's a little known fact for you humans: when female Akritirian *chaka* emus—a marsupial hybrid—die *before* the age of fifty-three, their brains become beans! Yes, this is true. Every third cell metastasizes into a real bean, with a rafinose cellular structure and protein comparable to any bean found on Earth. The great Akritiri chef Kok LaKok "The Kok" LaPokkok discovered this accidentally while experimenting with Akitirian roadkill during a famine many eons ago. Now, the brain beans, called "mool," are harvested regularly and form the basis for an outstanding dish that you can make at home. No need to sift through the brains of dead *chaka* emus because Earth's fava bean comes so close I doubt even old Kokky himself could tell the difference. And the Lebanese make a meal that utilizes the fava bean in a dish that approximates Akritirian mool. A word of caution: while delicious, and healthy, mool can cause some gas. Once I got stuck in a turbolift with Tuvok after he'd eaten three bowls of mool. Not a pleasant experience.

1½ cups dried fava beans *or* dried navy beans

1 small onion, chopped

½ pound thick-sliced bacon, diced (optional)

1 12-ounce bottle beer

¼ cup dark molasses

1 tablespoon dry mustard *or* 2 tablespoons Polish mustard

2 tablespoons Worcestershire sauce

1 teaspoon apple vinegar

salt and pepper to taste

This is a Crock-Pot dish or a kettle dish you can leave on a coal stove or Franklin stove the entire day. Prepare the night before, leave in your refrigerator, set it on the stove in the morning for slow cooking, and it will be ready by the evening.

The night before you want to serve this, simmer dried beans in just enough water to cover them for about 2 hours. Drain the beans, but preserve the cooking water, and add all of the other ingredients to the beans at the same time, including the diced bacon and bean water to cover. Follow your Crock-Pot directions for slow cooking, which should take anywhere from 8 to 10 hours at about 250 degrees. You can also bake these all day in a slow oven, 225 to 250 degrees, or in a heavy cast-iron kettle on your coal or woodstove. Serves four to six.

Ethan Phillips—My Talaxian Chili Stew for a Whole Crew

In real life as well as on the show, I sometimes have to cook for a whole bunch of people when they show up for a party that I didn't know about. But if you have some buffalo meat in the freezer, which I usually do, and spaghetti sauce and canned tomatoes on hand, you can make a Kansas-style chili stew with buffalo that's exotic and hearty at the same time.

2 15-ounce cans medium-sized stewed tomatoes

2 8-ounce cans spaghetti sauce

2 green bell peppers

1 large (or 2 small) onions

2 to 3 pounds buffalo burger

1 tablespoon chili powder

1 teaspoon salt

1 tablespoon olive oil to brown the meat

lime wedges for garnish

First brown buffalo burger in olive oil in a heavy skillet, then put meat into a large pot and add everything else, and simmer about 1 hour. Pour it over rice or quinoa, garnish with lime wedges, and serve. Serves six to eight.

THE LOST
RECIPES OF TALAX

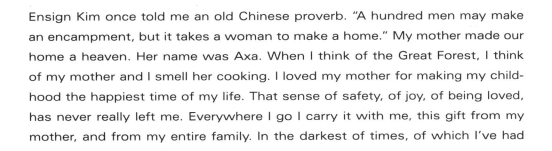

Ensign Kim once told me an old Chinese proverb. "A hundred men may make an encampment, but it takes a woman to make a home." My mother made our home a heaven. Her name was Axa. When I think of the Great Forest, I think of my mother and I smell her cooking. I loved my mother for making my child-hood the happiest time of my life. That sense of safety, of joy, of being loved, has never really left me. Everywhere I go I carry it with me, this gift from my mother, and from my entire family. In the darkest of times, of which I've had my share, I have never *fully* consented to despair. I've come very close, but the knowledge that I've experienced something so fulfilling has sustained me. My wish for everyone is a childhood like I had.

My home and my family were completely obliterated in the metreon cascade, soon after my spots came in. Rinax, the moon I lived on, was reduced to a cinder. Over three hundred thousand Talaxians died. I escaped physical harm, being on Talax at the time, but the rage I felt was in some ways just as toxic. It corrupted me for a great while. And though that fury is gone now, there remains a constant ache. Even in my dreams, I still grieve. The memory of my family is with me ceaselessly. I am and will always be homesick.

Before the horror came and broke everything, there were so many wonderful times! That's what I remember now, the faces of my sisters as they endlessly spoiled me; my papa, Eximar, teaching me how to fire a xeno cannon; my mother rocking me in her arms as the yute birds sang. That yute bird never shut up! My pet udox, Pixie. My hovercraft. My hut in the woods. Vaxi, the adorable sweet Vaxi who lived next door. And I remember the meals. The meals I've tried to re-create on *Voyager* for my new family, and that I want to share with you here.

Of all the meals I remember, it is the celebration of the holiday of Prixin I recall with the most delight. This traditional feast day, which actually lasted five full days, was a festival of family. From what I can surmise, it was similar to Love Day on Ocampa, Earth's Thanksgiving Day, the Evening of Hope on Hakos, and probably a myriad of other days throughout the universe that celebrate the bonds of family and the gratitude for the nourishment of good crops, shelter, peace, but most of all, love. It was my favorite time of the year.

Besides the unbearable anticipation, the joy of preparation, all the decorating with the garlands of fellin branches, the placing of the testle-scented candles, the long process of brewing the *moolt* nectar, the gathering in the chilly forests of the ghost wood for the ceremonial fires that blazed for the five days, and the giving and receiving of gifts, the singing of songs, the games, and the coming and going of friends and cousins—besides all this, there was the actual feast.

The centerpiece was always roast *thill*, a big delicious game bird that roamed in abundance throughout the Dalibardadian Plains of Central Talax. The way my mother cooked this must have been learned from the gods; it liquefied in your mouth, like meat-flavored butter. She served it with swarthy swamp tubers, *soral* stuffing, kekkleberry sauce, whipped violet, creamed butterweed pie, pudder beans, and always the fruit compotes soaked in *moolt*. I used to eat as much of the compote as I could because it made me feel silly and giddy and then I'd make everyone laugh. And Talaxians love to laugh.

Roast *Thill*

1 raw clean fresh or defrosted turkey (trim excess fat and puncture holes all over it with a knife)

½ cup butter, sliced

1½ tablespoons cornstarch

½ cup water

PREPARE A PASTE WITH THE FOLLOWING:

5 tablespoons minced fresh garlic

½ cup water

½ teaspoon ground black pepper

½ teaspoon ground cumin

1 cube Knorr chicken bouillon

juice of ½ lime

½ teaspoon salt

2 tablespoons melted butter

(NOTE: reserve ½ tablespoon of this mixture)

Preheat oven to 325 degrees. Put turkey into roasting pan and rub the mixture on the turkey inside and out and let marinate in a refrigerator for at least 4 hours.

In a bowl, mix the ½ tablespoon reserved from the mixture with:

1 cup water

1½ to 2 tablespoons of soy sauce

½ cube chicken bouillon dissolved in 1 teaspoon water

BASTING MIX

2 cups of regular *or* diet cola

3 tablespoons soy sauce

Pour this mix around the turkey just before you place it into the 325 degree oven, dot the turkey with little bits of butter, and cover roasting pan.

Bake turkey in a covered roasting pan at 325 degrees and baste every ten minutes for at least 1½ hours. Increase the temperature to 350 degrees and pour over the turkey a mix of cola and soy sauce. Save about ¼ cup of this mix.

Continue cooking at 350, basting every ten minutes until the bird is about done. A fully thawed or fresh turkey should cook for 30 minutes per pound. Check for doneness, first, by puncturing the skin with a fork and making sure the juices are running clear (without any blood). Also, make sure that the turkey leg wiggles freely in its socket. When the leg wiggles freely and the juices are running clear, pour the remaining ¼ cola and soy sauce mix on the bird to give the skin a dark color and increase the oven temperature to 400 degrees for no more than 10 minutes. Be careful not to burn the turkey.

To make the gravy, you can use the turkey juices in the bottom of the roasting pan. Remove turkey to platter to let it rest, and you can now start the gravy. First mix 1½ tablespoons cornstarch into ½ cup cold water, stirring to completely dilute the cornstarch and avoid lumps. Next, spoon out some of the turkey juices into a separate bowl and stir them into the cornstarch mixture, again, stirring constantly to avoid lumps. Now you can add the entire cornstarch mixture back to the turkey pan and let them heat for five minutes. If your gravy is too thick, add more water by the tablespoon, stirring through, until you reach the desired consistency. Each half pound of turkey will serve one gentle Talaxian or human.

Iced Neth

Even as a boy I was a wanderer. The woods by my house were the site of my unmapped expeditions and in my dreams I was a stowaway. Though I loved my family, I loved to leave them, too. In roaming, I found a freedom and excitement I couldn't find in my room. And though I so praise the gladness I felt in familial security, I think early on I became equally addicted to uncertainty, danger, and new shores.

My sister Alixia shared my wanderlust. I remember trekking with her for hours deep into the countryside. She would teach me the names of all the different plants and trees and birds. Alixia said it was important to know what to call everything that grows and roams around you because that would center you and steer you from confusion. To whatever extent I am today a naturalist, it is a gift from Alixia.

My sweetest sister always made sure we had plenty of treats for our getaways. We brought along ample portions of brillen, chilly tilotubs of iced neth, and my favorite, scarlet-flavored trove bars. For you backpackers and fellow ramblers, I present them to you here and remind you of a quote I came across while traveling through the vast isolinear deserts of Voyager's massive computer: "The world is a book, and those who do not travel read only a page."

Not only is this drink crackling cold, but you can make it sweet— with mangos and honey—or salty with spices like cardamom and cumin.

SWEET ICED NETH

1 cup plain yogurt and 1 cup milk

1 mango, processed in a blender

2 tablespoons honey

Combine yogurt, milk, honey, and mango slush in a blender and blend until smooth. You can make this by the glass or by the pitcher. Serves one.

SPICED ICED NETH

equal parts plain yogurt and milk (1 cup = 1 cup)

1 teaspoon ground ginger

1 teaspoon ground cardamom

½ teaspoon ground cumin seeds

1 teaspoon ground fennel

Combine spices and add to milk and yogurt mixture in your blender. Blend until smooth. Serves one.

In the yearly temperate spans, my family loved to picnic. We'd all pile into Papa's bobber transport and head for the sun fields (though Talax has three suns, only one, Mormo, shone directly on Rinax). There on those fuchsia velvet meadows, under the swift, sweet summer skies of my youth, I'd play spiral ring with my sisters and chase my pet udox through the terrows while my papa listened to the complex honeyed warblings of the oliara birds and my mother set up the repast. Then we'd banquet under the shade of the giant *zax* trees. What memories! What meals! *Etten*, a cold bean casserole my sister Mixin created only for those picnics, no matter how much I pleaded with her to make it more often. *Umsasia* (spider apple pudding), blooming dulcet dung fungus, wild hawk marrow patties, clementine shade brisket, *flemp* cookies, sundrops, frostberry scones. Everything was topped off and complemented with moon-ripened Talaxian champagne. I'll try to replicate some of these dishes here for you. Take some of these tasties on your next outing, compliments of Neelix.

Wild-Hawk Marrow Patties

On Talax we used a chopped meat made from the wing muscles and bone marrow of the wild hawk. There were plenty of wild hawks, but catching them was the tough part. For a culture based on barter, these birds were very costly. I've found that some of the texture, but not the least bit of the gaminess, of these patties can be replicated with the use of turkey or chicken muscle patties, which, lucky for you, you can buy at your local market.

1 to 2 pounds ground turkey (You can also replace with chicken
     if ground turkey is unavailable)

¼ cup chopped onions

¼ cup bread crumbs

1 teaspoon ketchup

1 teaspoon Worcestershire sauce

1 teaspoon garlic salt

1 teaspoon celery seed

black pepper to taste

¼ cup blue cheese *or* blue cheese salad dressing

1 round bun—my favorites are egg roll and potato roll as a bun—
     per burger

1 slice of tomato per burger

You can prepare these burgers on an outdoor grill, in a kitchen broiler, or on a skillet on a range top. Begin by mixing all the ingredients—except for the cheese and tomatoes, which go on at the end as toppings, and the rolls—in a medium-to-large mixing bowl. Knead vigorously to blend all of the ingredients and then shape the mixture into flat, 2-inch patties. Sear over high heat to seal in the juices, then let cook more slowly. Serve each patty on its own bun with a slice of tomato and a splash of blue cheese dressing. Each pound of meat yields four burgers.

Clementine Shade Brisket

Whenever we had leftover *sploth* brisket, as we would have after a hearty harvest banquet, we used to make sandwiches on long rolls or our version of what is called French bread, for dipping in a sauce made from the leftover *sploth* gravy and *sploth* consommé. If you have leftover roast beef or brisket of beef, you can have the same kind of sandwiches. Here's what you'll need:

> **1 to 2 pounds leftover roast beef or beef brisket**
> **1 dozen medium-sized long rolls or egg hot-dog rolls *or* even 1 long French bread, sliced into sandwich-sized portions**
> **1 8-ounce can beef bouillon *or* beef consommé**
> **sandwich condiments to taste (horseradish, mustard, steak sauce)**

Preheat oven to 250 degrees. Slice the leftover roast beef or brisket as thin as you can and warm in a saucepan or in your oven at 250 degrees—or you can use your microwave oven per manufacturer's recommendations—while you heat the consommé or bouillon in a small saucepan. Bring it to a boil, reduce to a simmer for 5 minutes, and spoon into individual serving bowls. Serve the meat on a platter and the rolls or French bread on another platter. Your guests will assemble their own sandwiches for dipping into the au jus bowls. Yields eight sandwiches.

Spider Apple Pudding

Unless you've grown up on Talax and were taken care of by a loving mother who served you spider apple pudding whenever you caught the Gorolian flu, how could you know that the Talaxian blue spider tastes just like two-day-old bread? Of course you have to have a lot of spiders, but once you get past the crunchiness of the legs, the lower stomach is surprisingly dough-like, especially when mashed and buttered and mixed with tart apples. I wouldn't recommend this on Earth, but, remembering the comforting taste of warm spider apple pudding with a little gnu cream on top, I feel I must share this with you. Replace the Talaxian blue spider with stale bread and make sure you use a tangy green apple like a Granny Smith, lots of cinnamon, and just a hint of vanilla extract and you're in business.

1 loaf stale white bread *or* (even better) day-old challah

8 ounces unsweetened applesauce

2 small green apples, peeled, cored, and sliced thin

½ cup (1 stick) butter

3 eggs

½ cup granulated white sugar

1 quart whole *or* skim milk

1 teaspoon light brown sugar

1 teaspoon cinnamon

1 teaspoon vanilla extract

¼ teaspoon salt

Slice apples and cover with water in a medium-sized saucepan; bring to a boil, cover, and reduce heat to simmer. Allow to stew for about 30 minutes. While the apples are cooking, beat the eggs slightly in a small mixing bowl and add granulated sugar, salt, milk, and vanilla. Now slice your stale bread into one-quarter inch slices and butter them. Arrange them in a deep dish and pour the egg mixture over them. Let stand for 30 minutes, by which time your apples should be tender and ready for the pudding. Now preheat oven to 275 degrees. Spread the apple mixture around the bottom of a lightly greased baking dish and top with the bread filling. Now arrange your cooked apple slices on top of the pudding and sprinkle with brown sugar and cinnamon. Bake for 30 minutes at 275, and serve topped with either vanilla ice cream or sweet cream. Serves eight to ten.

Etten

My aunt taught my mother who taught my sister how to make a casserole out of cooked beans that she served cold after marinating it for a week in rare oils and spices from wherever my uncle had been. In fact, they wouldn't let him back in the house unless the scan of his rickety old cargo vessel produced evidence of some exotic spice from a new, strange race of aliens he'd traded with. So every so often, depending upon how frequently my uncle returned from sectors unknown, we'd enjoy new variations of *etten* with different spices and oils. Were I to prepare this for my crewmates on *Voyager*—and now that I'm thinking about it, I probably will—I'd have a basic Earth recipe that I'd vary according to whomever we encountered. For my Earth recipe I'd begin by letting fresh apple cider turn to vinegar and store it for salads, and then marinate 5 cloves of garlic in one cruet of virgin olive oil; in another cruet of oil, the hottest red pepper I could find, split; and in a third, a sprig of rosemary. These I would combine as necessary for the marinade. To these basic ingredients, I would add whatever cooked beans I could find, onion, parsley, basil, and, every now and then, some oregano.

1 cup apple-cider vinegar (You can make your own by letting
    fresh apple cider turn in your refrigerator.)

1 cup specially marinated olive oil (garlic, rosemary, or pepper) *or*
    ⅓ cup of each

1 teaspoon sea salt

1 or 2 leaves fresh basil, minced

¼ cup fresh lime juice and some pulp

1 15-ounce can each of red kidney beans, white navy beans, and
    pinto beans, all of which should be rinsed and drained

1 small onion, chopped

3 scallions, chopped

1 teaspoon dried parsley

1 teaspoon coarse-ground black pepper

Drain the beans and spoon them into a very large mixing bowl or, better, a large covered jar. Combine all of the other ingredients and pour them over the beans. Cover and refrigerate for at least 24 hours and serve. Serves six to eight.

On Talax it was a tradition to share the history of a meal before eating it, in order to enhance the culinary experience. When I learned to cook at my mother's knee, I'd hear a tale for every dish. She made every course, every garnish come alive by making it a character in a story. Turnips became soldiers, radishes kings. Eggs carried weapons. Mushrooms missed their mommies, and potatoes were poets lost at sea. I sat enchanted while she minced and diced, seasoned and baked. Dinnertime was storytime. Years later I often entertained Kes with these little tales when I cooked for her. And I remember explaining to Mr. Vulcan about this tradition as well. I was just about to tell him my favorite story, the crustacean who ran away from home, when I was interrupted by a thermal surge caused while engineering made adjustments to the plasma conduits. I won't tell that story now either, but I will give you the recipe for this crusty old character my mother invented many years ago.

The Lost Crustacean

This is a dish made with a white sauce, which is nothing more than a little milk, flour, butter, and pepper mixed together and scalded in a saucepan and used to thicken foods, sauces, and soups. It is used as a base for my crustacean.

WHITE SAUCE

¼ cup milk

1 tablespoon all-purpose flour

1 tablespoon butter

black pepper to taste

Scald milk by heating it in a saucepan until the sides begin to bubble, melt butter in the milk, and add flour, stirring rapidly. Add enough coarsely ground black pepper to the thin white sauce so that you can taste the pepper. Allow the sauce to cool before using.

FOR THE LOST CRUSTACEAN YOU WILL NEED:

2 pounds boiled lobster meat, plus the shells

1½ cups white sauce

½ cup seasoned bread crumbs

¼ stick butter

2 teaspoons lemon juice

2 teaspoons Polish (spicy) mustard

½ teaspoon salt

¼ teaspoon red cayenne pepper

lemon wedges for each serving

1 to 1½ cups (2½ sticks) butter, melted

Remove lobster meat from shells and chop into bite-sized pieces. In a medium-sized saucepan place lobster pieces, white sauce, salt, cayenne pepper, mustard, and lemon juice, and heat for about 5 minutes. In a separate pan, melt butter and add bread crumbs. Arrange the lobster meat mix in the shells and top with buttered bread-crumb mixture. Arrange lobster shells—you can also use large clamshells, scallop shells, or even oyster shells—in shallow baking pan and broil for about 5 minutes or bake for 15 minutes until the bread crumbs are nice and brown. Serve with lemon wedges and melted butter. Serves four to six.

Uncle Zisky's Mandelbrot

The following is a special sweet recipe my mother made for my uncle Zisky whenever he came to stay with us. Let me tell you about that gentle little man. He was my favorite uncle. Whenever he visited, he'd tell us jokes. But as a little boy, I didn't really know they were jokes; I just thought funny things happened to him all the time. I'd sit at his feet in wonder at this enchanted, silly life he led. He'd always start his stories by saying, "Well, a funny thing happened to me . . ." and then launch into something that made me howl. It was magic! And I wanted that gift too. So I waited and watched all day for funny things to happen to me so I could come home from school and say, "Papa, a funny thing happened to me today . . ." It wasn't until I was around ten that I realized they were all made up in Uncle Zisky's nutty brain. But that didn't take away the appeal for me. I still loved to laugh at them, and I still loved Uncle Zisky.

For Uncle Zisky, my mother made a very sweet, cinnamon pastry that she spooned out into bread pans and topped with sugar and some special oranges. This looked like a bread, but we always had it for dessert.

1½ cups all-purpose flour

1 cup granulated white sugar

1 cup (2 sticks) butter, creamed

2 eggs

2 egg yolks

¼ cup plain yogurt *or* sour cream

2 teaspoons cinnamon

1 teaspoon double-acting baking powder

1 teaspoon light brown sugar

1 teaspoon grated orange rind

½ teaspoon vanilla extract

2 tablespoons butter, melted

Cream the butter in a mixing bowl; then slowly combine the white sugar with it, stirring as you do. These should be blended into a very creamy texture. Now beat in 1 egg yolk until it is completely blended, and then add the

2 whole eggs, again beating to make sure the ingredients are blended. Next add the sour cream or yogurt. Each provides a slightly different flavor. I suggest the yogurt because it's a touch lighter. But you may like the sour cream instead. When your mix is nice and creamy, slowly sift the flour into the mixture, stirring all the time. When this, too, is blended, it's time to add the baking powder, 1 teaspoon of the cinnamon, vanilla, and ½ teaspoon of the orange rind. Blend all the ingredients and knead it by hand into a kind of large dough ball. Chill for 3 hours. You can also make this the night before and let it sit in the fridge overnight or for a day before you bake the bread.

When you're ready to bake, preheat oven to 375 degrees and remove dough from refrigerator. Either spoon it into a loaf pan and top with melted butter and beaten yolk, the rest of the cinnamon and orange rind, and the brown sugar, or knead it into any shape you like and bake it on a greased flat sheet, also topped with butter, brown sugar, cinnamon, and orange rind. Bake for 20 to 25 minutes, testing for doneness after 20 minutes. When it's done, cut the bread into thick slices. Yields one loaf.

If you want to twist your dough into small shapes, such as letters of the alphabet or numbers or even animal figures, when you remove the dough from the refrigerator, form it into shapes on a floured cutting board. Then place the shapes on a greased 14-inch flat baking pan and bake for only 10 minutes. Yields ten to twelve depending on the shape.

Wild *Griggen*

Wild *griggin* is a dish my mother, Axa, prepared often, whenever a family member returned from a journey; when my sister Raxel returned from the Mazonian Conflict; when my father came back from the Scark; when my uncle Keenux was brought back by the Fraduus after being in their keep for many dark months. You want to know why she prepared it? Because when you're stuck in some transwarp continuum on these end-less selling trips back east you get a little heavy in the kishkes and need something to bring back your old self. That's the secret of wild *griggen*. It's truly a welcome-home dish, for a lot of reasons, whose main ingredient is love. Generously laced with *adoros* bulbettes (a rare tuberous fruit grown by Tenorphian monks that has magical digestive properties) and garnished with *prextly,* wild *griggen* reminds me more than anything of family bonds. It's so filling, too, at least initially. It originated on Doseph, a small moon of Rewad IV, where the Rewadians consume troughs of it but never grow very fat. Before they began eating wild *griggen,* they used to be so heavy their tailors took their measurements using longitude and latitude. They began eating wild *griggen* and became as thin as rails. This is a fact!

    2½ cups whole-wheat flour

    1½ cups pitted prunes right out of the can or package, thinly
           sliced or coarsely chopped, according to your taste (You
           can also use the entire contents of a 16-ounce package,
           can, or jar, but you have to drain any liquid.)

    1½ cups milk

    1 cup chopped walnuts

    1 cup cornmeal

    1 cup raisins or currants

    ¾ cup honey

    ½ cup soy oil

    ½ cup warm water

    3 eggs

2 tablespoons active dry yeast

1 tablespoon cinnamon

1 teaspoon salt

Begin by preheating your oven to 350 degrees and adding the yeast to the warm water in a small bowl and stirring. Wait for at least 5 minutes, possibly 10, for the yeast to bubble. As yeast begins to activate, beat the eggs and mix them with the milk, honey, and soy oil in a blender. Then with the blender on high, add and blend in the activated yeast mixture. Combine flour and corn-meal and add this to the blender, running it for 2 minutes on low. Now add prunes, walnuts, salt, cinnamon, raisins or currants, and blend on slow until smooth, but nice and thick. Using the soy oil, lightly grease a loaf pan or 2 inch muffin tin. You can also use waxed paper to line the bottoms of little individual muffin cups in the tin. Pour in the batter, fill halfway, and bake at 350 degrees. The loaf takes 1 hour, while the muffins should take only 30 minutes, but check them after 20 minutes to make sure they brown but don't burn.

Gaborsti Stew

Of all my sisters, Raxel was the best cook. Mixin was the prettiest, Xepha was the smartest, Melorix was the strongest, and Alixia was my favorite. But Raxel could create refections even my mother, the most extraordinary cook I've ever known, envied. And of all the dishes she made, *gaborsti* stew was my favorite. My only complaint was she didn't make it enough! I cannot describe this flavor to you in words, but even if I could take you to Rinax for a bite of Raxel's *gaborsti* stew, you would still not fully appreciate it. The reason is the little known fact that Talaxians have more taste buds than any other species in the Delta Quadrant. In fact, 65% of my mouth is taste bud, including my throat. I'm still tasting while I swallow! Is it any wonder I love to eat?

    Gaborsti stew has become one of the meals that pleases everyone on the ship—even Mr. Tuvok. It was so popular that when I ran out of seconds one night, the psychotic Suder tried to kill me with a fork. Luckily Chakotay was there (eating a tangerine tart) to quickly dispatch him. The stew is a slightly sweet dish my mom also made on Talax when the weather turned cold. We didn't have turkey, but we had *booky,* a game bird that flew near the equatorial dust shrouds, and she used *threkkles,* a sweet little berry that grew on the walls of the massive clam caves. I've given all the substitutions below for you Terrans.

    1¼ pounds ground turkey breast

    1 tablespoon olive oil

    1¼ cups chopped onions

    3 cloves garlic, finely chopped

    1 tablespoon chili powder

    2 teaspoons dried oregano

    1 teaspoon ground cumin

    ¼ teaspoon sea salt

    ¼ teaspoon ground red pepper

    2¼ cups water

    ¼ pound raisins

    1 14-ounce can of black beans, undrained

Cook the turkey in a skillet or a nonstick pan until it's brown and drain it. Heat the olive oil in a skillet over medium heat, add the onion and garlic, and sauté for 7 minutes. Add the oregano, cumin, chili powder, salt, and red pepper. Cook for a minute. Add the turkey and then stir in the water, raisins, and the contents of the can of beans. Let the stew come to a boil. Then lower the heat and cover it, while it simmers for about 5 minutes. Serve it over rice or millet. Serves four.

So we wander through the Delta Quadrant, crew of party guests and travelers from different planets, once strangers and enemies, now a family. And each and every day, well before the morning watch, I'm in my galley preparing the day's mess and making sure all the individual needs of my crew, my family, are met. At night I dream of the forests on my little moon far away, now only memories: the sound of a distant bird on a chilly winter morning, the voice of a sister arousing me out of half-sleep, the touch of my mother. All gone now, gone as if they'd never been, except for the dreams that come at night. But somewhere in nowhere time is the beep of a ship's computer breaking into the reveries that can flood your mind after a long day. And although I want to crawl back to my quarters, another watch is standing down and will want to be fed. So I have promises to keep and light-years to go before I sleep.

Acknowledgments

There are many people I'd like to thank for their help in the writing of this book. The following people took the time to write down and give me their favorite personal recipe. It was very kind of them and I am very grateful. Mike Westmore, Brad Dourif, Kate Mulgrew, Armin Shimerman, Jennifer Lien, Jonathan Frakes, James Doohan, Leonard Nimoy, Bobby Tyson, Roxanne Dawson, Jeri Ryan, Marina Sirtis Lamper, Ruth Olsen, Fannie Cash, Bea Mercadante, Anastasia Cibelli, Mary Allis, Joan Schieck, Tim Russ, Rene Auberjonois, Alexander Siddig, Nana Visitor, Garrett Wang, Robert Beltran, Marta Wheeler, Robert Duncan McNeill, Dwight Schultz, Robert Picardo, Mary Sandy, Jack Potter, Angela Cody, Andy Robinson, and Armin Shimerman.

Allan Sims, the prop guru on *Star Trek: Voyager*, took time from his busy schedule and was our primary resource who explained the look of *Star Trek* cooking and presentation, and I thank *Star Trek: Deep Space Nine*'s Joe Longo as well for his insight and advice. Both of these gentlemen define the look of *Star Trek* each and every week.

To Jeri Taylor, who very kindly allowed me a peek at her chapter on Neelix's past from the manuscript of her new book, I offer grateful thanks.

Also many people at Paramount deserve mention: Rick Berman, Michael Pillar, Brannon Braga, Merri Howard, Dave Rossi, Maril Davis, Wendy Neuss, Joe Menosky, Ken Biller, Lisa Klink, Bryan Fuller, Lolita Fatjo, Janet Nemecek, Brad Yacobian, Michael DeMeritt, Adele Simmons, Jerry Fleck, Richard James, Rick Sternbach, Michael Okuda, Jim Mees, and Guy

Vardaman. If I missed anyone, I love you and thank you, too! I send very special thanks to Dennis Boutsikaris, Tom Mardirosian, Diane Fitzpatrick, Scott Wheeler, and Bob Picardo.

Hal Bodner was very helpful. And Jill Poller. (Thank you Jill!) To my mom, whom I love and thank for her help, and to my dad, whose memory I will carry with me always.

To the cooks at Go Veggie in Los Angeles go my thanks for their help in creating kabocha squash *plomeek* soup as well as to Jan Higgins in Louisiana for her scholarly explanation of creole cooking, and Diana Rosen, editor of *Tea Talk*.

To my wonderful editor at Pocket Books, Margaret Clark, who piloted this cookbook through many copyedits, photo crises, and design decisions go my adulation and gratitude as well as to Gina Centrillo, Kara Welsh, Scott Shannon, Donna O'Neill, Donna Ruvituso, and Erin Galligan.

To a terrific partner in prose, my coauthor William J. Birnes, publisher of *UFO Magazine*, and to his lovely wife, author Nancy Hayfield. And finally to the very light of my life, my wife, Patty.

—ETHAN PHILLIPS

Index